Religion and Public Opinion in Britain

Religion and Public Opinion in Britain

Continuity and Change

Ben Clements

Lecturer, Department of Politics and International Relations,
University of Leicester, UK

First published 2015 by
PALGRAVE MACMILLAN

Palgrave Macmillan in the UK is an imprint of Macmillan Publishers Limited, registered in England, company number 785998, of Houndmills, Basingstoke, Hampshire, RG21 6XS.

Palgrave Macmillan in the US is a division of St Martin's Press LLC, 175 Fifth Avenue, New York, NY 10010.

Palgrave is the global academic imprint of the above companies and has companies and representatives throughout the world.

Palgrave® and Macmillan® are registered trademarks in the United States, the United Kingdom, Europe and other countries.

ISBN: 978-0-230-29389-2

This book is printed on paper suitable for recycling and made from fully managed and sustained forest sources. Logging, pulping and manufacturing processes are expected to conform to the environmental regulations of the country of origin.

A catalogue record for this book is available from the British Library.

A catalog record for this book is available from the Library of Congress.

For Kyriaki and Erini

Contents

List of Tables

List of Figures

Preface

This book provides a detailed treatment of religion and public opinion in Britain over recent decades. This covers a period when religion has declined in significance as a social force in Britain, with falling levels of identity, belief, attendance and of the traditional rites of passage. It analyses the opinions of the wider British public towards religious authority in an era of growing secularisation, before assessing areas of change and continuity in the socio-political attitudes of religious groups, examining political party support, ideology, abortion, homosexuality and gay rights, and foreign policy. As well as examining change and continuity across time, it also assesses the religious basis of contemporary socio-political attitudes. It uses a multifaceted approach for the analysis of micro-level religion, looking at the role of belonging, behaving and believing. It provides an important 'bottom-up' perspective on the historical and contemporary linkages between religion and politics in Britain, complementing recent research which has shed light on the role of religious actors in the political process and party system. The findings from the book speak to broader debates in political science, the sociology of religion and religious history.

Acknowledgements

I am very grateful to the following people for kindly reading and providing insightful feedback on earlier chapter drafts: Simona Guerra, Jim Guth, Clive Field, Steven Kettell, Richard Whitaker and Linda Woodhead. I would particularly like to thank Clive Field for providing some of the historical polling data used in some of the chapters. Clive should also be congratulated for creating and maintaining the invaluable source database included on the British Religion in Numbers website, which I used on several occasions to track down relevant data. I would also like to thank the University of Leicester for granting a period of study leave which enabled me to work at length on the manuscript. The Department of Politics and International Relations, at the University of Leicester, has always been a friendly, constructive and stimulating environment in which to work and undertake the research for the book. At Palgrave Macmillan, Andy Baird and Jemima Warren provided helpful and prompt editorial assistance, and I thank them also for their forbearance as several agreed deadlines came and went. I would also like to thank Shirley Tan for copy editing the book and Angela Hall for compiling the index.

Some of the material from Chapter 3 first appeared in the report, co-authored with Nick Spencer, published by Theos in early-2014: *Values and Voting in the UK: Does religion count?* I am grateful to Theos for granting me permission to allow this material to be reproduced. A few of the tables in Chapter 2 also appear in: '"Politics and religion don't mix." Or do they?', *Sociology Review*, 2014, (24) 1, pp. 30–3. I am grateful to Philip Allan Magazines for kindly granting permission to allow these tables to be reproduced (some albeit in a slightly extended format).

Most of all, I would like to thank my wife, Kyriaki, for all her support and encouragement during the long period of working on this book, and for offering her ideas and feedback at different stages of development. It is to her and to our wonderful daughter, Erini, to whom this book is dedicated.

Market Harborough, Leicestershire
September 2014

1
Introduction

A substantial body of scholarly research has examined in detail the interactions and interconnections between religion and politics in Britain in recent decades, in particular relations between the major Christian denominations and political parties during the era of Conservative government between 1979 and 1997 (Gover 2011; Filby 2010; Durham 1997; Martin 1989; Baker 1991; Clarke 1993; Moyser 1989; Medhurst and Moyser 1988; Machin 1998). More recent scholarly research has examined the role of religious institutions within public debate and the legislative process during the period of the Labour governments, 1997–2010, as well as the Conservative-Liberal Democrat coalition which entered office in May 2010 (Kettell 2009, 2013).

There have also been broader book-length assessments of the contemporary and historical linkages between religion and politics in Britain (Bruce 2012; Steven 2011a). The topics covered in this book and the associated empirical analyses of continuity and change in religious groups' attitudes should serve to complement some of the specific areas of religion and British politics given detailed historical and contemporary treatments in the works of Bruce (2012) and Steven (2011a), both published as part of the Routledge Studies in Religion and Politics. Steven argues that religion has been a 'neglected dimension' on the part of scholars of British politics (2011a).

While it is clear that more recent research has made an important contribution to elucidating the nature and extent of the engagement of religious actors within the political process, there is clearly a need for a broader assessment of the historical and contemporary links between *religion* and *public opinion* in Britain. In short, a more 'bottom-up' perspective is required to complement this existing body of scholarship. The detailed single-country focus of this research also complements studies with a broader cross-country focus on religion and politics, using comparative survey data, most notably that conducted by Norris and Inglehart (2012).

The research undertaken in this book provides this assessment and contributes to scholarship examining the complex and changing relationship between religion and the political process in Britain. It examines the social and political attitudes of religious groups across time, focusing on the overarching themes of change and continuity in public opinion. This book's central aim is to provide an in-depth and wide-ranging assessment – both historical and contemporary – of religion and public opinion in Britain. More specifically, in the area of public opinion, the book analyses the linkages between: religion and political party support, religion and ideological beliefs, religion and homosexuality and gay rights, religion and abortion, and religion and foreign policy. Some of the topics pursued in this book, moreover, concern two of the key ways – as identified by Heath et al. (1993a: 50) – in which religion can be important for politics. First, contemporary political issues, which although they may not be overtly religious, can engage to the core beliefs or teachings of particular religious traditions. The archetypal issues here include debates over human sexuality or abortion. Second, there can be historical and contemporary linkages between particular religious groups and specific political parties. This may be reflected in patterns of voting behaviour or through broader party affiliation. These long-standing denominational linkages are underpinned by particular social cleavages which became 'frozen' in European party systems (Heath et al. 1993a: 50; Lipset and Rokkan 1967). In analysing these topics the focus is on areas of continuity and change, divergence and convergence, in the opinions of religious groups across recent decades. Before these topics are analysed in depth and in order to address the broader theme of secularisation, however, the book assesses the nature and extent of religious change and declining religious authority in British society. How this is to be done, and with what scholarly materials, is set out in the next section.

Methodological approach and source material

This book examines and interprets changes and patterns in the attitudes of religious groups based on available recurrent social survey data. Its approach is to use multiple surveys rather than relying exclusively on one survey series as the source of attitudinal data. This evidence base available typically means that data on religious groups' attitudes are examined from the 1960s or 1970s onwards, with supplementary sources – commercial opinion polling and one-off surveys – used to provide other relevant data. The book takes the assessment of religious groups' attitudes up to the present day, using the most recently-released survey sources. It needs to be stated at the outset that this is an extensive exercise in secondary data analysis, in that much of the evidence used here comes from well-established, long-running social surveys which make datasets available in the public domain for wider usage by scholars and other interested parties. These generally constitute national sample surveys of the adult population, conducted from the 1950s onwards, which collectively represent a 'tremendous potential research resource for scholars of religious studies, modern history, and social science' (Field forthcoming: 12). By undertaking this, the book therefore makes a major contribution to the 'repurposing' of religious data using British social surveys and opinion polls (Field, forthcoming). Of course, while this book uses the best evidence available, it should be recognised that there are also challenges to using surveys to study religion, as discussed in existing research (Voas 2003, 2007; Field forthcoming). This study proceeds with such caveats in mind and thus avoids over-reliance on a single survey source. In sum, it uses a plurality of recurrent social surveys to more robustly establish patterns and trends, discern areas of divergence and convergence, and to map change and continuity in the social and political attitudes of religious groups.

The book is therefore deliberately data rich for three reasons. First, each chapter focuses in detail on a particular aspect of public opinion. Secondly, each chapter examines the historical evidence, often stretching back over several decades. Third, as already indicated, to provide a more robust and comprehensive treatment, it uses multiple survey sources – where data permit – to assess patterns and trends in the attitudes of religious groups in Britain.

Data sources

Two areas of omission should be noted here. First, the parameters of the book exclude consideration of public opinion in Northern Ireland, so the focus is on attitudes in Great Britain (England, Scotland and Wales), hereafter referred to as 'Britain'. Secondly, given the centrality of the over-time focus here and because many of the earlier surveys used here featured very few respondents who reported that they belonged to non-Christian minority faiths, reflecting their incidence within wider society, they have not been included in the classification of affiliation for the analysis of historical survey data. They are included in the samples when focusing on attitudes on the basis of religious attendance and belief; and when undertaking more detailed multivariate analysis of recent or contemporary data, when they are more numerous in the samples and in order to provide a wider base for assessing the impact of religion on attitudes. Moreover, a growing literature from political science and sociology has provided more in-depth analysis of the political attitudes, social beliefs and electoral behaviour of religious and ethnic minorities in recent years (see, for example, Clements 2013; Heath et al. 2013; Lewis and Kashyap 2013).

In terms of the data used in this book, five main survey series provide the major sources of nationally-representative, public opinion data (a full bibliographic list of the survey datasets used from each of these series, and any supplementary surveys, is provided). The surveys and the periods of time covered (relevant to the analyses in the book) are as follows:

- British Election Study (BES), 1963–2010
- British Social Attitudes (BSA), 1983–2012
- European Values Study (EVS), 1981–2008
- European Social Survey (EVS), 2002–2012
- Eurobarometer (EB), 1970–2006

Both because of the range of questions asked in various topic areas and their longevity, the BES, BSA and EVS surveys are used most extensively for the analyses undertaken in this book. The EB and ESS surveys are used less extensively: the EB because it is of greatest utility for its long-running coverage of questions on member state relations with the European integration process; and the ESS because it is a relative 'latecomer' to the survey world, beginning on a biennial basis in 2002.

Measurement of religion

As recent scholarship has observed, religion is a 'multifaceted phenomenon' (Smidt et al. 2009: 4–5) and it is important to examine how these different dimensions are consequential for politics – more specifically for this book, how these dimensions are associated with social and political attitudes concerning the aforementioned topics. The treatment of religion within this book therefore includes the three main areas commonly used for analysing religion: belonging, behaving and believing (Smidt et al. 2009; Leege and Kellstedt 1993). Each of these areas is generally analysed independently from the others, in that they are examined separately when looking at changes in attitudes over time and when assessing the contemporary social and religious factors shaping public opinion. More broadly, in classifying and applying the different aspects of religion to social and political attitudes, the book – an extensive exercise in secondary data analysis – has attempted to 'make the best use of available data' (Smidt et al. 2009: 9).

The questions used from the social surveys to operationalise these three areas of religion are listed in Appendix 1. This also shows where question wording has changed across surveys within a particular series (as, for example, has been the case with the measures of affiliation and attendance in the BES surveys). It should be noted that while the surveys have generally nearly always or always included measures of affiliation (belonging) and attendance (behaving), there has been less extensive coverage of religious beliefs. However, each EVS survey has included questions on traditional religious beliefs, while three BSA surveys have included sets of religious belief questions as part of specialist modules on religion (in 1991, 1998 and 2008). The BES and ESS surveys have not, however, administered any questions on religious belief. In the chapters that follow, the coverage of religious beliefs is necessarily less extensive than that for belonging and behaviour. To keep the analyses of the survey data more manageable where religious belief is concerned, only questions focusing on beliefs in and about and personal engagement with God are used. As far as the data allow, this enables an assessment of the nature and extent of any 'God gap' in popular attitudes in the areas of religious authority, ideological beliefs and social-morality issues in Britain. Other traditional beliefs asked about on the BSA and EVS surveys – such as belief in life after death, heaven and hell – are not analysed in the book.

The main measures used for belonging is that of respondents' current self-declared affiliation and, for behaving, that of attendance at religious services (normally treated as an indicator of group or communal practice – there has generally been less extensive coverage across time of private religious practices in the recurrent social surveys). Religious affiliation focuses on those with a Christian affiliation or no affiliation and is generally based on the following four categories:

- Anglican
- Catholic

- Other Christian (including all other Protestant denominations and those Christians with no denominational affiliation)
- No affiliation

The principal exception to this standard classification of religious affiliation is in the analysis of religion and party choice, where the classification is based on five categories in accordance with the traditional associations examined between denominations and political parties (Anglican, Catholic, Church of Scotland/Presbyterian, Nonconformist, no religion).

Measures of religious affiliation in the recurrent social surveys are generally divided into three categories:

- Frequent-attenders: those who attend once a month or more often
- Infrequent attenders: those who attend less often than once a month
- Non-attenders: those who never attend.

Other measures of religious belonging and behaving from the EVS and ESS surveys – which have been included over time – are also utilised for the purposes of analysis and further information on classification is provided in the relevant chapters. One limitation of the recurrent surveys is that the earliest of them dates to 1963 (the first survey in the BES series) and the two containing the most detailed range of questions about social-morality attitudes – the BSA and EVS surveys – did not start until the early 1980s. Therefore, those interested in looking at change and continuity in the attitudes of religious groups in the 1950s and 1960s are somewhat disadvantaged by the comparative lack of recurrent social survey data, which is a notable lacuna given the scholarly debate over the nature and extent of religious change in Britain in these decades (Yates 2010; McLeod 2007; Brown 2006; Machin 1996, 1998). In fact, the first BES questions on social-moral issues – such as abortion and homosexuality – did not feature until the 1974 surveys, with the exception of the issue of capital punishment (where questions were fielded from the outset – the 1963 survey). Moreover, while polling was often undertaken on these sorts of issues by organisations such as Gallup and NOP, data breakdowns for religious groups are generally not in the public domain and the published sources for these data (Gallup 1976a, 1976b) only tend to provide figures for the British public as a whole. Where they provide relevant measures of religion, one-off surveys and published data from major polling organisations are used to provide useful supplementary evidence, in particular to shed further light on the attitudes of particular religious groups and to furnish relevant data for years not covered by the recurrent social surveys. Where data are analysed from historical opinion polls, these tend to be limited to religious affiliation and, in particular, to those belonging to the main Christian traditions. Now that the methodological approach and source material has been introduced, the final section discusses the substantive topic addressed in each chapter.

Outline of chapters

There are six substantive chapters, all of which undertake extensive analysis of recurrent social surveys and supplementary polling sources. Each chapter focuses on a specific area of public opinion and makes liberal use of tables and figures in order to present data, whether charting religious groups' attitudes across time or analysing the religious basis of contemporary public opinion in greater depth. Taken together they cover the following topics: religious authority; party choice, ideology, abortion, homosexuality and gay rights, and foreign policy issues. In more detail, the aims and scope of each chapter are as follows:

Chapter 2 ('Religious Authority') looks at broader attitudes towards the role of religion (institutions and leaders) in public life. It provides a detailed assessment of whether there has been a 'decline in religious authority' in British public life (Chaves 1994), which provides a means of examining the extent of secularisation in public life, looking over time at public confidence in religious institutions. It looks at public perceptions of religious institutions in general as well as specific evaluations of the Anglican and Roman Catholic churches. It also looks at public attitudes on the appropriate role for religious leaders in the political process, examining which social groups are more or less receptive to the exercise of religious authority – towards governments and voters – and assesses whether views have changed over time.

Chapter 3 ('Religion and Party Choice') looks in detail at the survey data pertaining to the traditional denominational links between religious groups and political parties, particularly Catholics and Labour and Anglicans and the Conservatives. It looks at the voting behaviour of religious groups at general elections for the period 1959–2010, as well as general party support – expressed in inter-election periods – in recent decades. There is also consideration of how party support based on religious belonging may vary based on the socio-structural factors of social class and region, as well as by religious attendance. There is also a contemporary assessment of how religion is associated with party support in the context of examining other sociological factors which have traditionally been associated with party choice.

Chapter 4 ('Religion and Ideology') links with and follows on from the focus of Chapter 2, examining religious groups' ideological orientations and beliefs, which are thought to structure a broader range of issue preferences within public opinion. It looks at whether, in general, religious groups are more likely to exhibit politically-conservative attitudes on social and economic beliefs compared to those who are not religious. It also focuses on whether Anglicans are more *conservative* in their political beliefs as they are more *Conservative* than other groups in their traditional expressions of party choice. It looks at both general ideological orientations based on left-right, welfare and libertarian-authoritarian dimensions, as well as individuals' self-placement on ideological scales. It also looks in greater detail at authoritarian sentiment in two areas of particular relevance for religious groups' beliefs and concerns, that of support for capital punishment and censorship (in order to uphold moral standard and to protect religious beliefs).

Chapters 5 and 6 look at religious groups' attitudes towards two important social-morality issues, abortion and homosexuality, both of which were the subject of landmark legislation in the 1960s during 'a "permissive" period where several forms of social and moral regulation underwent a substantial liberalization' (Thorup Larsen et al. 2012: 114). Chapter 5 ('Religion and Abortion') examines views on legal abortion, one of the most important of the 'life' issues for religious groups. It looks at the views of religious groups both prior to and then in the decades after, the 1967 Abortion Act. It provides a detailed look at attitudes towards the different circumstances under which legal abortion can be carried out. Given the historical importance of this issue for the core teachings of the Roman Catholic Church and its leaders, and important findings from recent survey research about the growing gap between core social teachings and the attitudes of ordinary Catholics (Woodhead 2013b, 2013c), there is also a supplementary examination of which social groups in the Catholic community are more or less likely to hold traditional views on this subject.

Chapter 6 ('Religion, Homosexuality and Gay Rights') examines the historical and contemporary data pertaining to religious groups' views on the acceptance or approval of homosexuality, as well as more specific issues of equality for gays and lesbians, such as legal recognitions of their relationships, adoption rights and acceptance of their presence in particular roles and occupations. There is also a close attention to group attitudes towards same-sex marriage, which represents the most recent instance of religious, party-political and societal disagreement over legislation – recently enacted under the Conservative-Liberal Democrat coalition government – furthering the legal rights of gay and lesbian couples in Britain.

Chapter 7 ('Religion and Foreign Policy') shifts the focus to foreign affairs. It examines the attitudes of religious groups towards issues of *war* – recent military interventions in Iraq and Afghanistan; and *peace* – Britain's post-war involvement in the European integration process. It uses policy-specific examples of the types of attitudinal measures which fit into the broader public opinion dimensions of 'militant internationalism' and 'cooperative internationalism' (Guth 2013a, 2013b). On the long-running issue of Britain's involvement in European integration, it assesses in particular whether Roman Catholics in Britain have traditionally held a more supportive – or less Eurosceptic – stance on European integration and whether other groups have been more Eurosceptic. Given Britain's reputation as a member state where both party-based and public Euroscepticism have been particularly prominent, it also provides a cross-national focus by examining the views of, on the one hand, Anglicans and Catholics in Britain, and, on the other, Protestants and Catholics across the EU as a whole. It then looks at religious groups' attitudes towards military interventions undertaken in the post-9-11 era, looking at whether religious groups were less or more supportive of Britain's role in Iraq and Afghanistan. Opposition to the Iraq War was evident from the then leaders of the Anglican and Catholic churches and these conflicts may well have had moral or religious underpinnings or resonances for both supporters and opponents, the latter group including many from the Islamic community in Britain. The analysis therefore pays close attention to the opinions of minority, non-Christian faiths.

The findings from the individual chapters, based on empirical assessment of an extensive set of attitudinal data from multiple social surveys, build upon important earlier studies which based their empirical analyses on one or several waves from a particular survey series. The historical focus of the public opinion analyses also help to document and clarify key areas of change and continuity in the socio-political attitudes of religious groups in Britain over several decades, and therefore complement major surveys of religion and public attitudes in contemporary Britain, namely the Westminster Faith Debates surveys: firstly, on Religion and Public Life, undertaken in 2012; and, secondly, on Religion and Personal Life carried out in 2013. The chapters also undertake multivariate analyses to examine the relative impact of religious factors on socio-political attitudes and beliefs when accounting for other socio-structural factors which might also directly influence these attitudes and be correlated with religious identity and practice (details on the measurement of the most commonly-used independent variables are provided in Appendix 2).

It is hoped that the research findings presented here – in relation to religious groups and party support, ideology, social-moral issues, foreign policy, and broader views on religion in public life – contribute to the literature examining the role of religion in British politics and society, and therefore is of relevance to political scientists, sociologists of religion, and historians of religion in post-war Britain.

2
Religious Authority

This chapter analyses public opinion towards religious authority in Britain in an era of secularisation. Succinctly defined, secularisation refers to the 'process whereby religious thinking, practice and institutions, lose social significance' (Wilson 1966: xiv). In Britain, this has resulted in religion undergoing a process of privatisation, losing some of its social functions as well as authority and influence in the sphere of politics (Bruce 2012: 164). In terms of popular engagement with religion, Bruce has argued that 'every index of religious interest and involvement in Britain shows decline. It is the consistency of the data which is significant' (2013: 374). An important part of this is the decline in the 'social reach' or 'penumbra' of Christianity (Bruce 2013: 374). Field observes that:

> When all is said and done, however, the fact remains that organized Christianity has been in retreat between the 1960s and 2010s, and on any number of fronts ... Thus, on all critical performance indicators (membership, attendance, rites of passage, and affiliation) net commitment to institutional Christianity has decreased in contemporary Britain (2014c: 192 and 193).

In terms of public attitudes towards the role and status of Christianity, public opinion data from the 1960s onwards show that there have been considerable declines in the proportions of the public who agree with the statements that Britain *is a* Christian country or that it should *be a* Christian country (Field 2014a). More recently, there has also been a fall in the proportion in Britain who think that it is very or fairly important that you are Christian in order to be truly British (Clements 2014a).

11

Given this wider context, this chapter analyses public attitudes towards religious institutions and their leaders, broadly applying Chaves' thesis that 'secularization is best understood not as the decline of religion, but as the declining scope of religious authority' (1994: 750). Specifically, the chapter investigates popular attitudes towards the role of religion in broader society – in terms of confidence in religious institutions – and in the political process, looking at the appropriateness of religious leaders intervening in topical debate and potentially influencing government and citizens. It analyses overall trends in public opinion as well as examines which social groups tend to be more – or less – supportive of religious authority and the exercise of that authority. The analyses undertaken in this chapter build on recent research into trends in public perceptions of the church and clergy in Britain (Field 2014c) and studies of public opinion towards religion in the public sphere (Bruce 2012; Glendinning and Bruce 2011; Glendinning 2014).

The chapter is divided into three main sections, all based on extensive analyses of recurrent social surveys. The first section ascertains the extent of religious change in recent decades in the broad areas of belonging, behaving and believing. The second section provides an over-time analysis of confidence in religious institutions in recent decades. The third section examines public attitudes towards the role of religion leaders in politics, in terms of both elite-level influence and mass-level influence.

Religious change: Belonging, behaving and believing

Before examining in detail public attitudes towards religious authority, it is important to examine the survey-based evidence pertaining to religious change in Britain. This is done for multiple indicators of the three aspects of belonging, behaving and believing (question wordings are provided in Appendix 1). The analysis of religious change covers the same time periods used for the assessment of public opinion towards religious authority (following the approach of Kleiman et al. 1996). The periods cover, respectively, 1981–2008 for the EVS surveys and 1991–2008 for the BSA surveys. Using the two 'book-end' surveys of 1981 and 2008, Table 2.1 reports data for multiple indicators of religion from the EVS surveys, with the various indicators classified by whether they measure religious belonging, behaving or believing. The right-hand column in Table 2.1 reports the percentage point change over time for each of these indicators.

Looking first at belonging, religious affiliation shows a very sharp drop over the period (from around nine-tenths professing an affiliation in 1981 to just over half in 2008); while membership of churches or other religious organisation – a stricter measure of belonging – fell from 21.7 percent to 12.3 percent. The proportion calling themselves a religious person declined by around a quarter, from 59.2 percent to 45.0 percent. In terms of the indicators of behaving, the measure of regular attendance at religious services (declining from 22.2 percent to 19.2 percent) somewhat understates the degree of change, as most of the change across time has occurred between the groups *attending infrequently* or *not at all*. Specifically, between 1981 and 2008, the proportion reporting attending services infrequently (that is, less than once a month) declined from 30.5 percent to 24.3 percent. The proportion reporting that they did not attend services correspondingly rose from 47.3 percent to 56.6 percent. By way of a caveat with attendance data, it should be noted that, because of the social prestige factor, reported attendance at religious services from survey respondents tends to overstate the reality of attendance at worship services. Some change has also occurred in the extent of personal religious practice (not reported in Table 2.1). A question asking about how often an individual prays outside of religious services shows that the proportion saying 'never' has increased from 33.4 percent in 1990 to 50.5 percent in 2008 (it was not asked in the 1981 survey). A differently-worded question asking about whether respondents take moments for prayer or meditation shows an increase in those responding 'never' from 1981 to 2008, from 49.5 percent to 55.5 percent.

Believing shows a somewhat more mixed picture than belonging and behaving, albeit there are more indicators to utilise in the EVS surveys. Traditional beliefs in and the personal salience of, God, have declined in recent decades. The proportion believing in God fell from around three-quarters (75.1 percent) to less than six in ten (57.7 percent). There was also a decline in the proportion thinking there is a personal God – from 31.6 percent to 25.8 percent. The average importance of God in individuals' lives declined from 5.69 to 4.67 (on a scale ranging from 1 to 10). There have also been falls in traditional belief in 'sin' and 'heaven' over the same period (levels of belief in 'hell' and 'life after death' have generally held up, with very minor falls). Similarly, the proportion deriving comfort or strength from religion has also shown modest decline (from 45.5 percent to 37.5 percent). The data clearly show that, while there have been large falls in belonging over recent decades and some decline in religious behaviour, the pattern for

Table 2.1   Indicators of religious change in the EVS surveys, 1981–2008

	1981 (%)	2008 (%)	Change
Belonging			
Has a religious affiliation	90.6	55.0	–35.6
Is a religious person	59.2	45.0	–14.2
Behaving			
Member of a church or religious organisation	21.7	12.3	–9.4
Attends religious services once a month or more	22.2	19.2	–3.0
Believing			
Gets comfort or strength from religion	45.5	37.5	–8.0
Believes in God	75.1	57.7	–17.4
Believes in sin	68.2	57.2	–11.0
Believes in heaven	57.0	46.4	–10.6
Believes in hell	26.2	28.6	+2.4
Believes in life after death	45.2	44.3	–0.9
There is a personal God	31.6	25.8	–5.8
How important is God in your life[a]	5.69	4.67	–1.02

Source: EVS surveys.
[a]Mean scores based on a scale ranging from 1=not at all important through to 10=very important.

believing – the proportions holding traditional religious beliefs – is more mixed, with some beliefs in decline and some showing little or no change (see Davie 1994; Gill et al. 1998; Gill 2003; Voas and Crockett 2005; Clements, 2014c).

Table 2.2 presents data on religious change from the BSA surveys for the period 1991–2008. Much of the data comes from specialist modules on religion asked in the 1991 and 2008 BSA surveys as part of the cross-national International Social Survey Programme (also included in the BSA 1998 survey, which is not used here). Where available, data are also reported for the earliest and most recently-released BSA surveys – 1983 and 2012 – to provide greater comparability with the time period covered by the EVS surveys. Table 2.2 reports a range of measures of religious belonging, behaving and believing, and also presents recall data on the religious characteristics of respondents' parents. The data for belonging show a decline in the proportion with some form of affiliation from 64.6 percent in 1991 (68.4 percent in 1983) to 56.7 percent in 2008 (and lower again in 2012). Levels of belonging at the outset of the BSA series – about two-thirds – are lower than that

Table 2.2   Indicators of religious change in the BSA surveys, 1991–2008

	1991 (%)	2008 (%)	Change
Belonging			
Has a religious affiliation	64.6 (68.4)	56.7 (51.9)	–7.9
Brought up within a religious background	94.1 (94.2)	86.9 (79.5)	–7.2
Behaving			
Attends services once a month or more	20.6 (21.3)	17.7 (16.9)	–2.9
Takes part in church activities (other than attending services)[b]	11.1	10.0	–1.1
Prays once a week or more often	27.2	21.4	–5.8
Believing			
Beliefs about God (1)[a]	62.5	48.4	–14.1
Beliefs about God (2)[b]	52.7	42.4	–10.3
God concerns himself with humans: strongly agree or agree	33.8	27.7	–6.1
Life is meaningful because God exists: strongly agree or agree	19.3	14.2	–5.1
Believes in heaven: definitely or probably	48.3	42.5	–5.8
Believes in hell: definitely or probably	25.7	28.6	+2.9
Believes in religious miracles: definitely or probably	39.9	30.4	–9.5
Believes in afterlife: definitely or probably	48.3	47.1	–1.2
Parental religion			
Mother had a religious affiliation	96.3	87.1	–9.2
Father had a religious affiliation	90.8	79.0	–11.8
Mother attended religious services about once a month or more	39.4	33.8	–5.6
Father attended religious services about once a month or more	27.8	23.5	–4.3

Source: BSA surveys.
Note: The figures in parentheses refer to the corresponding data from the first and most recent BSA surveys (1983 and 2012), where equivalent measures are available.
[a]Those who answered 'I find myself believing in God some of the time, but not at others', 'While I have doubts, I feel that I do believe in God' and 'I know God really exists and I have no doubts about it'.
[b]Those who answered 'I believe in God now and I always have' or 'I believe in God now, but I didn't use to'.

reported in the first EVS survey in 1981, which showed around nine-tenths claimed some form of affiliation. Research has shown that, in British surveys and opinion polls, the overall level of affiliation recorded can be affected by survey-specific question wordings and response options (Field 2014b). There has also been a fall in the proportion raised in a family religion, albeit the levels are generally very high across surveys – falling from 94.2 percent in 1983 to 79.5 percent in 2012, with a decline in the 1991–2008 period from 94.1 percent to 86.9 percent.

Behaving is measured by both group and personal practices: religious attendance, involvement in other church activity, frequency of prayer and service attendance when aged 11–12 years. The measure of current attendance shows a small decline similar to the EVS surveys (from 20.6 percent to 17.7 percent), with regular attendance always a minority activity. Over the longer 1983–2012 period, the decline is from 21.3 percent to 16.9 percent. Those praying frequently (once a week or more) constitute a minority in both surveys, which has declined from 27.2 percent in 1991 to 21.4 percent in 2008. Taking a regular part in other forms of church activity (beyond attending services), which is consistently the preserve of a small minority, shows a small drop from 11.1 percent to 10.0 percent.

As with the EVS surveys, a wide range of measures of believing can be used from the BSA surveys. Taking into account that they span across a shorter period than the EVS data and rely on different question wordings and response options, the BSA measures of belief tend to show a similar picture of decline – albeit of varying magnitudes – with a couple of exceptions. The exceptions concern a slight rise in belief in hell (from 25.7 percent to 28.6 percent) and a very small decline in belief in an afterlife (from 48.3 percent to 47.1 percent). However, there are clear declines in belief in heaven and religious miracles; the former declining from 48.3 percent to 42.5 percent, the latter from 39.9 percent to 30.4 percent. The four questions asking about beliefs in or conceptions about God all register a decline over this period. Based on one question, those expressing a firm or somewhat less clear sense of belief in God have declined from 62.5 percent to 48.4 percent. Based on another question, the proportion always believing in God or who believe now but did not earlier in their lives has fallen from 52.7 percent to 42.4 percent. Focusing just on those with a consistent belief in God throughout their lives or who say that God exists and have no doubts, the proportions have fallen, respectively, from 46.6 percent to 37.2 percent and from 23.7 percent to 17.0 percent.

The proportion agreeing that God concerns himself with humans fell from 33.8 percent to 27.7 percent. The proportion in agreement with the statement that life is meaningful because God exists – only a small minority in each survey – also declined somewhat, from 19.3 percent to 14.2 percent.

Finally, declines are also registered for respondents' recollections about their mothers' and fathers' religious characteristics, relating to affiliation and attendance. Specifically, between 1991 and 2008 the proportion of respondents whose mother or father had a religious affiliation declined, respectively, 96.3 percent to 87.1 percent and from 90.8 percent to 79.0 percent. The proportions of mothers and fathers attending religious services on a frequent basis, while always a minority, also fell over time based on individual recollections (although regular attendance was always higher for mothers).

In summary, it is clear that nearly all of the BSA indicators tend to move in the same direction; that is, towards lower personal engagement with religion. As with the EVS surveys, those indicators which show little change or stay the same relate to specific beliefs. The decline in levels of religious belonging can be seen as part of a wider pattern of decline in traditional social identities (Heath et al. 2007), and much of the decline in belonging is due to waning Christian identification in recent decades, in particular amongst Anglicans (Clements 2014a). The data on religious belonging, from both survey series, are in accordance with recent research into historical and contemporary trends in affiliation, which observed that, in contemporary British society, 'between one-quarter and one-half the population now make sense of their lives without a religious identity' (Field 2014b: 379). Clearly, then, the decline in an extensive set of indicators of belonging, believing and behaving within the British public in recent decades would lead to the expectation that public acceptance of religious authority has also declined. Has this, indeed, happened?

Religious authority in Britain

As well as measures of belonging, behaving and believing, another way of examining the thesis of secularisation in Britain is to look at the extent of decline in the authority of religious institutions and leaders. This analytical approach originated with Chaves, who theorised that 'secularization is best understood not as the decline of religion, but as the declining scope of religious authority' (1994: 750). Since then there has been relatively little empirical research on attitudes towards religious authority in Britain (an exception is Field 2014c), although there have been several analyses undertaken of this aspect of public opinion in the US (Hoffman 1998, 2013; Kleiman et al. 1996). This section provides an over-time perspective on religious authority, analysing public confidence in religious institutions in Britain. It uses confidence in religious institutions as the specific measure of religious authority (Hoffman 1998, 2013). An advantage of focusing on confidence in religious institutions is that, as Kleiman et al. observe, the 'wording of this item distinguishes between confidence in religious leaders and the individual's faith in religious ideals or belief systems. A person could consider himself or herself religious, yet have low confidence in the persons involved in leadership positions within religious organizations' (1996: 81). As well as looking at aggregate trends in public opinion, this section analyses change and continuity in the perceptions of a range of social groups, including those classified on the basis of religious characteristics. This section uses data from the British component of the EVS surveys, which offer the longest and richest set of recurrent questions on religion.

Confidence in religious institutions: Aggregate-level trends

Given this wider context of many indicators of micro-level religion trending downwards – with some showing substantial declines – in recent decades, it would also be expected that levels of confidence in religious institutions would see a similar decline. The EVS surveys have posed the following question on this topic:

> Please look at this card and tell me, for each item listed, how much confidence you have in them, it is a great deal, quite a lot, not very much, or not at all?

Responses to this question can be compared over time. The overall distribution of opinion for each survey is shown in Table 2.3.

Note that the EVS question refers to 'the church' rather than to religious institutions. The data clearly show a decline in the proportion of people who have either a 'great deal' or 'quite a lot' of confidence in the church (falling from 48.6 percent to 35.0 percent). The proportion having 'none at all' almost doubles over the period covered by the surveys (between 1981 and 2008), from 10.5 percent to 19.2 percent. Interestingly, the decline in confidence mainly occurred up to 1999. For example, looking at the proportions who respond 'a great deal' at each time point, the decreases are as follows: from 19.3 percent to 16.1 percent between 1981 and 1990; from 16.1 percent to 9.3 percent

Table 2.3   Confidence in the church, 1981–2008

	1981 (%)	1990 (%)	1999 (%)	2008 (%)	Change
A great deal	19.3	16.1	9.3	10.4	–8.9
Quite a lot	29.3	26.7	23.8	24.6	–4.7
Total agree	48.6	42.8	33.1	35.0	–13.6
Not very much	40.9	44.1	44.3	42.2	+1.3
None at all	10.5	13.2	19.0	19.2	+8.7
Total disagree	51.4	57.3	63.3	61.4	+10.0
Don't know	0.0	0.0	3.5	3.6	+3.6

Source: EVS surveys.

between 1990 and 1999; and rising slightly from 9.3 percent to 10.4 percent between 1999 and 2008. Similarly, for those saying 'none at all', the decreases happened between 1981–90 and 1991–99, with barely any change between 1999 and 2008. Trend data from Gallup surveys provide some corroboration for the EVS data. They show a decline in the proportion of the British public with a great deal or quite a lot of confidence in the church for the period 1983–2000, falling from 52.0 percent to 37.0 percent (Field 2014c: 197). Moreover, other trend data show those tending to trust religious institutions in Britain decreasing from 53.0 percent in 1997 to 36.0 percent in 2010 (Field 2014c: 199); while another series showed the proportion having a great deal or quite a lot of trust in the church fell from 42.0 percent in 2003 to 30.0 percent in 2013 (Field 2014c: 200).

Group attitudes

While looking at the overall picture sheds light on general attitudes towards religious institutions in British society, it is also important to look at which particular social groups have shown the greatest change in their views of religious institutions. Data are presented in Table 2.4 for groups classified by the following sociological and attitudinal variables: sex, age group, educational attainment, social grade, party supported and left-right ideology (the left-right scale ranges from 1 = most left-wing through to 10 = most right-wing. Values between 1 and 4 are classed as left-wing, 5–6 classed as centre and 7 to 10 as right-wing).

Table 2.4 shows the proportion in each social group who say they have a 'great deal' or 'quite a lot' of confidence in the churches, for the period 1981–2008. The final column again reports the level of change for each social group across the entire period (showing whether group attitudes have moved in the direction of more or less confidence). The

Table 2.4   Percent with confidence in the church, by socio-demographic group, 1981–2008

Variable	Category	1981 (%)	1990 (%)	1999 (%)	2008 (%)	Change[a]
Sex	Men	41.5	33.0	27.5	31.8	–9.7
	Women	55.3	51.7	37.8	38.1	–17.2
Age group	18–24 years	34.6	30.1	34.2	29.3	–5.3
	25–34 years	36.6	35.4	25.5	34.0	–2.6
	35–44 years	43.7	35.2	28.5	29.1	–14.6
	45–54 years	45.6	47.1	32.6	30.5	–15.1
	55–64 years	68.5	43.9	36.8	33.3	–35.2
	65–74 years	63.8	54.5	46.8	43.9	–19.9
	75+	67.0	69.6	41.0	54.5	–12.5
Education	Degree-level	51.4	43.3	34.1	38.7	–12.7
	Below degree-level	48.3	39.0	32.2	33.9	–14.4
Social grade	AB	46.4	41.3	43.3	–	–3.1
	C1	44.9	38.8	34.5	–	–10.4
	C2	48.4	40.4	34.0	–	–14.4
	DE	51.3	51.6	27.5	–	–23.8
Party support	Conservative	–	43.8	47.2	41.6	–2.2
	Labour	–	41.4	36.8	36.9	–4.5
	Liberal Democrat	–	48.1	36.8	49.3	+1.2
	Other party	–	45.0	15.1	28.5	–16.5
	No party	–	41.1	24.0	29.9	–11.2
Ideology	Left	38.2	33.0	21.0	34.8	–3.4
	Centre	45.8	44.2	36.5	34.5	–11.3
	Right	64.4	41.5	37.3	40.4	–24.0

Source: EVS surveys.
[a]For the social grade categories, the differences are calculated between 1981 and 1999. For party support, the differences are calculated between 1990 and 2008.
Note: Combines 'a great deal of confidence' and 'quite a lot of confidence'.

picture is invariably, if not inevitably, one of declining confidence across social groups. Even so, the extent of the decline varies considerably across groups. Looking first at demographic groups, it is evident that the absolute decline is larger amongst women compared to men (falling from 55.3 percent in 1981 to 38.1 percent in 2008). Given generational explanations of religious decline, whereby each successive generation should be less religious in their belonging, beliefs and behaviour, what are the findings for age? It is clear that there are wide variations in the levels of decline in confidence in the church, which reflects the higher levels of confidence expressed at the outset in 1981 by the older age groups. The largest absolute declines occur for those aged 55–64 years (at 35.2 percentage points) and those aged 65–74 years (19.9 percentage points). Those aged 35–44 years, 45–54 years and 75 and over all register declines in the range of 12–15 percentage points. The smallest falls in confidence occur for those aged 18–24 years and 25–34 years, who had the lowest levels of confidence in 1981. Also, the 'confidence gap' between the youngest and oldest age groups has shrunk somewhat over time (calculated by subtracting the level of confidence of the youngest age group from that of the oldest age group). The difference was 32.4 percentage points in 1981 and 25.2 percentage points in 2008. In 1981, the three oldest groups had confidence levels in the church in excess of 60.0 percent, whereas in 2008 only a majority of the oldest group (aged 75 and over) expressed 'a great deal' or 'quite a lot' of confidence (54.5 percent).

In terms of socio-economic background, respondents are classified by the highest qualification they have obtained (degree-level or below) and social grade (AB, C1, C2 and DE).[1] There are similar falls in confidence for education, but based on social grade, the largest decline is seen amongst those in the DE group (comprising the unskilled working class and those not in work). Interestingly, those in the lowest socio-economic grouping therefore shift from having the highest level of confidence in the church in 1981 to having the lowest level in 1999. Those in the AB grade move from having a similar level of confidence to those in the C1 and C2 groups in 1981 to being the most positive in their assessment in 1999.

The more limited coverage for party political supporters shows small reductions for supporters of the major parties, with much larger falls for those who support a minor party or none at all (at 16.5 and 11.2 percentage points, respectively). The only exception is for supporters of the third political party, the Liberal Democrats (which shows a very small increase, of 1.2 percent). The absence of party support data from the 1981 survey negates an examination of whether religious interventions against the policies of the Conservative governments in the 1980s had shifted supporters' attitudes in any way by 1990.

There is marked variations in the decline in confidence across groups classified according to their self-positioning on a left-right ideological scale. The largest decline is found among those with a right-wing position, who had the most confidence in 1981 (falling from 64.4 percent to 40.4 percent). This is a societal grouping that might be expected to traditionally support established social institutions. This ideological grouping may have grown disillusioned with religious bodies as they perceived them to be bastions of liberal or progressive thinking who do not stand up for traditional social values. They may have reacted negatively to the Church of England as a source of religious authority, in particular, after its public disagreements with the Conservative governments' social and economic policies during the 1980s (Martin 1989; Baker 1991; Filby 2010). As Machin notes:

> ... many Church leaders became known from 1980 as outspoken critics of government economic and social policy. They have appeared as defenders of the former party political 'consensus' and the State interventionist attitudes to social policy which was condemned by the Thatcherite, 'New Right', free-enterprise approach in the late 1970s and 1980s (1998: 226).

In contrast, smaller declines are evident amongst those with left-wing and centrist positions on this scale (3.4 and 11.3 percentage points, respectively).

In Table 2.5, equivalent data are shown for groups classified by various measures of belonging, behaving and believing. In broad terms, there are declines in confidence across nearly all groups, regardless of the measure used. Amongst religious traditions, the largest absolute decrease has been amongst Catholics (at 10.0 percentage points), although they are more likely in 2008 to have confidence than Church of England affiliates (as is also the case in every survey year). Averaging the differences between Catholics and Anglicans over the four surveys, the score is 18.0 percentage points. In recent decades, then, Catholics have consistently expressed higher confidence in the church than have Anglicans.

Bucking the main trend, those who belong to some other religious tradition (whether Christian or non-Christian) actually showed an increase in levels of confidence, rising from 58.9 percent in 1981 to 65.6 percent in 2008. Examining the group in more detail shows that members of non-Christian religions have somewhat higher levels of confidence than other Christians (respectively, 69.7 percent and 58.6 percent in 2008). Overall, this group shows more positive evaluations than both Anglicans (by a long way) and Catholics (by some way) on the most recent reading. There has been hardly any change in the views of those with no religion over time, which is not unexpected given this group's very low levels of confidence from the outset (16.5 percent in 1981 and 15.6 percent in 2008). In terms of attending services, the largest declines come from those who report attending infrequently (12.9 percentage points) or not at all (10.5 percentage points), compared to a smaller fall for those attending often (at

Table 2.5 Percent with confidence in the church, by religious group, 1981–2008

Variable	Category	1981 (%)	1990 (%)	1999 (%)	2008 (%)	Change
Belonging	Church of England[a]	48.5	56.7	30.1	42.0	−6.5
	Catholic	66.4	69.3	57.1	56.4	−10.0
	Other religion	58.9	56.5	38.2	65.6	+6.7
	No religion	16.5	21.2	7.1	15.6	−0.9
	Member of a religious organisation	85.3	76.6	33.9	83.1	−2.2
	Not a member of a religious organisation	38.4	36.3	31.9	28.3	−10.1
	Is a religious person	67.5	64.9	62.4	61.5	−6.0
	Is not a religious person/is a convinced atheist	24.6	16.9	15.6	14.8	−9.8
Behaving	Frequent-attender	83.0	81.0	83.2	78.2	−4.8
	Infrequent-attender	56.2	46.2	39.0	43.3	−12.9
	Non-attender	27.3	21.1	13.7	16.8	−10.5
Believing	Believes in God	60.3	56.9	47.8	52.5	−7.8
	Does not believe in God	7.7	8.2	8.9	9.2	+1.5
	There is a personal God	71.0	69.9	60.8	67.1	−3.9
	There is no personal God/other response	38.2	29.3	21.3	24.3	−13.9

Source: EVS surveys.
[a]Note that this category for the 1981 survey covers Protestant traditions apart from Nonconformists. For all subsequent surveys, Nonconformists and other Christian traditions fall within the 'other Christian' category.
Note: Combines 'a great deal of confidence' and 'quite a lot of confidence'.

4.8 percentage points). There has been a greater decline in confidence amongst those who do not belong to a religious organisation (10.1 percentage points) and those who do not consider themselves to be a religious person (9.8 percentage points) compared to, respectively, those who belong to a religious group and those who see themselves as a religious person. There has been a greater decline in confidence amongst those who believe in God (7.8 percentage points) compared to those who do not, but this is partly due to the very low levels of confidence held by the latter group (just 7.7 percent in 1981 and 9.2 percent in 2008), the lowest of any group in Tables 2.4 and 2.5.

However, for belief in a personal God, the decline has been largest amongst those who do not believe in a personal God (at 13.9 percentage points), and confidence has held up reasonably well amongst those who do think there is a personal God.

Confidence in the church and other institutions

Next, overall public confidence in the church is compared to the levels expressed in other societal institutions. Previous studies have argued that any measurable declines in confidence in religious institutions may form part of a broader social climate in recent decades of growing disillusionment with national institutions in various spheres – politics and public administration, civil society, the economy, as well as religion. Indeed, Hoffman's analysis of public attitudes towards societal institutions in the US showed that 'There is little evidence that declining confidence is unique to religious organisations and their leaders' (2013: 22). He further notes that:

> In general, then, secularization, if it has occurred among some groups, is not a unique or independent trend in American society. Instead, it is simply one element of a more complex process that has led to a general decline in confidence and trust in institutions (2013: 22).

The EVS surveys can be used to perform a similar exercise for Britain, as they have all asked about confidence in various national institutions. The number of institutions asked about has varied across surveys, but there are a core of nine institutions (including the church) included in each survey. These are shown in Table 2.6, which again presents the combined percentages having 'a great deal' or 'quite a lot' of confidence in each institution. The final row also reports a 'pan-institutional' average (excluding the church), which shows overall confidence across the other eight bodies included in each survey. It is evident that, in each survey year, levels of confidence vary dramatically, being very high for the armed forces, police and education system, and much lower for the press and trade unions. Some institutions see a clear decline in levels of confidence between 1981 and 2008, such as the press, police, parliament, justice system and, less so, the civil service. Others see little change or a slight improvement in their fortunes, such as the armed forces, education system and the trade unions. The church belongs in the former group, experiencing a clear decline in levels of confidence, from 48.6 percent in 1981 to

Table 2.6   Percent with confidence in national institutions, 1981–2008

	1981 (%)	1990 (%)	1999 (%)	2008 (%)	Change
Church	48.6	42.8	33.1	35.0	−13.6
Armed forces	82.1	81.2	81.8	86.8	+4.7
Education system	61.6	47.4	65.0	67.6	+6.0
The press	29.5	13.8	15.7	15.2	−14.3
Trade unions	26.8	26.0	25.7	27.3	+0.5
Police	86.8	77.1	68.8	68.0	−18.8
Parliament	41.2	46.1	34.2	22.5	−18.7
Civil service	49.5	44.4	42.0	40.5	−9.0
Justice system	66.5	53.6	48.0	49.5	−17.0
Inter-institutional average[a]	55.5	48.7	47.7	47.2	−8.3

Source: EVS surveys.
[a]Excluding confidence in the 'church'.
Note: Combines 'a great deal of confidence' and 'quite a lot of confidence'.

35.0 percent in 2008. Relative to the institutional average, it performs worse in the two later surveys. Its confidence levels are always lower than the institutional average but more so for 1999 (33.1 percent compared to 47.7 percent) and 2008 (35.0 percent compared to 47.2 percent). Another way of looking at this is to note the stability in the overall average between 1990, 1999 and 2008, while confidence in the church falls markedly between 1990 and 1999 (from 42.8 percent to 33.1 percent), only recovering slightly between 1999 and 2008. The averages fall for both the church and pan-institutionally between 1981 and 1990. The church occupies the same relative ranking in 2008 as in 1981: at sixth place, enjoying higher confidence levels than the press, trade unions and parliament, but lower levels than all other institutions.

Therefore, the EVS surveys tend to show that declining confidence in the church seems to be part of a broader shift towards greater scepticism towards – and the declining credibility of – other, though not all, national institutions. The EVS data seem to show a trend similar to that found by Hoffman (2013) for US public opinion. On the one hand, there is no uniform and consistent trend of a major decline confidence in every institution over time, but, on the other, there is little evidence that declining confidence is unique to the church as a social institution in recent decades. What has occurred to the church has also happened to parliament, the police, the press, the civil service and the justice system.

Next, a more detailed profile of contemporary attitudes is undertaken. Specifically, multivariate analysis is conducted to see which individual characteristics correlate with confidence in the church in Britain, using data from the 2008 EVS survey. This survey had a sample size of 1,549 and the data are weighted. The factors examined are socio-demographic traits, religious factors (measures of belonging, behaving and believing) and party-political support. The dependent variable is a binary measure constructed by scoring the responses 'a great deal' and 'quite a lot' as 1 and 'not very much' and 'none at all' as 0. 'Don't know' responses (3.6 percent of the sample) are treated as missing data and omitted from the analysis. Given the nature of the dependent variable, binary logistic regression is used. Details on how the independent variables are measured are provided in Appendix 2. Note that the measure of social class differs from that used in Table 2.4 (which is based on the ABC1C2DE scheme), as a different classification was used in the 2008 survey. Two separate models are estimated: first, a parsimonious specification which includes socio-demographic factors (namely: sex, age, marital status, presence of children in the household, education and occupation), some of which are traditionally associated with higher levels of religious identity and religiosity; second, a fuller specification which includes different measures of religious orientation, as well as party-political support. The results are presented in Table 2.7.

Looking first at the results for the limited model specification, collectively socio-demographic factors account for little of the variance in trust in religious institutions (just 4.0 percent). Some factors do have significant effects, however. Men are less likely to have confidence in the church than women, while older people are more likely to have higher levels of confidence. Those who are married are also more likely to have confidence in the church. There are no significant effects for the measures of socio-economic status (education or occupation), or for having children in the individual's household.

Next a fuller model is estimated, which includes a set of variables measuring religious orientations as well as measures of party support. The first thing to notice is that the effects of the socio-structural variables from the limited model disappear once the effects of religion are accounted for. That is, age, sex and marital status do not have a significant impact in the second estimation. However, with the other variables added, the proportion of variance explained increases tenfold, to 43.0 percent (as reported in the Nagelkere R Square statistic). There are only weak effects for religious affiliation. The only significant

Table 2.7 Binary logistic regression analyses of confidence in the church

Variable	Limited model B (SE)		Limited model Odds ratio	Full model B (SE)		Full model Odds ratio
Sex	.29*	(.11)	1.34	−.09	(.14)	.92
Age	.01*	(.00)	1.02	.00	(.00)	1.00
Marital status	.28*	(.12)	1.32	.03	(.15)	1.03
Children in household	−.07	(.14)	.93	−.08	(.18)	.92
Education	.22	(.14)	1.24	.09	(.18)	1.10
Occupation	.02	(.13)	1.02	−.15	(.16)	.86
Anglican				.21	(.18)	1.23
Catholic				.28	(.24)	1.32
Other Christian				.18	(.32)	1.20
Other religion				.55	(.30)	1.74
Attendance				.29*	(.05)	1.34
Membership				.88*	(.27)	2.41
Identity				−.89*	(.17)	.41
Belief in God				.95*	(.19)	2.60
Conservative				−.08	(.18)	.93
Labour				.38	(.20)	1.46
Liberal Democrat				.56*	(.25)	1.75
Other party				−.18	(.27)	.83
Constant	−1.58* (.18)		.21	−.98*	(.45)	.37
Weighted N	1,459			1,431		
Nagelkerke R Square	.04			.04		

Note: *$p<.05$ or lower.
Reference categories: no religion; non-party identifier.
Source: EVS 2008 survey.

impact is for those affiliated with non-Christian faiths, who are more likely to have confidence in religious institutions compared to those with no religion (odds ratio: 1.75). There are stronger effects for behaving (attendance), believing (belief in God), broader identity (being a religious person) and membership of a church or other group (a stricter measure of belonging). Those who attend religious services more frequently are more likely to have confidence in religious institutions, as are those who are members of religious organisations (odds ratio: 2.41) and those who believe in God (odds ratio: 2.59). Interestingly, those who possess a religious identity in general terms are less likely to have confidence in religious institutions (odds ratio: 0.41). Greater personal engagement with faith tends to usually – if not always – underpin higher confidence in religious institutions.

The results for the party support variables show that, compared to those with no party affiliation, it is clear Liberal Democrat supporters are more likely to have confidence in the church. However, Conservative Party supporters do not significantly differ from the reference category (those who do not support a party), and neither do supporters of minor parties. The left-right ideological scale was omitted from the multivariate analyses presented here due to the considerable proportion of missing data for this measure (20.5 percent of the sample). Additional multivariate analysis, which included the left-right scale as an additional independent variable, showed it did not have a significant impact on confidence in religious institutions. Based on the evidence from the EVS survey, contemporary British attitudes towards trust in religious institutions are driven largely by religious factors, although there are also differences based on party-political affiliations.[2]

Attitudes towards the Church of England and the Roman Catholic Church

So it is clear that there has been both aggregate change and group variation in levels of confidence in the church in Britain in recent decades. What about contemporary public views towards specific religious institutions, namely the Church of England and the Roman Catholic Church? It is important to explore appraisals of the two largest pillars of institutional Christianity. As Field observes in relation to the Church of England:

> But since the 1990s Anglicanism's struggle to 'modernize' its thinking about sexual orientation and gender roles has adversely affected public attitudes to the church of England, its stances on same-sex marriage and women bishops latterly being especially problematical for many adults (2014c: 202).

Similarly, the Catholic Church's 'reputation has undoubtedly diminished, largely in consequence of negative reactions to the Church's conservative social ethics ... Even more damaging have been revelations of child sex abuse at the hands of priests and the Church's perceived inadequate responses to them' (Field, 2014b: 203).

Analysis is undertaken of contemporary attitudes towards both institutions using data from a nationally-representative survey conducted by YouGov in March 2013. This posed separate questions about the Church of England and the Roman Catholic Church, asking whether

Table 2.8 Attitudes towards the Church of England and the Roman Catholic Church

	Church of England (%)	Roman Catholic Church (%)
Very in touch	1.6	0.7
Fairly in touch	19.2	8.6
Fairly out of touch	39.5	29.9
Very out of touch	21.4	47.2
Not sure	18.2	13.6

Source: YouGov survey of adults in Britain adults, 14–15 March 2013.

they are 'in touch' or 'out of touch', which can be used as another indicator of the public standing of religious institutions. The overall distribution of responses to these questions is shown in Table 2.8.

For both institutions, the picture is a gloomy one. The proportion of the British public thinking that either church is 'in touch' to some degree is just 20.8 percent for the Church of England and, even lower, 9.3 percent for the Roman Catholic Church. While positive assessments of the Church of England are very low, more than double think it is 'in touch' compared to the Roman Catholic Church. Of course, the overall distribution of opinion can hide group variation, so data for social and attitudinal factors (including religious affiliation) are shown in Table 2.9. As might be expected, the most positive assessments are found amongst 'the faithful' for each denomination. Amongst those affiliated to the Church of England, around a third believe it to be 'in touch' compared with a quarter of Catholics expressing this sentiment for their institution. Large majorities of both Anglicans and Catholics therefore have negative views of their respective institutions' relevance to modern society. Negative assessments are even higher for those belonging to other denominations or non-Christian faiths and higher still for those with no religion (at 11.6 percent and 3.7 percent).

Are there also group variations based on other social factors? Results are reported for sex, age, ethnic background, education, social class and political party supported. In terms of evaluations of the Church of England, those more likely to think it is 'in touch' include older age cohorts (particularly those aged 75 and over), those from a minority ethnic group and those in the AB social group. Differences of view are much less evident based on sex or educational attainment. Differences between supporters of major parties are less evident – so, on this indicator at least, there is little support for the popular and

Table 2.9   Percent saying the Church of England and Roman Catholic Church are in touch, by socio-demographic group

		Church of England (%)	Roman Catholic Church (%)
Sex	Men	19.4	8.8
	Women	22.2	9.8
Age group	18–24	21.5	9.1
	25–34	17.0	8.2
	35–44	19.4	10.2
	45–54	19.6	7.3
	55–64	22.7	8.8
	65–74	24.6	14.0
	75+	32.6	7.0
Ethnic group	White British	19.8	8.2
	Other group	28.1	19.2
Education	Degree-level	22.5	10.6
	Below degree-level	20.4	9.1
Social grade	AB	25.3	11.4
	C1	20.9	9.9
	C2	17.6	5.2
	DE	18.3	9.9
Party support	Conservative	22.5	9.7
	Labour	20.8	9.6
	Liberal Democrat	26.5	12.6
	Other party	12.3	12.3
	No party	17.2	6.5
Religious affiliation	Anglican	33.2	11.7
	Catholic	23.8	25.0
	Other Christian	22.9	15.1
	Other religion	23.9	14.4
	No religion	11.6	3.7

Source: YouGov survey of adults in Britain adults, 14–15 March 2013.
Note: Combines 'very in touch' and 'fairly in touch'.

long-standing description of the Church of England being the 'Conservative Party at prayer'! However, minor party supporters are less likely to think the Church of England is 'in touch'. There is generally less variation across social groups in terms of views of the Catholic Church, with favourable impressions peaking amongst those aged 65–74 years and older (14.0 percent) and those from minority ethnic groups (19.2 percent). Again, there is little variation in opinion between men and women or based on having a degree-level qualification or not.

Separate multivariate analyses were undertaken for perceptions of the Church of England and the Roman Catholic Church, including all of the factors shown in Tables 2.8–2.9. The results (not reported in detail here) showed that *all* religious groups – Christian or otherwise – were more likely to think that, respectively, the Church of England and the Roman Catholic Church were in touch, compared to those with no religion. Additionally, men and those belonging to a white ethnic group were less likely to perceive the Church of England as being in touch, while supporters of the Liberal Democrat party had more positive views (compared to those who did not support a party). Those with a white ethnic background were also less likely to have positive views of the Catholic Church. Again, Liberal Democrat supporters held more positive perceptions.

The very low levels perceiving the Catholic Church to be 'in touch' will of course reflect recent events which have not reflected well on the institution or its leaders, such as its perceived mishandling of child sex abuse scandals in various countries as well as unpopularity amongst grassroots adherents of its moralistic social teachings on issues such as contraception, celibacy, homosexuality and abortion (see Clements 2014e; Woodhead 2013a). Similarly, other polls tend to show negative perceptions of the church and its leaders heavily outweighing favourable evaluations. A cross-national poll undertaken in February 2013 in the wake of the resignation of Pope Benedict found that, in Britain, 33.0 percent of those polled perceived Catholic leaders to play a negative role in their country's life (much lower for Catholics, at 14.0 percent, who differed from other Christians, at 29.0 percent). For Protestant bishops and archbishops, the proportion with a negative stance was considerably lower, at 22.0 percent (at 13.0 percent for other Christians and 15.0 percent for Catholics) (YouGov 2013).

Public attitudes towards the involvement of religious leaders in politics

One aspect of secularisation involves religion losing authority and influence in the sphere of politics (Bruce 2012: 164). Long-term polling data indeed show that religion has been perceived by the public to have lost influence in the post-war era. When asked 'Speaking generally, which would you say has more influence on the way people live and their circumstances, religion or politics?' in the period between 1948 and 1996, the proportion who thought religion had more influence on the way people lived and their circumstances halved from 26.0 percent to 13.0 percent, while the proportion thinking this about politics nearly doubled, rising from 37.0 percent to 68.0 percent.

Between 1948 and 1964, the proportion mentioning 'religion' stayed reasonably constant, with values of 27.0 percent (1948), 30.0 percent (1957) and 26.0 percent (1964). The decline occurred in the lengthy period between 1964 and 1996.

In recent decades, successive governments of different party-political stripes have had to respond to concerns or criticisms made in the public domain about actual or proposed policies by, most prominently, senior Anglican or Catholic archbishops. These often high-profile and sometimes controversial interventions have ranged across different policy areas, both domestic and foreign. Notable instances of intervention by bishops in recent times include: opposition from within the Church of England to the Thatcher governments' economic and welfare policies in the 1980s (Martin 1989); opposition to the invasion of Iraq in 2003 from leaders of the Anglican and Catholic churches (Bates 2003; Alden 2002); and opposition to recent government's same-sex equality measures from leaders of Christian denominations and minority faiths (such as gay adoption rights, civil partnerships and, most recently, same-sex marriage).

Other issues may periodically arouse the attention and ire of the leaders of particular traditions, such as the question of abortion for the Catholic Church. In recent years, religious leaders have also made pronouncements about the alleged growing marginalisation and disrespect for religious belief and institutions present in wider society and, related to this, the supposed ill-effects of processes of secularisation (Butt 2011). What, then, does the British public currently think about the involvement of religious leaders or institutions in British politics? Building on recent research (Glendinning and Bruce 2011; Glendinning 2014), the detailed modules on religion included in the 1991, 1998 and 2008 BSA surveys are used to analyse public attitudes towards the role of religion in politics. As already stated at the outset, one of the ways in which religion loses its social significance through secularisation is through the diminishing of its political power (Bruce 2012),

Aggregate-level trends

To look in more detail at public opinion on the political role of religion, two questions from the BSA surveys are used which asked about levels of agreement or disagreement with religious leaders influencing the government (what might be labelled *elite-level influence*) or voters (what might be termed *mass-level influence*). The question wordings are as follows:

Religious leaders should not try to influence government decisions. Strongly agree. Agree. Neither agree nor disagree. Disagree. Strongly disagree. Can't choose.

Religious leaders should not try to influence how people vote in elections. Strongly agree. Agree. Neither agree nor disagree. Disagree. Strongly disagree. Can't choose.

Agreement with either of the propositions contained in these questions therefore indicates opposition to religious leaders influencing political leaders or how citizens vote. The overall distribution of opinion for these two questions is given in Table 2.10 (for government) and Table 2.11 (for voters). At the outset there is a clear majority opposition to religious leaders exerting influence in the political process; unfortunately, earlier data are not available in order to ascertain whether this represents a change from opinion in previous decades.

In terms of religious leaders influencing government, there has been a clear increase in the proportion disapproving of this elite-level channel of influence (who either 'strongly agree' or 'agree'): rising from 57.3 percent in 1991 to 64.6 percent in 1998; and then increasing to 68.9 percent in 2008. Conversely, the proportion who 'strongly disagree' or 'disagree' with the proposition has fallen from 23.4 percent in 1998 to 14.2 percent in 2008. There has been a more modest increase in the overall proportion that agree or strongly agree that it is wrong for religious leaders to influence voting behaviour (by 4.2 percentage points between 1991 and 2008). The proportion disagreeing to some extent has fallen by 5.9 percentage points. In all survey years, there is greater opposition to religious leaders attempting to influence voters than governments, but the gap narrows by 2008. While 71.6 percent disagree with the influencing of voters in 1991 compared to 57.3 percent opposed to influencing government (a gap of 14.3 percentage points), in 2008 levels of opposition are, respectively, 75.8 percent and 68.9 percent (with the gap more than halving to 6.9 percentage points).

The greater degree of agreement with the question on religious leaders may partly reflect heightened public perceptions of religious groups actively campaigning to influence government policy in recent years on social or equality issues (Kettell 2009), where legislation has been perceived by faith groups to be undermining particular moral beliefs or traditions or impinging on their freedom of conscience. Based on the evidence presented in Tables 2.10 and 2.11, there is

Table 2.10   Attitudes towards religious leaders influencing government, 1991–2008

	1991 (%)	1998 (%)	2008 (%)	Change
Strongly agree	22.0	32.4	39.1	+17.1
Agree	35.3	32.2	29.8	–5.5
Total agree	57.3	64.6	68.9	+11.6
Neither	15.9	12.0	14.2	–1.7
Disagree	16.4	15.8	9.5	–6.9
Strongly disagree	7.0	5.5	4.7	–2.3
Total disagree	23.4	21.3	14.2	–9.2
Can't choose	3.3	2.1	2.8	–0.5

Source: BSA surveys.

Table 2.11   Attitudes towards religious leaders influencing how people vote, 1991–2008

	1991 (%)	1998 (%)	2008 (%)	Change
Strongly agree	32.7	40.6	45.2	+12.5
Agree	38.9	32.1	30.6	–8.3
Total agree	71.6	72.7	75.8	+4.2
Neither	7.9	9.6	10.0	+2.1
Disagree	10.7	10.2	6.4	–4.3
Strongly disagree	6.9	5.4	5.3	–1.6
Total disagree	17.6	15.6	11.7	–5.9
Can't choose	2.8	2.2	2.5	–0.3

Source: BSA surveys.

evidence for 'declining religious authority' (Chaves 1994), as expressed in greater disapproval for religious leaders' exerting influence in the political process, at the elite and mass levels.

Group attitudes

Given this change in aggregate-level opinion, it is worthwhile analysing group variation in attitudes, as already undertaken for the EVS data on religious authority. In particular, is there evidence to lend support to a generational pattern of religious change, with successive generations less religious than the next, thereby implying some inevitability about long-term decline regarding religion's political power and authority. Do younger age groups prove to be less accepting of religious involvement in the political process?

Table 2.12 (socio-demographic characteristics) and Table 2.13 (religious factors) present a breakdown of attitudes towards influencing government. Looking first at the results for age groups, there is no real evidence supporting a generational pattern of change, whereby the younger cohorts show the greatest change on this question. There has, in fact, been an increase in opposition to religious leaders influencing government across all age groups. Specifically, while those aged 18–24 increased their agreement by 8.7 percentage points, this was half as much as those aged 25–34 (at 16.6 percentage points). There were similar increases to the latter amongst the 35–44 and 55–64 cohorts. Agreement rose only slightly amongst those aged 45–54, at just 2.9 percentage points. Agreement also increased, by modest amounts, amongst those aged 65–74 and 75 and older (respectively, 5.3 and 7.3 percentage points).

In Table 2.12, the groups exhibiting the largest increases in agreement include men (15.9 percentage points), those with a degree-level qualification (31.5 percentage points), and Labour and Liberal Democrat supporters (21.0 and 16.3 percentage points, respectively).

Table 2.12 **Percent who disagree with religious leaders trying to influence government, by socio-demographic group, 1991–2008**

		1991 (%)	1998 (%)	2008 (%)	Change
Sex	Men	54.6	65.1	70.5	+15.9
	Women	59.7	64.1	67.2	+7.5
Age group	18–24	54.4	80.6	63.1	+8.7
	25–34	56.4	70.1	73.0	+16.6
	35–44	52.9	60.2	70.3	+17.4
	45–54	64.3	59.4	67.2	+2.9
	55–64	51.8	60.0	68.5	+16.7
	65–74	60.5	62.2	65.8	+5.3
	75+	65.5	67.7	72.8	+7.3
Education	Degree-level	37.3	45.3	68.8	+31.5
	Lower than degree-level	59.5	66.7	68.8	+9.3
Occupation	Non-manual	54.5	63.8	69.4	+14.9
	Manual	61.5	64.2	69.9	+8.4
Party support	Conservative	66.6	72.0	69.9	+3.3
	Labour	49.5	63.9	70.5	+21.0
	Liberal Democrat	51.5	58.0	67.8	+16.3
	Other party	60.7	52.6	64.4	+3.7
	No party	53.4	61.3	66.1	+12.7

Source: BSA surveys.
Note: Combines 'strongly agree' and 'agree'.

Table 2.13 **Percent who disagree with religious leaders trying to influence government, by religious group, 1991–2008**

		1991 (%)	1998 (%)	2008 (%)	Change
Belonging	Anglicans	56.8	59.8	68.0	+11.2
	Catholic	56.3	55.7	61.0	+4.7
	Other religion	48.7	51.2	60.1	+11.4
	No religion	63.2	74.0	75.3	+12.1
Behaving	Frequent-attender	42.0	41.0	52.4	+10.4
	Infrequent-attender	58.3	65.0	65.7	+7.4
	Non-attender	62.5	72.2	74.4	11.9
Belief in God (1)	Believes in God	51.1	56.7	62.6	+11.5
	Does not believe in God	68.6	75.8	76.5	+7.9
Belief in God (2)	Believes in God	46.4	48.0	51.9	+5.5
	Other response	59.0	68.9	71.0	+12.0
	Does not believe in God	69.7	70.5	77.7	+8.0
Concerned God	Agree	47.6	54.2	55.4	+7.8
	Neither	61.6	67.2	69.1	+7.5
	Disagree	63.8	73.3	80.5	+16.7
Life is meaningful	Agree	45.3	43.1	51.0	+5.7
	Neither	54.8	62.6	62.5	+7.7
	Disagree	62.0	71.8	77.0	+15.0

Source: BSA surveys.
Note: Combines 'strongly agree' and 'agree'.

The increase for Conservative partisans is comparatively minor, at 3.3 percentage points, along with 3.7 percentage points for minor party supporters. The relatively high levels of agreement for Conservative Party supporters expressed in Table 2.12 from the first survey conducted in 1991 might reflect an aversion to political interference from church leaders which is partly related to the high-profile criticisms of the domestic policies of the Thatcher governments during the 1980s, most notably from leading clergy within the Church of England (Filby 2010).

Based on the data for religious groups, Table 2.13 shows that, perhaps surprisingly, there are also clear increases across the religious groups, with similar rises for Anglicans, members of non-Christian faiths and those with no religion. Catholics register the smallest increase (at 4.7 percentage points). There are similar increases by frequency of attendance at religious services (slightly lower in magnitude for infrequent attenders). Even so, in 2008, those who attend services often are much less likely to agree compared to those who attend less often or not at all. This difference by attendance is larger than that which exists between those with a religious affiliation and those without. All of the measures of belief in and conceptions of God show increases in levels of agreement over time. Even so, in 2008, as in previous years, those who believe in God, who believe there is an engaged God, and for whom live is meaningful only because of God's existence, are less likely to agree that it is wrong for religious leaders to try and influence the government. Further evidence for belief is provided by several additional questions first included in the BSA 2008 survey which asked about belief in and personal engagement with God (attitudinal data based on these questions for this and subsequent chapters are reported in Appendix 3). The highest levels of agreement are expressed by those who answered don't believe in God in response to the questions asking about the involvement of God in the respondents' affairs and whether God is angered by human sin. There is little variation in attitudes in response to the question asking whether individuals have their own way of connecting with God outside of more formal religious settings.

Table 2.14 (for socio-demographic factors) and Table 2.15 (for religious factors) present data for attitudes towards religious leaders trying to influence voters. They show more modest increases over time across social groups. Some groups do stand out for increasing their levels of agreement, including men (7.1 percentage points), those with a degree (12.6 percentage points), Labour supporters (12.8 percentage points) and minor party supporters (9.1 percentage points). The increases for age are smaller in Table 2.14, but again there is increased agreement across the younger and older age groups. The increase is largest for those aged 25–34 (11.8 percentage points).

In terms of religious factors (shown in Table 2.15), all groups show small increases over time, but these are generally lower in absolute terms than those evident in Table 2.13. Again, based on the 2008 survey, the gap in levels of agreement is larger for attendance at religious services than it is for religious affiliation. For the different measures of believing, the differences are evident for all four indicators, with those who believe in god, who think there is an engaged God, and for whom God makes life meaningful, less likely to express agreement in 2008, as in the previous years. Nearly all groups classified by belief show some increase in agreement over time, although they are generally of a small or very small magnitude. Finally, looking at the additional questions on God in the BSA 2008 survey, it is clear that, with regards to the question on influencing voters, agreement is

Table 2.14   **Percent who disagree with religious leaders trying to influence how people vote, by socio-demographic group, 1991–2008**

Variable	Category	1991 (%)	1998 (%)	2008 (%)	Change
Sex	Men	70.1	70.9	77.2	+7.1
	Women	73.0	74.0	74.6	+1.6
Age group	18–24	72.5	86.1	69.4	–3.1
	25–34	66.1	71.4	77.9	+11.8
	35–44	74.2	72.3	75.5	+1.3
	45–54	78.1	70.8	74.8	–3.3
	55–64	72.7	73.2	79.5	+6.8
	65–74	67.8	71.1	76.3	+8.5
	75+	69.0	65.1	76.1	+7.1
Education	Degree-level	67.5	64.6	80.1	+12.6
	Lower than degree-level	72.2	73.6	74.8	+2.6
Occupation	Non-manual	74.4	75.4	77.9	+3.5
	Manual	69.3	69.4	73.7	+4.4
Party support	Conservative	81.4	79.9	80.8	–0.6
	Labour	62.2	69.0	75.0	+12.8
	Liberal Democrat	72.6	73.6	72.1	–0.5
	Other party	70.0	73.7	79.1	+9.1
	No party	67.0	72.7	70.7	+3.7

Source: BSA surveys.
Note: Combines 'strongly agree' and 'agree'.

highest amongst those who do not believe in God – for the questions on an involved God and an angry God – and particularly when compared to those who think that God is directly involved in their affairs and those who think that God is angered by sinful activity (shown in Appendix 3).

Building on this analysis of over-time BSA survey data, contemporary attitudes are analysed in greater detail. Data are employed from a nationally-representative survey undertaken by YouGov in March 2013. Bruce's review of polling in Britain in the last two decades or so showed that there was a:

> Strong preference in favour of religious leaders speaking out on 'political issues which they are concerned about', *though we cannot know if this reflects likely agreement with church views or a principled commitment to free speech* (2012: 66) (emphasis added).

Given this important caveat is stressed, therefore, caution needs to be exercised when using a single indicator of attitudes towards the

Table 2.15 Percent who disagree with religious leaders trying to influence how people vote, by religious group, 1991–2008

		1991 (%)	1998 (%)	2008 (%)	Change
Belonging	Anglican	71.5	69.5	75.2	+3.7
	Catholic	69.5	64.8	73.2	+3.7
	Other religion	67.7	66.2	73.2	+5.5
	No religion	74.8	78.2	78.1	+3.3
Behaving	Frequent-attender	62.4	61.8	68.8	+6.4
	Infrequent-attender	75.5	72.2	75.7	+0.2
	Non-attender	72.9	76.4	77.5	+4.6
Belief in God (1)	Believes in God	68.2	69.7	73.4	+5.2
	Does not believe in God	78.2	78.1	79.5	+1.3
Belief in God (2)	Believes in God	63.0	64.7	67.0	+4.0
	Conditional response	74.2	75.5	77.5	+3.3
	Does not believe in God	78.7	71.2	79.3	+0.6
Concerned God	Agree	66.6	67.7	69.3	+2.7
	Neither	73.9	75.0	76.0	+2.1
	Disagree	79.4	77.4	82.6	+3.2
	Agree	65.2	60.7	65.9	+0.7
Life is meaningful	Neither	71.3	69.6	71.2	−0.1
	Disagree	76.6	80.0	81.6	+5.0

Source: BSA surveys.
Note: Combines 'strongly agree' and 'agree'.

involvement of religious leaders in politics. The question wording from the YouGov survey is as follows:

> More generally, do you think it is right or wrong for Bishops and senior clergyman to comment on political issues and government policies?
> Right – the church has a useful and important role to play in public discussion of government policies and should be free to speak its mind
> Wrong – it is not appropriate for unelected bishops to speak on political issues, they should remain neutral and not comment on politics and government policies

Public opinion was evenly distributed on this question, with 43.5 percent thinking it is right and 43.1 percent thinking it is wrong (with a small proportion unsure, at 13.4 percent). This question followed one asking respondents about a specific and topical instance of intervention in political debate by the Archbishop of Canterbury. This occurred over proposals to reform the welfare system put forward by the Conservative-Liberal Democrat coalition government, with public criticism of the proposals made by the Archbishop (specifically in relation to the imposition of a cap on social security benefits to keep them rising below the level of inflation).

Again, it is worthwhile examining the attitudes of various social groups, again defined by social, religious and political factors. Table 2.16 presents the proportion saying 'right' for each group. Specifically, it shows results for the following factors: sex, age group, ethnic background, education, social class, party support (measured as current vote intention) and religious affiliation.

Table 2.16   Percent saying it is right for religious leaders to comment on political issues and government policies, by socio-demographic group

Variable	Category	%
Sex	Men	45.9
	Women	41.2
Age group	18–24	35.3
	25–34	36.6
	35–44	45.1
	45–54	47.2
	55–64	43.7
	65–74	49.6
	75+	60.5
Ethnic group	White British	43.0
	Other group	46.1
Education	Degree-level	55.4
	Below degree-level	39.6
Social grade	AB	47.5
	C1	41.5
	C2	39.5
	DE	45.0
Party support	Conservative	31.7
	Labour	54.8
	Liberal Democrat	53.8
	Other party	45.7
	No party	3.8
Religious affiliation	Anglican	48.3
	Catholic	57.7
	Other Christian	46.7
	Other religion	51.3
	No religion	36.5

Source: YouGov survey of adults in Britain adults, 14–15 March 2013.

Table 2.17   Binary logistic regression of public attitudes towards the
involvement of religious leaders in politics

Variable	B (SE)		Odds ratio
Sex	.11	(.11)	1.12
Ethnic group	.03	(.22)	1.04
Age	.00	(.00)	1.00
Degree	.72*	(.13)	2.05
Social grade: AB	−.16	(.16)	.85
Social grade: C1	−.29	(.16)	.75
Social grade: C2	−.22	(.17)	.80
Anglican	.81*	(.13)	2.24
Catholic	.98*	(.21)	2.66
Other Christian	.54*	(.23)	1.71
Other religion	.75*	(.26)	2.11
Labour	1.46*	(.15)	4.31
Lib Dem	1.21*	(.21)	3.36
Other party	.81*	(.18)	2.24
None	.71*	(.16)	2.04
Constant	−1.52*	(.32)	.22
Weighted N		1,586	
Nagelkerke R Square		.15	

Note: *p<.05 or lower.
Reference categories: social grade: DE; does not have a religion; Conservative Party supporter.
Source: YouGov survey of adults in Britain 2013.

Higher support for the involvement of church leaders in politics
comes from those aged 65 and over, those with a degree-level education, and those supporting the Labour and Liberal Democrat parties.
The differences are much less evident for sex and ethnic group. As
might be expected, given the wider party-political context at the time,
with their party the major partner in the coalition administration,
there are lower levels of approval of the Archbishop's intervention
from Conservative supporters. In terms of attitudes based on religious
belonging, approval is highest amongst Catholics (at 57.7 percent), followed by members of non-Christian faiths (at 51.3 percent). Anglicans
and other Christians show similar levels of support (at, respectively,
48.3 percent and 46.7 percent), while those with no religion are much
less likely to support the intervention of religious leaders or senior
clergy (36.5 percent). There is somewhat of a division therefore
between those with a religious affiliation and those without.

Given these religious divisions in group attitudes and the content
and political context of the question being asked, as a final step multivariate analysis is undertaken to see whether any other explanatory

factors – beyond religious belonging – affect opinion. Table 2.17 reports the results from a binary logistic regression analysis, where those who expressed a positive view of religious leaders' involvement in politics are coded as 1 and those who held a negative viewpoint are coded as 0. The expected effects are present for the religious groups. That is, there is a religious-secular divide with all religious groups (odds ratios: Anglicans: 2.24; Catholics: 2.66; other Christians: 1.71; and non-Christian minority faiths: 2.11) more supportive of religious leaders' involvement compared to those with no religion. Even though the religious affiliation variables have strong effects, other factors still have a significant impact. Specifically, those with a degree-level qualification are more likely to support political involvement by religious leaders, as are all party-political groups (compared to Conservative Party supporters).

Conclusion

This chapter provided a detailed analysis of public confidence in religious institutions, as well as attitudes towards the role played by religious leaders in the political process (at both the elite and mass levels). It examined both aggregate-level shifts over time as well as paying attention to group variation. The latter focus certainly showed that invariably, if not inevitably, social group changes in attitude were in the directions of less confidence in the church and less acceptance of a role for religious leaders in exerting influence at the elite or mass levels. It should be reiterated that while the direction of change was usually the same, the magnitude of change fluctuated from sizeable shifts to very minor fluctuations. Taken together, there was evidence in the British context, therefore, for the thesis that secularisation represents the 'decline of religious authority' (Chaves 1994; Hoffman 1998, 2013; Kleiman et al. 1996). This was manifested in falling levels of confidence in 'the church' for the 1981–2008 period, as well as greater disapproval of religious leaders influencing government and instructing individuals how to vote (for the 1991–2008 period). In short, the trend in British attitudes here shows that, to quote Hoffman (1998: 339), 'movement toward secularization has occurred'. The evidence presented here forms an important part of a broader, longer-term picture of declining religious authority in terms of institutional Christianity in Britain – both church and clergy – which has been delineated by existing research (Field 2014b).

The declining level of public confidence in the church occurred alongside a general pattern of wide-ranging decline across indicators of micro-level religious orientations – tapping into belonging, behaving and believing. However, the decline in popular standing of the church has not occurred in isolation; rather, it forms one aspect of a broader loss of reputation by some – but not all – national institutions in recent decades. Even so, more detailed analysis of contemporary attitudes also showed that religious factors formed the main explanatory underpinnings of confidence (or lack of) in religious institutions. The chapter has helped to both broaden and deepen understanding of one of the several levels of secularisation, namely 'general societal disenchantment with religious organisations and the authority that their leaders claim to have' (Hoffman 2013: 20).

3
Religion and Party Choice

This chapter looks in detail at the historical associations between religious groups and support for political parties in the post-war period. Throughout it mainly focuses on support for the two major parties in post-war British politics – Conservative and Labour – but also looks at support for the third party: the Liberal Party up to the 1970s, its 1980s alliance with the SDP, and its successor from 1988, the Liberal Democrats.[1] The relationship between religious groups and political parties represents one of the key pathways through which religion can affect politics. Heath et al. (1993a: 50) observe that:

> [M]embers of particular religions or denominations may nonetheless continue to identify with and support specific political parties, perhaps as a result of longstanding loyalties or associations ... In this sense the persistence of religious cleavages in contemporary political behaviour may be a relic of past political controversies.

For analysts of voting and elections in Britain, social class has been the primary social division structuring how votes are cast at general elections in the post-World War 2 era. As Pulzer famously summed up the key influence on voting and elections in this period: 'Class is the basis of British party politics; all else is embellishment and detail' (1967: 102). However, historically, religion has been an important social cleavage which structured party politics and electoral competition. Prior to social class becoming the dominant social cleavage, religious divisions had important consequences for electoral behaviour, being 'once the principal source of party division' (Butler and Stokes 1974: 155). Class and religion were two of the sources of 'frozen' social cleavages structuring party systems and electoral competition which

Lipset and Rokkan applied to countries in Western Europe, although religion was seen as of less importance for Britain compared to other nations (1967).

In Britain, the historic competition between Tories and Whigs reflected the division between the Church of England and Nonconformism. The Tories consistently opposed Whig efforts to remove Nonconformist disadvantages. From the 19th century and into the 20th century, there was a strong association between Nonconformism – that is, belonging to one of the free churches, such as the Methodists, Baptists, Congregationalists and Quakers – and electoral support for the Liberal Party (Koss 1975; Catterall 1993: 668). In the 20th century, with the decline of the Liberal Party as a major political force, Catholics were an important source of support for the Labour Party. As Hornsby-Smith observes: 'For historical reasons, largely grounded in differences between the political parties with respect to the Irish question, Catholics have disproportionately given their allegiance to the Labour Party' (1987: 164–5). Given this wider context, this chapter provides a longitudinal focus on the association between religion and voting behaviour in post-war Britain, building on and extending previous work in this area (Seawright 2000; Kotler-Berkowitz 2001; McAndrew 2010; Steven 2011a; Raymond 2013; Tilley 2014).

The chapter is divided into four main sections. The first section uses data from non-recurrent surveys to examine the association between religious affiliation and party choice in the early post-war period, the late 1940s and 1950s. The second section, using data from the BES surveys, provides a systematic assessment of the associations between religious groups and voting behaviour at post-war general elections, looking at the period 1959–2010. The third section, using data from the BSA surveys, then provides an assessment of religion and inter-election party support for the period 1983–2012. The fourth section provides a more detailed analysis of the contemporary associations between religion and party choice, undertaking multivariate analysis of BES and BSA data and assessing the relative impact of religious belonging and behaving within broader sociological models of party support.[2]

Religion and party support in the 1940s and 1950s

Limited survey sources can be used to examine the relationship between religious affiliation and party choice in the early post-war decades. Two sources are particularly useful for this task. First, data are used from two large-scale surveys (of over 6,000 respondents) of adults in Britain undertaken by Mass Observation for the *Daily Telegraph* in April–May 1948 and December 1955–January 1956. The data clearly illustrate the historical links between religious groups and the political parties in the early post-war period. The question asked did not specifically refer to voting behaviour but instead was worded as follows:

Which political party, if any, do you support?

The associations between Anglicans and the Conservative Party and Catholics and Labour are apparent in both surveys. Based on the 1948 survey, 52.0 percent of those who affiliated with the Church of England said they supported the Conservative Party (compared to 23.0 percent for Labour), while 41.0 percent of Catholics supported Labour (compared to 25.0 percent for the Conservatives). Church of Scotland affiliates were more likely to support the Conservative Party than Labour (40.0 percent and 28.0 percent, respectively). Across all groups, Nonconformists were most likely to say they supported the Liberal Party (at 18.0 percent). Similar associations were evident in the 1955–56 survey. Church of England affiliates divided 46.0 percent for the Conservatives and 30.0 percent for Labour, while Catholics were about twice as likely to support Labour (47.0 percent compared to 24.0 percent for the Conservatives). Nonconformists again showed the highest level of support for the Liberal Party (though at just 10.0 percent), while Church of Scotland affiliates were equally split between the two main parties (35.0 percent for both Labour and Conservative).[3] In both surveys, a plurality of those who did not have a religious affiliation supported the Labour party (38.0 percent in 1948 and 45.0 percent in 1955–56, compared to, respectively, 30.0 percent and 24.0 percent favouring the Conservative Party).

Second, the cross-country Civic Culture Study, conducted in 1959–60, with fieldwork for the British sample taking place in June–July 1959, can help shed further light on religion-party choice associations in the early post-war period. In the survey, respondents were asked about which party they had voted for at the last three national elections (information was also collected on religious affiliation). The fieldwork therefore occurred before the October 1959 general election (the three previous general elections having occurred in 1950, 1951 and 1955). Subject to some typical error in voter recall in social surveys, it can reasonably be presumed that many of the respondents were thinking of general elections in the 1950s (although 'national elections' could potentially elicit party choice in local elections taking place nationwide). The introductory question wording was as follows:

If you can remember, will you tell me how you voted in the last three national elections.

Respondents were then asked about the 'last national election', 'second election' and 'third election'. Party vote shares by religious affiliation are shown in Table 3.1, for 'Protestants' (the data cannot be further separated into Anglicans and Nonconformists), Catholics and those with no religion. The distribution of vote choice is fairly evenly split between Conservative and Labour at each of the three elections for Protestants. At the first national election, 49.1 percent of Protestants supported the Conservatives with 46.6 percent opting for Labour, while at the third election support for Labour was marginally higher at 48.7 percent (48.0 percent for the Conservatives). At each election, a clear majority of Catholics reported that they supported the Labour Party. At the first election they divided 57.1 percent voting Labour and 39.3 percent voting Conservative, while the differences were even more emphatic in the two other elections, with around two-thirds

Table 3.1   Vote choice in the last three national elections by affiliation

	Protestant (%)	Catholic (%)	None (%)
First election			
Con	49.1	39.3	40.0
Lab	46.6	57.1	56.2
Lib	3.4	3.6	3.8
Other	0.9	0.0	0.0
Second election			
Con	48.9	34.1	37.0
Lab	47.3	64.6	61.7
Lib	3.0	1.2	1.2
Other	0.9	0.0	0.0
Third election			
Con	48.0	31.2	38.0
Lab	48.7	64.9	60.8
Lib	2.4	2.6	1.3
Other	0.9	1.3	0.0

Source: Civic Culture Study, 1959–60.

having said they voted for Labour and around a third having supported the Conservatives. Those with no religion, who comprised a small proportion of the British sample, also showed majority support for Labour at each election, which was again more pronounced at the second and third contests.[4]

Religion and voting behaviour at general elections

This section addresses the evidence bearing upon the traditional associations between religious affiliation and voting in the post-war era, looking at every general election from 1959 to 2010. The source of data for this section is the long-running BES survey series, which began in 1963 to conduct fieldwork with nationally-representative samples of the British electorate. Specifically, it examines the voting behaviour of five groups classified by religious affiliation. Information on the religious affiliation of respondents has been collected since the inception of the BES. The categories used here for the BES survey data differ somewhat from the standard classification for religious affiliation used in other chapters. The categories used are as follows:

- Anglican
- Roman Catholic
- Nonconformist
- Church of Scotland/Presbyterian
- No religious affiliation

Member of non-Christian faiths are not compared here in detail as they often comprised very small numbers of respondents in the earlier BES survey samples. It is important to reiterate that the geographical coverage of the BES surveys excludes Northern Ireland, so all of the data reported here relate to voting behaviour of the British – not the United Kingdom – electorate. Information on vote choice in the BES surveys has traditionally been ascertained by the following two questions:

> Did you manage to vote in the (last) general election? *If 'yes':*
> Which party did you vote for in the general election?

In order to first look at the broader historical picture for each group, Figures 3.1–3.5 chart the proportions voting for the largest parties – Conservatives, Labour and the third party (Liberal Party and its predecessors) – between 1959 and 2010. Due to changes in the wider party-political landscape the voting data refer to the Liberal Party for the 1959–79 elections, the Alliance (comprising the Liberal Party and Social Democratic Party) for the 1983 and 1987 elections and to the Liberal Democrats for the 1992–2010 elections. The percentage base used here includes those voting for minor parties (the number and nature of which have varied over time) but their vote share is not shown in the figures. All of the voting data presented here comes from the BES post-election cross-section surveys – in other words, it is based on *reported voting behaviour* rather than *current vote intention* as is commonly measured by inter-election opinion polls and pre-election surveys.

Figure 3.1 looks at voting behaviour amongst Anglicans, who bear – or did bear, it might be argued – the historical label of 'the Conservative Party at prayer' (which referred specifically to the Church of England). As Peele observes:

> Historically, there used to be a marked divide between the political stance of the Church of England (which was thought conservative in outlook) and the radicalism of the Roman Catholic and nonconformist churches which in part reflected their very different adherents (2012: 87).

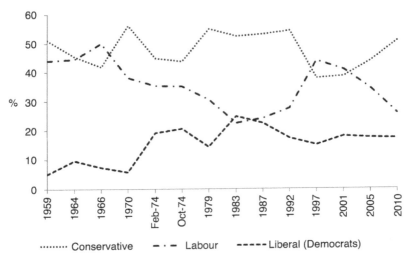

Figure 3.1 Voting behaviour of Anglicans at general elections, 1959–2010
Source: BES surveys.

Taking this historical context into account, it is apparent that, across elections, Anglicans have – invariably, if not inevitably – been more likely to vote Conservative than Labour. The exceptions are 1966 and 1997, both clear Labour victories. The characterisation of the Church of England as the 'Conservative Party at prayer' is more apposite for those elections when the Conservatives gained significant victories – such as those in 1979, 1983, 1987 and 1992. The Conservative Party's share of the Anglican vote also increased at the most recent elections of 2005 and 2010.

Roman Catholics represent an interesting example of a denomination whose strict religious beliefs and teachings, it has been observed, should have predisposed them to vote for the more morally traditionalist right-wing party in Britain, as their co-religionists traditionally did in continental European countries such as France and Germany (Bruce 2012). However, as Bruce (2012: 23–4) has observed, the broader economic disadvantages and socio-political discrimination they suffered as migrant communities, meant that their 'natural party' was Labour. Catholics therefore traditionally supported the Liberal Party and, with the 'replacement of religion by class as the principal cleavage' (Harrop and Miller 1987: 180) and the emergence of Labour Party as a political force in the early 20th century, voted preponderantly for the party of the trade unions and the working classes.

Looking at the voting behaviour of Catholics in Britain in the post-war era, charted in Figure 3.2, it is clear that, although the level of support for Labour has fluctuated, at most contests Catholics have supported Labour and often by large margins. Support declined somewhat in the 1970s – and the only contest at which Catholic support for Labour was eclipsed by that for the Conservatives was the 1979 election. Support for Labour increased during the 1980s–90s, but has fallen away at recent elections. The data here are interesting in the context of Steven's observation that 'The Labour Party – rationally – continues to be conscious of the Catholic vote, knowing that it is still a secure base for electoral support' (2011a: 143). It is also worth noting that support for the third party amongst Catholics has been generally lower than that evident for Anglicans (and Nonconformists).[5]

The next group comprise those who affiliate with the Nonconformist or 'free churches'. Given that this group has tended to comprise small numbers of those who belong to a Christian tradition – or who have a religious affiliation – in the BES surveys, this precludes a more finely-grained look at the voting behaviour of the different free churches (whether Methodist, Baptist or other tradition). However, given the

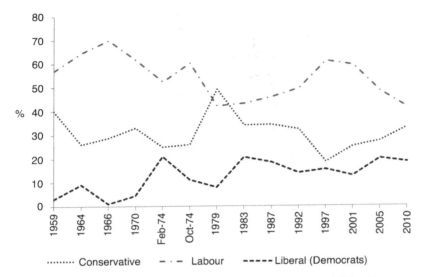

Figure 3.2 Voting behaviour of Catholics at general elections, 1959–2010
Source: BES surveys.

historical linkages between adherents of the dissenting churches and the Liberal Party (Koss 1975; Bebbington 1982), the over-time voting data are reported in Figure 3.3, combining those who reported an affiliation with any of the free churches. Higher support for the Conservatives is generally evident in the 1970s and 1980s, and into the 1990s. As with the other groups looked at here, the Liberal Party and its successor have been very much the 'third party' in the voting behaviour of Nonconformists, although in 1983 and 1987 the vote share for the Alliance did eclipse that of Labour for second place behind the Conservative Party. These two elections aside, support for their traditional 'home' – the Liberal Party, the Alliance and then the Liberal Democrats – has been in the region of 15.0–25.0 percent.

Figure 3.4 next charts the party vote share for those who report an affiliation with the Church of Scotland or as Presbyterian. Historically, adherents of the Church of Scotland showed variation in party support based on their class location: in the early 1960s Butler and Stokes found that those in higher occupational grades were much more likely to support the Conservatives and those in the lower grades more likely to support Labour (1969: 158). There is a mixed picture in their post-war voting behaviour, whereby at some elections a greater proportion

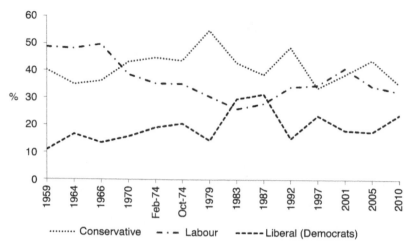

Figure 3.3 Voting behaviour of Nonconformists at general elections, 1959–2010
Source: BES surveys.

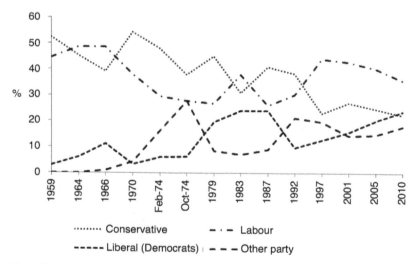

Figure 3.4 Voting behaviour of Church of Scotland affiliates or Presbyterians at general elections, 1959–2010
Source: BES surveys.

has voted for Labour, while at other contests, the Conservatives have won more votes from this group. There is no evidence of consistent voting in favour of a particular party, Labour or Conservative. It is also notable that support for the third party has fluctuated over time (particularly during the time of the 'Alliance', at the 1983 and 1987 elections, as well as more recently for the Liberal Democrats).

Finally, Figure 3.5 charts party vote shares for those with no religion (from 1983 onwards). It is clear that the voting behaviour of those with no religion has fluctuated somewhat over time. As with other religious groups, both Labour and the Conservatives have secured greater vote share in different post-war contests. One interesting trend has been the growing support for the Liberal Democrats at recent elections, (which has been on a par with or slightly higher than support for the Conservatives). This is probably partly attributable to the fact that those with no religion in British society are more likely to be in a younger age group than those who report having some form of religious affiliation (Lee, L. 2012).

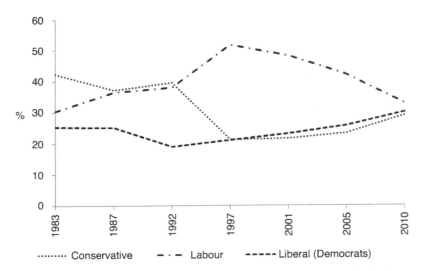

Figure 3.5   Voting behaviour of those with no religion at general elections, 1983–2010
Source: BES surveys.

Religion, parental socialisation and voting

Another way of examining the historical links between religion and party choice at elections is to use data on parental voting behaviour, based on 'recall' questions asked of respondents in BES surveys up until 1997. Earlier research into electoral behaviour and party choice in Britain stressed the role of processes of political socialisation in transmitting partisan identities from parents through to their children within the family environment (Butler and Stokes 1969: 66–78), similar to the transmission of denominational affiliations. However, before looking at the longitudinal data on the voting preferences of respondents' fathers and mothers, recall data from the earliest BES study (the 1963 cross-section survey) is analysed, where respondents were asked about the party their parents usually voted for, providing separate answers for their father and mother. Respondents were also probed as to the religious affiliation of their parents, and so parental party preference and religious affiliation data are presented in Table 3.2. The question wordings, which refer to party preference rather than specifically to voting behaviour, are as follows:

> [Father] Did he have any particular preferences for one of the parties when you were young? Which party was that?
> [Mother] Did she have any particular preferences for one of the parties when you were young? Which party was that?
> When you were young, what was your parents' religion?

Results are shown for four categories: Anglican, Catholic, Nonconformist and Church of Scotland/Presbyterian/Protestant. Figures are not shown for those with no religion or who belong to a non-Christian faith as both groups comprise very few respondents in the 1963 cross-section survey.

Mothers and fathers with an Anglican affiliation show similar levels of support for the Conservatives (39.6 percent and 39.2 percent, respectively), but the former are less likely to have supported Labour – at 27.7 percent compared to 38.4 percent for the latter. Based on parents being Roman Catholic, *both mothers and fathers* were much more likely to have a party preference for Labour than for the Conservatives. For mothers, 38.5 percent usually supported the Labour Party, with just 16.2 percent regularly supporting the Conservative Party. Fathers show a more pronounced bias towards Labour, with 51.3 percent usually supporting them compared to a fifth tending to

Table 3.2   Parental party preference by parental religious affiliation

	Anglican (%)	Catholic (%)	Nonconformist (%)	Church of Scotland/ Presbyterian/ Protestant (%)
Father				
Conservative	39.6	22.7	17.7	32.9
Labour	38.4	51.3	35.0	36.6
Liberal	14.0	5.0	35.0	19.9
Other response[a]	8.0	21.0	12.4	10.6
Mother				
Conservative	39.2	16.2	17.9	28.9
Labour	27.7	38.5	26.4	23.6
Liberal	8.1	5.1	23.6	8.7
Other response[a]	24.9	40.2	32.1	37.9

Source: BES 1963 cross-section survey.
[a]Including: other party, no preference, or mixed preferences.

support the Conservative Party (22.7 percent). Turning to those respondents whose parents belonged to a Nonconformist denomination, it can be seen that both fathers and mothers show the highest level of support for the Liberal Party of any religious group, at, 35.0 percent and 23.6 percent respectively. Even so, a general tendency to have supported Labour rivals that of the Liberal Party for both mothers and fathers, but support for the Conservative Party was much lower in each case (17.7 percent and 17.9 percent, respectively). Finally, based on parental affiliation as Church of Scotland or Presbyterian, fathers were slightly more likely to favour Labour (36.6 percent) over the Conservatives (32.9 percent) whereas mothers were slightly more likely to support the Conservatives (28.9 percent compared to 23.6 percent for Labour). As shown by the 'other response' category, it is evident that, based on respondents' recall of their family circumstances, mothers were much more likely than fathers to have had mixed party preferences, to have had no particular preference or to have tended to support some other party. This is evident across all of the four religious groups (highest for mothers with a Catholic affiliation, at 40.2 percent, compared to 21.0 percent for Catholic fathers).

Tables 3.3 and 3.4 extend this analysis – for respondents' fathers and mothers, respectively – using data from later BES surveys, encompassing the period from 1974 (1979 for mothers) to 1997. The data here are

Table 3.3   Party father usually voted for, by respondent's affiliation, 1974–1997

	Anglican (%)	Roman Catholic (%)	Other Christian (%)	No religion (%)
October 1974				
Conservative	44.1	25.6	33.9	29.5
Labour	44.0	64.4	40.3	60.9
Liberal	11.2	5.6	24.2	8.3
Other party	0.7	4.4	1.7	1.2
1979				
Conservative	45.6	28.6	35.7	29.4
Labour	45.8	63.9	43.2	63.3
Liberal	8.4	6.8	21.1	6.1
Other party	0.2	0.8	0.0	1.1
1983				
Conservative	36.0	19.9	27.1	31.2
Labour	52.9	73.1	54.2	61.0
Liberal	9.4	3.7	17.1	4.7
Other party	1.7	3.4	1.6	3.0
1987				
Conservative	38.7	23.1	33.4	29.1
Labour	51.9	72.0	47.2	63.0
Liberal	8.4	3.4	16.9	7.2
Other party	1.1	1.5	2.5	0.7
1992				
Conservative	38.7	16.3	32.0	32.7
Labour	53.2	78.6	56.7	59.9
Liberal Democrat	7.2	2.0	7.4	5.2
Other party	0.9	3.1	3.9	2.2
1997				
Conservative	40.6	27.0	35.0	32.9
Labour	53.1	71.7	52.2	58.4
Liberal Democrat	5.5	1.3	9.6	5.9
Other party	0.7	0.0	3.2	2.9

Source: BES surveys.
Note: Excludes those who answered 'can't remember/don't know', 'did not vote', 'refused to disclose voting', 'not applicable/not brought up in Britain'.

different in that recall data on parental religious affiliation is not available. As a result, data on parental voting behaviour (party usually voted for) was related to information on the survey respondents' current religious affiliation, which is used as a proxy measure. This is less than ideal, but it seems reasonable to presume that a significant proportion of respondents shared the religious identity of their parents through

Table 3.4 Party mother usually voted for, by respondent's affiliation, 1979–1997

	Anglican (%)	Roman Catholic (%)	Other Christian (%)	No religion (%)
1979				
Conservative	48.5	34.1	42.0	33.9
Labour	43.4	57.9	40.5	58.5
Liberal Democrat	7.4	7.9	17.5	6.7
Other party	0.7	0.0	0.0	0.9
1983				
Conservative	39.1	22.7	30.4	34.6
Labour	49.9	71.5	48.0	55.6
Liberal Democrat	9.3	3.6	19.7	7.3
Other party	1.6	2.1	1.8	2.4
1987				
Conservative	42.5	26.9	35.9	30.2
Labour	47.0	66.2	44.2	59.7
Liberal Democrat	9.8	4.7	16.7	8.8
Other party	0.7	2.5	3.2	1.3
1992				
Conservative	41.5	21.7	36.1	36.4
Labour	48.9	71.0	47.9	56.6
Liberal Democrat	8.2	3.9	14.0	5.4
Other party	1.4	3.4	2.0	1.5
1997				
Conservative	43.7	30.1	37.6	33.3
Labour	48.0	65.1	46.6	55.4
Liberal Democrat	7.4	4.4	11.7	8.4
Other party	0.9	0.4	4.1	2.8

Source: BES surveys.
Note: Excludes those who answered 'can't remember/don't know', 'did not vote', 'refused to disclose voting', 'not applicable/not brought up in Britain'.

processes of generational transmission within families (even if they were only 'nominal' adherents of a particular denomination). As a result, the broader picture and patterns across time are of greater interest rather than the specific details of a particular survey. Respondents were first asked the following question about their father's party preference:

Did he have any particular preferences for one of the parties when you were young? Which party was that?

Subsequently, they were then asked whether their mother had any particular party preference (though the wording of this follow-up question varied slightly across BES surveys). In general terms, respondents who identified themselves as Catholic reported that both their fathers and mothers were preponderantly Labour voters (usually higher than 60.0 percent). The figures for Anglicans are not so distinctive, with a more even split between voting for Labour and the Conservatives. The proportion of Anglicans who report their mother and father generally voting for the Conservatives is noticeably higher for the 1983–92 elections than for other contests, which may be suggestive evidence of respondents projecting their support for that (election-winning) party onto their parents' preferences. Interestingly, those who belong to another Christian denomination are much more likely to report that their mother or father voted for the third party, the Liberals, which ties in with the historical links between this party and Nonconformist allegiance (while again cautioning that recall data on parental religious affiliation is not available). The proportions reporting parental voting for the third party is higher for the earlier elections covered in Tables 3.3 and 3.4. There is also a consistent pattern for those of no religion: they report that both their mothers and fathers were much more likely to vote for Labour than the Conservatives.

Overall, some association between religion and party choice at postwar general elections is clear from the data presented so far. There is particularly clear evidence for Catholics' traditionally higher levels of support for the Labour Party, and this is the case for both respondents' own voting behaviour and their recall of how their parents' tended to vote. These associations can be examined in greater depth by looking at how religion intersects with other social factors, namely social class, region and attendance at religious services which show how the relationship between religion and party choice is modified by the presence of other sociological characteristics.

Religion, other social factors and voting

First, voting patterns amongst Anglicans and Catholics on the basis of social class is examined, an area of considerable interest to previous studies of electoral behaviour in Britain (Butler and Stokes 1969: 162–5; Heath et al. 1991: 86–7). This research examined whether the associations between denomination and party support varied according to location in the middle or working classes. For clarity of presentation and to aim for a broad consistency of categories across surveys, a dichotomous classification of social class is used, based on more detailed categorisations of occupational grades used in each BES survey. In each survey, respondents have been classified as being either in non-manual or manual employment, traditionally labelled as 'white-collar' or 'blue-collar' work, respectively (excluding those who said they did 'other' work and who are not readily classifiable, or who said they had never worked).

The data are shown in Figure 3.6, which shows levels of Conservative voting amongst non-manual and manual Anglicans and levels of Labour voting amongst non-manual and manual Catholics. Based on social class, there are clear variations in party support amongst Anglicans and Catholics, which persist over time. Anglicans in non-manual occupations are generally more likely to support the Conservative Party over time, while Catholics in manual occupations were much more likely to support the Labour Party. Conversely, Anglicans in manual occupations have been more likely to support the Labour Party and Catholics in non-manual employment have shown a greater propensity to vote for the Conservatives. In 1964, 67.0 percent of Anglicans in non-manual occupations voted for the Conservative Party compared to 31.1 percent of their co-religionists in manual work. In 2010, the figures were, respectively, 56.7 percent and 35.6 percent. The figures for Labour voting amongst Catholics at the 1964 election were, respectively, 78.8 percent and 35.5 percent for those in manual and non-manual occupations. In 2010, the difference was considerably narrower but in the same direction: 47.1 percent for manual occupations and 39.7 percent for those in non-manual positions.

Another important factor which intersects with religious denomination and may cause different patterns of party support is region, specifically the historically variegated geographical distribution of religious communities in Britain and the differing religious complexion of England, Wales and Scotland (Bruce 2012). Again, this is an important aspect of electoral geography for Britain's Catholic population. Traditionally, historical patterns of emigration and settlement have seen Roman Catholics concentrated in urban areas in Scotland and in London and north-west England. The overall levels of party support for British Catholics shown in Figure 3.6 therefore may hide important regional variation. Data from Budge and Urwin's study (1966: 61) showed that in Scotland, 76.0 percent of Catholics surveyed voted Labour at the 1955 general election compared to 51.0 percent of Catholics in England. Their local survey of the electorate in Cathcart in Glasgow found that 81.0 percent of Catholics voted Labour at the 1964

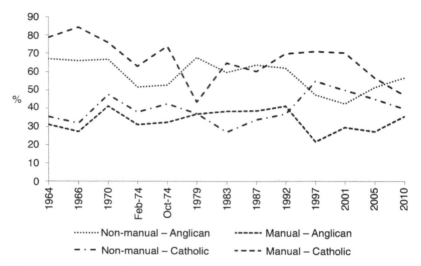

Figure 3.6   Voting behaviour of Anglicans (percent voting Conservative) and Catholics (percent voting Labour), by social class, 1964–2010
Source: BES surveys.

general election compared to 36.0 percent of Protestants; just 19.0 percent of Catholics voted Conservative compared to 64.0 percent of Protestants (Budge and Urwin 1966: 61). Figure 3.7 presents the separate vote shares for Labour and Conservative for Catholics living in England and Scotland, for the 1970–2010 general elections (taking advantage of data from several Scottish election studies which provide larger samples for those living in Scotland and ran alongside the main BES survey at several elections).

There is a clear geographical division in the levels of support for Labour amongst those Catholics residing in Scotland and England. Levels of support for Labour are consistently higher in Scotland. This can also be shown by calculating a difference score for each election, by subtracting the Catholic vote share for Labour in Scotland from the Catholic vote share for Labour in England. A positive figure indicates higher Catholic voting for Labour in Scotland and a negative figure indicates higher voting in England. The differences show much higher levels of Catholic support for Labour in Scotland, ranging from a low of 18.4 percent in the 1970 and 1992 elections to a high of 38.3 percent in the 1979 election. It is also worth noting the much lower levels of support across time for the Conservatives and the third

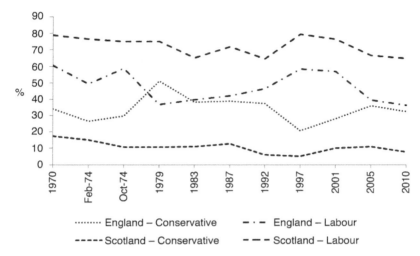

Figure 3.7　Percent voting Conservative and Labour, Catholics in England and Scotland, 1970–2010
Source: BES surveys.

party amongst Catholics in Scotland, partly explained by Labour's traditional electoral dominance here and by the presence of the SNP as a fourth party (and Catholics' greater willingness to vote for the latter at recent elections). The former feature is shown by large majorities of the vote secured by Labour at each general election – reaching around three-quarters or four-fifths of vote share in 1992 and 1997 – even in those contests where the Conservatives won an overall victory by a considerable margin. Indeed, support for the Conservatives amongst Catholics in Scotland has dipped well below 10.0 percent at several recent elections (1992, 1997 and 2010). Of course, given the much higher levels of support for Labour amongst Catholics in Scotland, Catholics residing in England have traditionally registered higher levels of support for the Conservative Party at general elections.

Earlier research showed differences in party support within different denominations according to level of attendance at religious services; with, for example, church-going Anglicans showing a greater propensity to support the Conservatives (Butler and Stokes 1969; McKenzie and Silver 1968). Here, the historic data are assessed by looking at vote share based on religious attendance *within denominations*. Anglicans and Catholics are subdivided in this way. Data from the BES surveys can be utilised which often – if not always – collected information on frequency of attendance at religious services. This measure of religious practice or 'behaviour' can be used as a proxy indicator of the degree of religious commitment or involvement. The response options for this question in the BES surveys have usually ranged, on the one hand, from do not attend religious services at all through to, on the other, attends once a week or more. In order to provide greater clarity of presentation, the response options for attendance were combined into two broader groups (based on the classification used in Heath et al. 1993a):

- Frequent attenders: those who go to religious services once a month or more.
- Infrequent attenders: those who go to services less often or do not go at all.

The data on religious belonging and behaviour are combined to compare the voting behaviour of frequent and infrequent attenders within the two largest denominational groups – Anglicans and Catholics. Data are reported separately for regular and irregular attenders in Figure 3.8 (Anglicans – support for the Conservatives) and Figure 3.9 (Catholics – support for Labour).

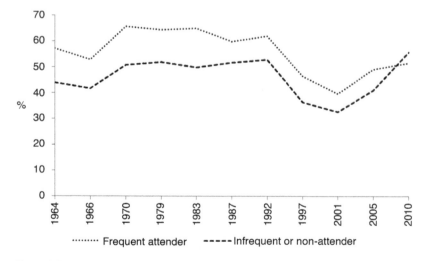

Figure 3.8 Percent voting for the Conservative Party by attendance, Anglicans, 1964–2010
Source: BES surveys.

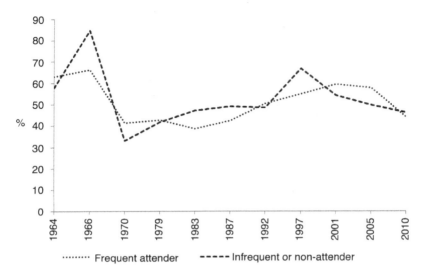

Figure 3.9 Percent voting for the Labour Party by attendance, Catholics, 1964–2010
Source: BES surveys.

Figure 3.8 shows that there are noticeable differences in levels of support for the Conservatives amongst Anglicans at general elections. Although the levels of support fluctuate from election to election, the relative ordering of regularly-attending and irregularly-attending Anglicans does not. At nearly every contest, regularly-attending Anglicans are more likely to have voted for the Conservative Party, although the gap has closed at the most recent election. Moreover, although not shown here, irregularly-attending Anglicans also show a greater tendency to vote for Labour *at every election* in this period. For Catholics, when differentiated by attendance at services, there is not a clear pattern evident at post-war general elections. Indeed, at some elections, the levels of support for Labour are very close or are higher for those who attend services less often or not at all. When classified by their religious attendance, Catholics also do not exhibit consistent differences in levels of support for the Conservatives in this period.

Religion and party support in recent decades

While the BES surveys provided the most authoritative evidence on voting behaviour at each general election, data from other recurrent surveys can be used to look at party support in recent decades. The BSA surveys provide an important source of supplementary data on the association between religious belonging and party support. The BSA data differ from the BES in several respects. First, they provide a more regular – specifically, a yearly – barometer of public opinion (with the exceptions of 1988 and 1992), supplying valuable information for the periods between general elections. Secondly, while they provide more frequent data points, they cover a shorter period than the BES series, starting in 1983, with latest data available from the 2012 survey. Thirdly, the measure of party support is based on several related questions and therefore is not as straightforward a measure as a single probe eliciting recent voting behaviour. Fourth, the question is applicable to the entire sample, whereas the BES question by definition excludes those who have already declared they did not vote at the respective general election. The following set of questions has been used to produce an overall measure of party support in the BSA surveys:

> Generally speaking, do you think of yourself as a supporter of any one political party?
> Do you think of yourself as a little closer to one political party than to others?
> If there were a general election tomorrow, which political party do you think you would be most likely to support?

These questions are used as the basis for analysing party support over time, concentrating in this section on the two most important historical linkages discussed above with contemporary resonance: Anglicans and the Conservative Party and Catholics and the Labour Party. Figures 3.10 and 3.11 therefore show levels of support for the three main parties amongst, respectively, Anglicans and Catholics. Figure 3.10 shows that support for the Conservatives amongst Anglicans was higher in the earlier and later stages of the time series. Support for Conservatives and Labour runs very close in the 1990s and early 2000s. Support for the third party is much lower over time, as was also the case in Figure 3.1 based on the BES survey data. A clearer pattern emerges in the equivalent time series for Catholics' party support. Over time fluctuation notwithstanding, Catholics always evince higher support for the Labour Party, with larger differences during the 1990s and early 2000s, shown in Figure 3.11. The differences are narrower at the earlier and later stages of the time period.

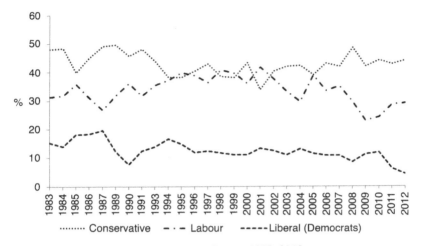

Figure 3.10   Party support amongst Anglicans, 1983–2012
Source: BSA surveys.

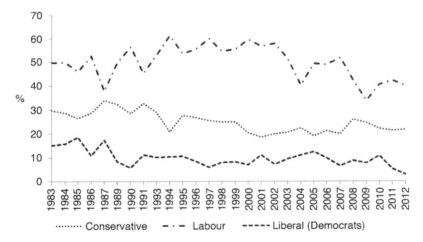

Figure 3.11   Party support amongst Catholics, 1983–2012
Source: BSA surveys.

Two other noteworthy points are that Catholics' support for the Conservatives is lower than Anglicans' support for the Labour Party, while support for the third party is usually somewhat lower than that of Anglicans, again features noted in the BES data analysed already.

As with the BES data, the BSA surveys can be used to investigate whether there is any variation in levels of support for the Conservative and Labour parties on the basis of social class and attendance at religious services. First, differences in party support amongst Anglicans and Catholics are assessed using a classification on the basis of occupational grade. That is, as with the BES surveys, they are classed as being in either a non-manual ('white-collar') or manual occupation ('blue-collar'). The relevant data are charted in Figure 3.12, which shows the proportions supporting the Conservatives amongst Anglicans in non-manual and manual occupations. The levels of support by affiliation do differ depending on occupational grade. Anglicans in non-manual occupations exhibit much higher support for the Conservative Party over time than do their co-religionists in manual employment. This gap persists over the period covered here.

Similar data for Catholics are presented in Figure 3.13, but this time charting support for the Labour Party. Interestingly, while there is traditionally a clear differential between Catholics in manual and non-manual work in levels of support for the Labour Party, with manual workers expressing higher levels of support, this gap has changed in more recent years, with the lines broadly converging.

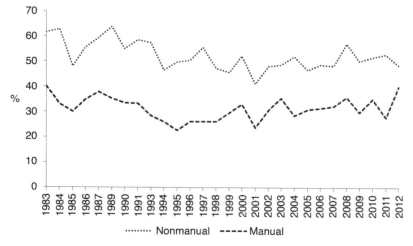

Figure 3.12 Percent supporting the Conservative Party by social class, Anglicans, 1983–2012
Source: BSA surveys.

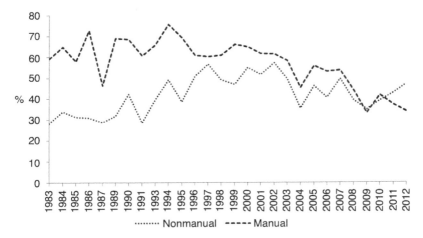

Figure 3.13 Percent supporting the Labour Party by social class, Catholics, 1983–2012
Source: BSA surveys.

Second, differences in party support amongst Anglicans and Catholics can be examined based on levels of attendance at services. As with the BES surveys, a dichotomous categorisation is used, whereby those attending monthly or more often are classed as 'frequent' attenders and those who attend less often or not at all are classed as 'infrequent' attenders. The data are shown in Figure 3.14 (Anglicans) and Figure 3.15 (Catholics). As was evident with the BES voting behaviour data charted in Figure 3.8, Anglicans who regularly attend services are somewhat more likely to express support for the Conservative Party compared to those who attend less often or not at all. This gap is evident across time, although it fluctuates from survey to survey. A similar sort of pattern is not apparent for Catholics when divided by religious attendance. There is no clear evidence across time that more religious involvement amongst Catholics is associated with a higher propensity to support Labour. This tends to underline what was found in Figure 3.9.

Religion and contemporary party choice

The previous section undertook a detailed examination of the historical associations between religious belonging and party choice. The contemporary associations of religion with party support in Britain are

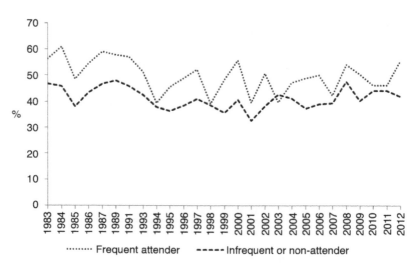

Figure 3.14   Percent supporting the Conservative Party by attendance, Anglicans, 1983–2012
Source: BSA surveys.

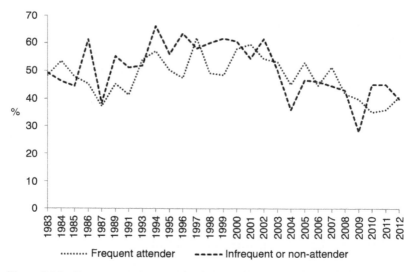

Figure 3.15   Percent supporting the Labour Party by attendance, Catholics, 1983–2012
Source: BSA surveys.

now assessed in greater detail. Two sets of multivariate analyses are undertaken. The first is based on data on voting at the 2010 general election taken from the BES 2010 election study. The second is based on general party support and comes from the BSA 2012 survey. By undertaking multivariate analysis, the independent effect of religion can be assessed when accounting for the relative impact of a range of sociological factors which (i) might be associated with having a religious identity – particularly sex and age – and (ii) have also been traditional determinants of party choice in Britain.

First, analysis is undertaken of voting behaviour using the BES 2010 Campaign Internet Panel Study (CIPS), which provides a much larger sample size than the traditional in-person cross-section survey. The analysis is based on the weighted post-election cross-section from the CIPS.[6] This means that separate analysis of geographically-defined sub-samples is feasible. Separate models are therefore estimated to examine how religion is associated with support for the major parties in Britain and Scotland. A series of binary logistic regressions are estimated which examine the factors that increase or decrease the probability of having voted for each of the major parties. This involved regressing a series of independent variables on the dependent variable, which in each case is a dichotomous measure, scored as 1 if a respondent voted for the party in question and 0 if the respondent voted for any other party (major or minor). In other words, separate models are estimated for those who supported the Conservative Party, Labour Party and Liberal Democrats (as well as the SNP in Scotland). A series of dummy variables are used to measure religious affiliation. The analysis excludes those respondents who reported they did not vote in the election and the very small proportion which could not remember or did not want to say which party they supported. The focus here is on the direction and significance of the effects of religious affiliation. The role of religion is examined in the context of assessing a 'sociological model' of voting behaviour (Denver et al. 2012: 23–4). In particular, controlling for other social factors:

- What, if any, is the association between Anglicans and voting for the Conservative Party in Britain?
- What, if any, is the association between Catholics and voting for the Labour Party in Britain (and Scotland)?
- What, if any, is the association between Nonconformism and voting for the Liberal Democrats in Britain?

Results from the analysis of voting in Britain are presented in Table 3.5. For religious affiliation, the omitted reference categories for the three models are: voted Conservative: Anglican; voted Labour: Catholic; voted Liberal Democrat: Nonconformist. The results from these model estimations generally confirm the expected associations between religious affiliation and party support, even when accounting for the influence of different indicators of socio-economic status (housing tenure, occupational grade and education) and other social characteristics.

Looking at the model of voting Conservative versus all other parties, it can be seen that all religious groups are less likely to report voting Conservative in 2010 compared to Anglicans, with the exception of those who affiliate as Church of Scotland or Presbyterian. Compared to Anglicans, Catholics (odds ratio: .60), those belonging to other religions (odds ratio: .70) and those with no religion (odds ratio: .56) were all less likely to report voting Conservative at the 2010 election (the odds ratio for Nonconformists was .92). The results are similarly clear-cut when looking at voting for Labour: all groups are less likely to have supported Labour compared to Catholics, while accounting for the influence of voters' social characteristics. More specifically, the odds ratios are .60 for Anglicans, .84 for Nonconformists, .67 for Church of Scotland/Presbyterian, .57 for other religions and .62 for those with no religion. The traditional association is partly upheld for Nonconformism and support for the Liberal Democrats. In this model, both Catholics and Anglicans are less likely to have voted Liberal Democrat (odds ratios of, respectively, .65 and .75). Interestingly, there are no significant differences between, on the one hand, Nonconformists and, on the other, members of other religions and those with no affiliation. Based on the sociological models of voting presented here, there are significant effects for the religious affiliation categories, which are generally in the expected direction. These effects are present when accounting for socio-demographic factors which are established correlates of religious belonging and vote choice.

Closer attention can also be paid to regional patterns of religion and party support by examining voting behaviour of the Scottish sub-sample within the BES 2010 CIPS. Research into voting behaviour at recent Scottish elections has found that religion influences party choice (Surridge et al. 1999). Historically, as Kendrick and McCrone note:

Religion has always mattered in Scottish politics but it dominated the nineteenth century and structured its cleavages to a quite

Table 3.5 Binary logistic regression analyses of voting at the 2010 general election, Britain

Variable	Voted Conservative		Voted Labour		Voted Liberal Democrat	
	B (SE)	Odds ratio	B (SE)	Odds ratio	B (SE)	Odds ratio
Sex	-.10* (.04)	.90	-.01 (.05)	.99	-.01 (.05)	.99
Ethnic group	.68* (.13)	1.97	-.74* (.11)	.48	-.01 (.11)	.99
Age 18–24 years	-.58* (.11)	.56	.23* (.11)	1.26	.61 (.11)	1.83
Age 25 to 34 years	-.19* (.08)	.83	.08 (.09)	1.08	.47* (.08)	1.60
Age 35 to 44 years	-.37* (.07)	.69	.36* (.08)	1.43	.26* (.08)	1.30
Age 45 to 54 years	-.48* (.07)	.62	.40* (.08)	1.50	.23* (.08)	1.25
Age 55 to 64 years	-.23* (.06)	.79	.05 (.07)	1.05	.17* (.07)	1.19
Manager or senior administrator	.21* (.07)	1.23	-.02 (.08)	.99	-.25* (.07)	.78
Clerical	-.01 (.07)	.99	.16* (.08)	1.18	-.20* (.07)	.82
Sales or services	-.34* (.09)	.71	.39* (.09)	1.48	-.16 (.09)	.85
Small business owner	.35* (.12)	1.42	-.27 (.14)	.76	-.34* (.13)	.72
Foreman or supervisor of other workers	-.10 (.13)	.91	.23 (.13)	1.26	-.37* (.14)	.69
Skilled manual work	-.28* (.10)	.76	.36* (.10)	1.44	-.39* (.10)	.68
Semi-skilled or unskilled manual work	-.33* (.09)	.72	.42* (.09)	1.52	-.32* (.09)	.73
Other	-.03 (.08)	.97	.18* (.09)	1.19	-.15 (.08)	.86
Never worked	.21 (.19)	1.23	-.03 (.19)	.97	-.03 (.18)	.97
Below degree-level	.24* (.07)	1.27	-.12 (.08)	.89	-.15* (.08)	.86
A-levels or equivalent	.28* (.07)	1.32	-.08 (.08)	.92	-.15 (.07)	.86
GCSEs or equivalent	.34* (.06)	1.41	-.04 (.07)	.96	-.33* (.06)	.72
No qualifications	.26* (.08)	1.30	.07 (.08)	1.07	-.33* (.08)	.72
Tenure: private rental	-.36* (.07)	.70	-.03 (.07)	.97	.27* (.07)	1.31
Tenure: public rental	-.56* (.07)	.57	.42* (.07)	1.52	-.11 (.07)	.89
Midlands	-.06 (.05)	.95	.24* (.06)	1.28	-.21* (.06)	.81
North	-.59* (.05)	.56	.89* (.06)	2.44	-.21* (.06)	.81

Table 3.5 Binary logistic regression analyses of voting at the 2010 general election, Britain – *continued*

Variable	Voted Conservative		Voted Labour		Voted Liberal Democrat	
	B (SE)	Odds ratio	B (SE)	Odds ratio	B (SE)	Odds ratio
Wales	-.88* (.11)	.42	.74* (.10)	2.10	-.14 (.10)	.87
Scotland	-1.31* (.11)	.27	1.00* (.08)	2.73	-.55* (.09)	.58
Anglican	–	–	-.51* (.08)	.60	-.43* (.11)	.65
Catholic	-.52* (.08)	.60	–	–	-.28* (.13)	.75
Nonconformist	-.08* (.03)	.92	-.17* (.04)	.84	–	–
Church of Scotland/Presbyterian	-.26 (.17)	.77	-.40* (.15)	.67	-.09 (.19)	.92
Other religion	-.36* (.10)	.70	-.57* (.12)	.57	-.05 (.14)	.96
No religion	-.58* (.05)	.56	-.48* (.08)	.62	.13 (.10)	1.14
Constant	-.41* (.15)	.66	-0.57* (.15)	.57	-.64* (.16)	.53
Reference category	Anglican		Catholic		Nonconformist	
Weighted N	11,405		11,405		11,406	
Nagelkerke R Square	.11		.09		.06	

Note: *$p<.05$ and lower.

Other reference categories: aged 65 and over; professional or higher technical work; degree-level qualification; owner-occupier; lives in southern England.

Source: BES 2010 CIPS.

remarkable extent. These influences continued well into the twentieth century, albeit in a much altered form (1989: 595).

Given the presence of multi-party competition in Scotland, there is also an examination of the factors which predict support for the SNP. Therefore, four separate binary logistic regression models were estimated, also using a different set of categories for religion given Scotland's differing religious fabric (Catholics, Church of Scotland or Presbyterian, other denomination or religion, and no religion). The omitted reference categories for religion are: voted Conservative: Church of Scotland/Presbyterian; voted Labour: Catholic; voted Liberal Democrat: no religion; voted SNP: no religion. The models include a similar set of sociological characteristics to those used in Table 3.5, with the obvious exception of regional location as well as omitting ethnic group (with very few survey respondents in Scotland reporting having a non-white ethnic background). Social class is measured as a single dummy variable (whether a member of the salariat or not), given the much smaller sample size of respondents living in Scotland.

Results from the analysis of voters in Scotland are presented in Table 3.6. The main finding in the results for voting in Scotland in 2010 is the effect for Catholics, as indicated by the evidence presented in the previous chapter. All groups are less likely to have voted Labour compared to Catholics in 2010. Specifically, the odds ratios are .45 for Church of Scotland/Presbyterian, .27 for other religions and .37 for those with no affiliation. Catholics are much less likely to have voted either Conservative (compared to Church of Scotland/Presbyterian; odds ratio: .45) or Liberal Democrat (compared to those with no religion; odds ratio: .27) in 2010. The only notable finding for support for the SNP is that those belonging to the other religion group (odds ratio: .45) are less likely to have cast their ballot for the nationalists compared to those with no religion.

As well as looking specifically at religious belonging and voting behaviour, religion and general party support are assessed using data from the most recently-available BSA survey (2012), again specifying similar 'sociological models'. This enables a further contemporary assessment of the expectations outlined earlier on. Three binary logistic regressions are estimated to assess the factors underpinning support for the Conservative, Labour and Liberal Democrat parties. Those who support the particular party are scored as 1 and all others are scored as 0 (*including* those who said they did not support any party or who did not know). In order to provide a robust test of the impact of religion,

Table 3.6 Binary logistic regression analyses of voting at the 2010 general election, Scotland

Variable	Voted Conservative B (SE)	Odds ratio	Voted Labour B (SE)	Odds ratio	Voted Liberal Democrat B (SE)	Odds ratio	Voted SNP B (SE)	Odds ratio
Sex	.03 (.19)	1.03	-.03 (.14)	.98	-.12* (.16)	.89	.10 (.17)	1.11
Age 18–24 years	-1.12* (.54)	.33	1.17* (.36)	3.22	.51 (.42)	1.66	-.91* (.48)	.40
Age 25 to 34 years	-.56 (.34)	.57	.59* (.27)	1.81	.53 (.31)	1.70	-.47 (.32)	.63
Age 35 to 44 years	-.46 (.30)	.63	.85* (.25)	2.34	.20 (.31)	1.22	-.61* (.30)	.54
Age 45 to 54 years	-.73* (.30)	.48	.97* (.24)	2.65	.06 (.30)	1.06	-.64* (.29)	.53
Age 55 to 64 years	-.69* (.27)	.50	.24 (.23)	1.27	.38 (.27)	1.46	.08 (.25)	1.08
Salariat	.28 (.22)	1.33	-.09 (.17)	.92	.11 (.19)	1.12	-.07 (.20)	.94
Below degree-level	.37 (.28)	1.45	.44* (.22)	1.55	-.88* (.25)	.41	.16 (.25)	1.18
A-levels or equivalent	.38 (.32)	1.46	.85* (.24)	2.33	-1.15* (.31)	.32	-.14 (.29)	.87
GCSEs or equivalent	.38 (.29)	1.46	.82* (.22)	2.28	-.95* (.26)	.39	-.15 (.26)	.86
No qualifications	.02 (.36)	1.02	.93* (.25)	2.54	-.35 (.28)	.70	-.64 (.33)	.53
Tenure: private rental	.25 (.32)	1.28	-.30 (.26)	.74	.14 (.27)	1.15	-.01 (.32)	1.00
Tenure: public rental	-.15 (.29)	.86	.06 (.20)	1.06	-.65* (.29)	.53	.47 (.24)	1.60
Catholic	-.80* (.41)	.45	–		-1.31* (.37)	.27	-.01 (.28)	.99
Church of Scotland/ Presbyterian	–		-.79* (.25)	.45	-.22 (.20)	.80	.00 (.20)	1.00
Other religion	.52 (.30)	1.68	-1.32* (.31)	.27	.15 (.26)	1.16	-.80* (.34)	.45
No religion	-.20 (.23)	.82	-.98* (.23)	.37	–		–	
Constant	1.47 (.35)	.23	-.52 (.33)	.60	-.83* (.32)	.44	-1.08* (.32)	.34
Reference category	Church of Scotland/ Presbyterian		Catholic		No religion		No religion	
Weighted N	992		993		992		993	
Nagelkerke R Square	.05		.13		.12		.05	

Note: *p<.05 and lower.
Other reference categories: aged 65 and over; degree-level qualification; owner-occupier.
Source: BES 2010 CIPS

a set of sociological factors are included in the models – again, some of which have traditionally been associated with party choice in Britain.

The models include a series of dummy variables measuring affiliation, slightly different from those used in the analysis of CIPS data to reflect the smaller sample for the BSA 2012 survey (Anglican, Catholic, other Christian, other religion or no religion). A measure of attendance at services is also included, which was not available in the BES 2010 CIPS. The results are presented in Table 3.7. The following groups serve as the reference categories for religious affiliation in the models: Anglican: support Conservative Party; Catholic: support Labour Party; other Christian: support Liberal Democrats.

The strongest net effects for the religious affiliation variables are apparent in the first model, examining support for the Conservative Party. Specifically, *all groups* – Catholics, other Christians, non-Christians and those with no religion – are less likely to support the Conservative Party compared to Anglicans. The odds ratios are .45 for Catholics, .59 for other Christians, .31 for non-Christian traditions and .41 for those with no religion. In the second model, there are no significant net effects for the religion variables, and so the findings do not lend further evidence to the traditional association between Catholics and Labour net of other sociological variables. In the third model, the only significant association found is for those with no religion (odds ratio: 1.79), who are more likely to express support for the Liberal Democrats than are other Christians (which, out of necessity, comprises a more encompassing group than the Nonconformists used as the reference group in the analysis of BES data). Attendance has significant effects in two of the three party support models (with more frequent attendance associated with supporting the Conservatives and the Liberal Democrats). Therefore, there is no clear evidence that, in Britain, religiosity – as operationalised by attendance – is exclusively associated with support for the main centre-right political party (van der Brug et al. 2009: 1276). The evidence from the BSA 2012 survey, like that already presented from voting behaviour at the 2010 general elections, supports one of the traditional associations between religious denominations and political parties; that is, Anglicans being more likely to affiliate with the Conservative Party. This association remain when controlling for a wide range of other social background variables, including socio-economic factors such as social class, housing tenure and education. It is interesting to note that, collectively, sociological factors, including religion, explain Conservative support (19.0 percent)

Table 3.7 Binary logistic regression analyses of party support in Britain, 2012

Variable	Conservative Party B (SE)	Odds ratio	Labour Party B (SE)	Odds ratio	Liberal Democrats B (SE)	Odds ratio
Sex	.31* (.09)	1.37	.10 (.08)	1.10	-.69* (.16)	.50
Age	.01* (.00)	1.01	.01* (.00)	1.01	.01 (.01)	1.01
Ethnic group	.94* (.23)	2.55	-.79* (.16)	.45	-.01 (.32)	.99
Marital status	.25* (.10)	1.28	-.26* (.09)	.77	.12 (.18)	1.13
Children	-.18 (.10)	.83	.04 (.09)	1.04	-.35 (.18)	.71
Northeast	.72* (.29)	2.06	.36 (.22)	1.44	.93 (.60)	2.53
Northwest	.51* (.24)	1.67	.76* (.17)	2.14	.82 (.51)	2.26
Yorkshire and Humberside	.83* (.25)	2.30	.36 (.18)	1.43	1.05* (.51)	2.85
East Midlands	.99* (.25)	2.69	.21 (.19)	1.24	.84 (.53)	2.32
West Midlands	1.09* (.24)	2.98	.04 (.19)	1.04	.39 (.56)	1.48
Southwest	.92* (.24)	2.50	-.34 (.19)	.71	1.67* (.48)	5.29
Eastern	1.43* (.23)	4.17	-.34 (.19)	.71	1.45* (.48)	4.27
Inner London	1.25* (.30)	3.50	.05 (.23)	1.05	1.69* (.52)	5.43
Outer London	1.19* (.25)	3.28	.19 (.19)	1.20	.90 (.52)	2.45
Southeast	1.45* (.22)	4.27	-.22 (.17)	.80	1.34* (.47)	3.81
Wales	.23 (.30)	1.25	.53* (.21)	1.71	.24 (.68)	1.27
Degree qualification	.09 (.12)	1.09	.07 (.11)	1.07	.80* (.20)	2.22
Salariat	.26* (.10)	1.30	.13 (.09)	1.13	.20 (.18)	1.22
Owner-occupier	.83* (.12)	2.30	-.35* (.09)	.70	.02 (.19)	1.02
Anglican	–	–	-.33* (.16)	.72	-.16 (.29)	.85
Catholic	-.80* (.18)	.45	–	–	-.67 (.43)	.51
Other Christian	-.53* (.14)	.59	-.09 (.16)	.92	–	–
Other religion	-1.18* (.31)	.31	-.34 (.23)	.71	.73 (.27)	2.08
No religion	-.89* (.12)	.41	-.29 (.15)	.75	.58* (.40)	1.79

Table 3.7 **Binary logistic regression analyses of party support in Britain, 2012** – *continued*

Variable	Conservative Party		Labour Party		Liberal Democrats	
	B (SE)	Odds ratio	B (SE)	Odds ratio	B (SE)	Odds ratio
Attendance	.05* (.03)	1.05	−.04 (.02)	.96	.10* (.05)	1.10
Constant	−3.72* (.37)	.02	.20 (.29)	1.23	−4.79* (.64)	.01
Reference category	Anglican		Catholic		Other Christian	
Weighted N	3,192		3,192		3,193	
Nagelkerke R Square	.19		.07		.10	

Note: *p<.05 or lower.
Other reference category: Scotland.
Source: BSA 2012 survey.

to a greater extent than they do supporting either Labour (7.0 percent) or the Liberal Democrats (10.0 percent). This was also the case for the models of voting behaviour in Britain based on the BES CIPS data. Overall, analysis of BSA data shows that the effects of religion on party support in Britain are channelled through belonging and behaving.

Conclusion

This chapter has provided a detailed assessment of the historical relationship between religious affiliation and party support in Britain, in particular using two recurrent survey sources (BES and BSA). The historic data bear out the two most historically important associations between Christian denominations and major political parties in 20th-century British electoral politics: Anglicans and the Conservatives, Catholics and Labour. Those with no religious affiliation (a growing segment of the BES samples over time) also show a tendency to support Labour over the other parties. Analyses of these associations also needs to show an appreciation for the other social factors which intersect with religious belonging. That is, Catholics living in Scotland have traditionally shown higher levels of support for Labour than their co-religionists in England. In relation to social class, Anglicans in non-manual occupations have displayed higher levels of support for the Conservatives than those in manual work. Catholics in manual employment have registered higher party vote shares for Labour compared to those in non-manual occupations. It is worth also remarking that the historical evidence does not show any evidence of monolithic 'bloc voting' amongst religious traditions at post-war general elections; that is, a significant proportion of Anglicans and Catholics have voted for, respectively, the Labour and Conservative parties. That said, the levels of support for the Labour Party registered amongst Catholics in Scotland have approached very high levels, frequently exceeding 70.0 percent, always higher than the equivalent vote share in England.

Religious belonging and party choice also varied on the basis of religious behaviour. Anglicans who attended religious services on a frequent basis were also more likely, historically, to support the Conservatives compared to those who attended less often or not at all; such a pattern was not evident for Catholics, though. These associations were also evident from party support data based on BSA surveys conducted in recent decades. Further analysis of contemporary data from the BSA also showed that these associations held up when accounting for a range of other sociological characteristics. Overall, then, the analysis of party support data from the BES and BSA surveys tends to support the assertion of Heath et al. (1993a: 50) that, as far as Anglicans and Catholics are concerned: '[M]embers of particular religions or denominations may nonetheless continue to identify with and support specific political parties, perhaps as a result of longstanding loyalties or associations'. So while it may be archaic to characterise Anglicans as the 'Conservative Party at prayer', and the party itself has moved on from being the 'church party' in the 1980s (Filby 2013), Anglicans continue to show a greater propensity to support the Conservative Party compared to other religion traditions, as Catholics do for the Labour Party. The traditional linkages between parties and religious groups which were established by and endured because of a 'frozen' religious cleavage in British society may still exercise influence over contemporary patterns of party support in wider society (Lipset and Rokkan 1967; Tilley 2014).

4
Religion and Ideology

This chapter examines the over-time relationship between religion and political ideology in Britain. Public debate and party-political contestation over socio-economic issues 'are at the core of contemporary European politics' (Davis and Robinson 1999: 1633). The chapter focuses mainly on three core dimensions of ideology, which can be said to be highly relevant for public attitudes and party contestation in post-war British politics. These are the left-right (or socialist-laissez-faire) axis, related to the class structure traditionally underpinning British party politics (Sanders 1999; Heath et al. 1996), welfare ideology, and the libertarian-authoritarian axis, which might be said to cover broadly non-economic issues. The case for examining the relationship between religion and political ideology on socio-economic issues is clear, as Wilson observes:

> ... there is perhaps no command more universally normative in the world's great religious traditions than the imperative of charity towards the poor. Thus, it would seem natural to assume a powerful nexus between religious belief and economic policy issues (2009: 191).

Previous research has noted that 'there tends to be the general assumption that "traditional" religious beliefs are naturally compatible with conservative political attitudes' (Froese and Bader 2008: 690). Davis and Robinson note that because of this it is often left unstated that 'conservative religious beliefs go with conservative political beliefs and progressive religious beliefs with progressive politics' (1999: 1632). However, both cross-national and single-country research has qualified this widely-held assumption in important respects, particularly in relation to beliefs and values concerning socio-economic policies (Froese and Bader 2008; Davis and Robinson 1999; Wilson 1999). Other cross-national studies have looked at the role played by religious affiliation, practice and beliefs in underpinning public attitudes towards redistribution and welfare provision (VanHeuvelen 2014; Jordan, 2013; Stegmueller et al. 2012; Scheve and Stasavage 2006).

This chapter aims to examine the evidence on religion and core ideological beliefs in Britain. Are those belonging to particular religious traditions and those who attend services frequently, or show their religious engagement in other ways – belief or salience – more likely to hold right-wing economic beliefs and socially-authoritarian attitudes compared to those with no religion and those who infrequently or never attend religious services? Another important link to explore between religion and ideological beliefs lies in the historical links between denomination and political party explored in the previous chapter. Given their traditional association with the Labour Party, manifested in voting behaviour and party affiliation (as examined in Chapter 3), their historical status as a migrant community with lower socio-economic status, as well as the social justice tradition of Roman Catholic teaching (Wilson 2009), do Catholics hold more left-wing views in socio-economic debates? Similarly, given the established support for the Conservative Party expressed by Anglicans, do they tend towards more right-wing or individualist views on socio-economic policy questions? This is also a pertinent area for investigation given the opposition to aspects of the Conservative governments' economic and welfare policies expressed by senior clergy within the Church of England in the 1980s (Gover 2011; Martin 1989; Baker 1991). As Filby observes for this period: '... Church leaders heralded the welfare state, redistributive taxation and government responsibility for the disadvantaged as the correct political manifestation of the Biblical doctrine of Christian fellowship' (2010: 14). Moreover, there has been recent controversy over critical remarks made by leading Catholic and Anglican bishops concerning the ramifications of the coalition government's welfare reforms (Boffey 2011; Bingham 2014).

The first section of the chapter examines the evidence relating to left-right ideology. The second section looks at religious groups' belief on welfare. The third section assesses beliefs relating to libertarian-authoritarian beliefs. The fourth section investigates authoritarian beliefs in greater detail, looking at two debates of historical and contemporary relevance for the beliefs and identities of religious traditions in Britain – application of the death penalty, where religious groups played a prominent role in the post-war debate over abolition, and the use of censorship for upholding moral standards and on religious grounds.

Left-right ideology

Questions of redistribution and the role of government have been at the heart of post-war debates in British politics and citizens' core beliefs and values have been consequential in influencing party choice at general elections (Sanders 1999). Moreover, 'these enduring core beliefs can account in part for the individual's attitudes towards the more transient political issues of the day' (Heath et al. 1993b: 115). In post-war British politics, the left-right ideological dimension or axis of political competition has encompassed a range of shifting debates and policies:

> Issues like privatization and the free market can be thought of as belonging to the conventional left-right dimension around which British politics has largely been organized in the postwar period. Other left-right issues include unemployment and inflation, economic inequality, trade unions and government spending. Attitudes towards these different issues tend to go together (Heath et al. 1991: 173).

Different indicators can be utilised to assess whether there are differences in left-right orientations based on religious affiliation and attendance. The types of survey instrument used here fall into two distinct types. Firstly, surveys have posed questions which ask about more abstract beliefs concerning left-right ideology, concerning what government should or should not do, and what should be core societal objectives. Second, surveys have asked respondents to locate themselves on a scale (acting as an ideological continuum) which ranges from the most left-wing point through to the most right-wing point. These scales usually range from 1 to 10 or from 0 to 10. It is worth noting that the latter type of measure often engender a proportion of missing data, as some respondents, particularly those with lower levels or education or who are politically disengaged, are unable to easily locate themselves using an abstract scale (Heath et al. 1993b; see also Butler and Stokes 1969).

Attitudes are first examined using the BSA surveys, which carried a battery of five questions since 1986 (with the exception of the 1997 survey), which together form valid and reliable left-right scales (Park et al. 2012: 163). The questions are worded as follows:

> How much do you agree or disagree that ... big business benefits owners at the expense of workers.
>
> How much do you agree or disagree that ... government should redistribute income from the better-off to those who are less well off.
>
> How much do you agree or disagree that ... management will always try to get the better of employees if it gets the chance.
>
> How much do you agree or disagree that ... ordinary working people do not get their fair share of the nation's wealth.
>
> How much do you agree or disagree that ... there is one law for the rich and one for the poor.

Response options come in the form of Likert-style scales, with five substantive options, which range from 'strongly agree' through to 'strongly disagree'. A neutral position can be registered by answering 'neither agree nor disagree'. Note that all questions are consistently-worded so that agreement always denotes *a left-wing position*. The mean scores on this scale (which ranges from 1 to 5 with a mid-point of 3) are charted for both religious affiliation and attendance. These are displayed in Figure 4.1 (affiliation) and Figure 4.2 (attendance). Are there differences in group mean scores when looking more closely at the beginning and end time-points for the series (1986 and 2012)?

In 1986, during the era of the Thatcher governments and when 'many Church leaders became known from 1980 as outspoken critics of government economic and social policy' (Machin 1998: 226), by a narrow margin Anglicans had the most right-wing score, at 2.61, compared to 2.56 for other Christians. Catholics and those with no religion registered slightly more left-wing scores, at 2.49 and 2.47, respectively (with a gap of 0.14 between the lowest and highest scores). In 2012, a similar pattern is evident, with average scores of 2.56 for other Christians and 2.57 for Anglicans, and 2.47 for Catholics and 2.45 for those with no affiliation).

Any single reading of left-right orientations is of limited use, so a more robust picture of group mean scores can be produced by averaging them over the 1986 to 2012 period. This gives overall scores as follows: Anglicans: 2.61; Catholics: 2.47; other Christian: 2.57; no religion: 2.49. Over the period as a whole, then Anglicans have more right-wing orientations (or, less left-wing orientations), followed

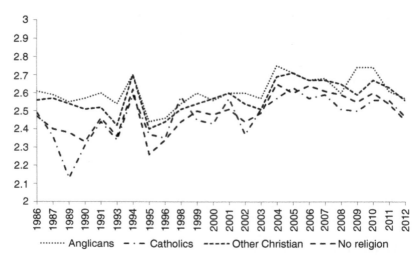

Figure 4.1   Mean scores on the left-right scale, by affiliation, 1986–2012
Source: BSA surveys.

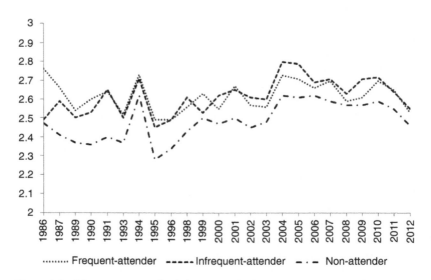

Figure 4.2   Mean scores on the left-right scale, by attendance, 1986–2012
Source: BSA surveys.

closely by other Christians. Catholics and those with no affiliation held less right-wing, or more left-wing, orientations. More broadly, all groups are positioned on the left-side of the scale (given that the mid-point is 3), and in no survey does any of the groups register a score of 3 or higher.

Turning next to religious attendance (Figure 4.2), in 1986 those who attended services frequently had the most right-wing score (at 2.73) compared to very similar scores for frequent and non-attenders (respectively, 2.49 and 2.47). In 2012, the differences are narrower, with frequent and infrequent-attenders registering almost identical scores (2.53 and 2.55, respectively), and those who never attend lower – and slightly more left-wing – at 2.46. When averaging the scores across the time period, those who do not attend services are less right-wing overall (2.48) than frequent or infrequent-attenders (both at 2.62). More broadly, all groups again have a slightly left-wing stance overall; and, as with religious affiliation, no score in any of the surveys reaches the mid-point value of 3 or above. Overall, then, whether classified by affiliation or attendance, religious groups have generally adopted slightly left-of-centre stances in terms of left-right ideology, based on evidence from the BSA surveys.

The left-right scale used in the BSA surveys comprises five separate questions, as outlined already, which, while through aggregation provides a more reliable measure of underlying attitudes, can also serve to obscure more finely grained differences. The scale can therefore be 'unpacked' to see if there are notable differences of attitudes by affiliation and attendance for any of these questions. This is done for the most recent survey (BSA 2012). Table 4.1 shows the proportions who agree (either strongly agreeing or agreeing) for each of the five statements (remembering that, for this scale, this always denotes the left-wing position). There is no consistent pattern of differences across most or all of the questions. That said, it is apparent that Anglicans (53.8 percent) and other Christians (53.6 percent) are somewhat less likely to agree with the statement that 'management will always try to get the better of employees' than are Catholics (62.5 percent) and those with no religion (58.5 percent). But based on the 'one law', 'fair share', 'big business' and 'redistribute income' items, there is less variation in levels of agreement across the three Christian groups. On some of the other questions, those with no religion are slightly more likely to agree – that is, to hold more left-wing beliefs. Across the questions, the lowest levels of agreement are registered for the item on the government redistributing income, with around two-fifths in each group

Table 4.1   Left-right scale: Percent who agree, by affiliation and attendance

	Redistribute income (%)	Big business (%)	Fair share (%)	One law (%)	Management (%)
Affiliation					
Anglican	38.5	52.7	57.1	64.1	53.8
Catholic	40.5	56.7	61.0	64.0	62.5
Other Christian	39.3	51.3	59.3	61.0	53.6
No religion	43.1	55.7	64.4	67.1	58.5
Attendance					
Frequent-attender	48.6	55.8	59.0	57.1	50.9
Infrequent-attender	37.4	51.5	58.2	64.4	56.6
Non-attender	41.6	55.3	64.0	67.8	59.6

Source: BSA 2012 survey.
Note: Combines 'strongly agree' and 'agree'.

supportive of this. Of course, support may be lower because of the particular phrasing of this question, referring to the government. A question that does not refer to the role of government may attract higher levels of agreement. Overall, based on a more finely-grained analysis of left-right attitudes, there are no consistent differences either between Christian traditions or between those with a religious affiliation and those without.

There is much similarity in levels of agreement across groups divided by frequency of attendance, although one clear exception is the statement on whether 'there is one law for the rich and one for the poor', where those who never attend are more likely to express agreement (67.8 percent) than those who attend frequently (57.1 percent). On several of the other questions those who do not attend services are slightly more likely to agree with the statement proposed; that is, they are more likely to hold left-wing views in relation to the questions on 'fair share' and 'management'. In terms of levels of agreement with the statement, they are lowest in relation to the question on redistribution, with around two-fifths of non-attenders and infrequent-attenders in agreement, rising to nearly half for frequent-attenders. Overall, though, when disaggregating the left-right scale, group attitudes are characterised more by convergence than divergence in levels of agreement with individual statements, although there are some exceptions.

Table 4.2   Linear regression of the left-right scale, BSA 2012

Variable	B (SE)		Beta
Constant	2.43*	(.05)	
Sex	−.07*	(.03)	−.04
Age	.00*	(.00)	−.11
Marital status	.10*	(.03)	.06
Children in household	.00	(.03)	.00
Degree qualification	.02	(.04)	.01
Salariat	.20*	(.03)	.13
Owner-occupier	.19*	(.03)	.11
Anglican	.14*	(.04)	.08
Catholic	.01	(.06)	.00
Other Christian	.11*	(.04)	.06
Other religion	−.29*	(.07)	−.08
Attendance	.01	(.01)	.02
Weighted N		2,739	
Adjusted R Square		.06	

Note: *$p<.05$ or lower.
Reference category: no religion.
Source: BSA 2012 survey.

Multivariate analysis is undertaken of the BSA 2012 survey data, to see the impact of affiliation and attendance on left-right beliefs when accounting for other social factors. Several indicators of socio-economic circumstances are included given that these are expected to be particularly important underpinnings of public attitudes towards left-right and social welfare orientations. As Heath et al. noted in their earlier research: '... it may be sensible to regard attitudes towards these issues as reflections, in part, of class interests' (1991: 173). Religion is measured by five dummy variables (Anglican, Catholic, other Christian, other religion and no religion), with those expressing no affiliation as the omitted reference group. Attendance is measured as a scale ranging from 1 (never attends) through to 7 (attends once a week or more). Linear regression was used for the model estimation and results are presented in Table 4.2. To reiterate, higher scores on the dependent variable indicate more right-wing orientations.

It is evident that, even when controlling for different indicators of socio-economic background as well as demographic variables, religion has a significant effect on left-right beliefs. First, Anglicans are more likely to have right-wing orientations compared to those with no religion (Beta: .08), as are other Christians (Beta: .06). Therefore, there is some evidence that their ideological orientations are in line with their greater disposition to support the Conservative Party, both historically and on the basis of contemporary assessments undertaken in Chapter 3. However, Catholics are not significantly different from the reference category. Members of non-Christian religions are less likely to have right-wing beliefs (Beta: −.08). Net of affiliation, frequency of attendance has no significant impact on left-right beliefs.

As already discussed, left-right orientations can also be ascertained using self-placement scales, which have featured in every EVS survey as well as in some BES surveys. First, data from the EVS are analysed, which included a self-placement scale in each survey (1981, 1990, 1999 and 2008). The data are based on a left-right self-placement scale where 1 represents the most left-wing stance and 10 the most right-wing position.[1] The question asked was as follows:

> In political matters, people talk of 'the left' and 'the right'. How would you place your views on this scale generally speaking.

The data are presented in Table 4.3, with an advantage here being that, given the EVS's extensive battery of questions on religion, other measures of religious belief can also be examined. Specifically, respondents can also be classified by whether they are a member of a religious group or not, whether they consider themselves to be a religious person or not, and whether they believe in God.

Looking at affiliation, Anglicans show more right-wing scores than the other religious groups, particularly Catholics and those with no affiliation. This is the case for 1981, 1990 and 2008, with 1999 being somewhat of an anomaly (with other Christians scoring the highest). The evidence for attendance shows that those who never attend services register less right-wing positions on the scale in each survey than those who attend either infrequently or often. Those who belong to a religious organisation or group also evince more right-wing self-placement scores in every survey compared to those who do not. A similar pattern is evident for those who perceived themselves to be religious, with those who do not consider themselves a religious person more left-wing based on self-placement, in each survey. There is also consistent evidence for two belief measures. That is, those who express a belief in God or who think there is a personal God register higher (more right-wing) scores on the self-placement scale. Again, the direction of the difference is consistent over time. Based on the EVS survey data, and regardless of whether religion is measured by belonging,

Table 4.3   Mean scores on a left-right self-placement scale, by religious group, 1981–2008

	1981	1990	1999	2008
Affiliation				
Anglican[a]	5.91	5.81	5.13	5.64
Catholic	5.36	5.44	5.02	4.95
Other Christian	5.74	5.41	5.24	5.43
No religion	4.50	5.08	4.82	5.03
Attendance				
Frequent-attender	6.10	5.7	5.45	5.37
Infrequent-attender	5.83	5.71	5.14	5.33
Non-attender	5.39	5.12	4.91	5.20
Membership				
Member of a religious group	6.29	5.70	5.63	5.44
Not a member of a religious group	5.52	5.39	5.05	5.24
Identity				
Is a religious person	5.93	5.68	5.36	5.53
Is not/is a convinced atheist	5.36	5.16	4.88	5.05
Beliefs				
Believes in god	5.90	5.57	5.27	5.44
Other response	5.07	5.11	4.76	5.01
Personal God	6.06	5.66	5.25	5.35
Other response	5.54	5.33	5.01	5.11

Source: EVS surveys.
[a] Note that this category for the 1981 survey covers Protestant traditions apart from Non-conformists. For all subsequent surveys, Non-conformists and other Christian traditions fall within the 'other Christian' category.

behaviour or belief, religious engagement is associated with more right-wing dispositions based on self-placement scales. Is this general pattern evident for the self-placement scales asked on the BES surveys (1997, 2001, and 2005), for which a more limited set of religion measures is available. The BES question was worded as follows:

> In politics people sometimes talk of left and right. Where would you place yourself on a scale from 0 to 10, where 0 means the left and 10 means the right?

Table 4.4 presents the mean scores based on left-right self-placement scales administered in three BES surveys (1997–2005). Scores are produced based on affiliation (for all three surveys) and attendance (for

Table 4.4   **Mean scores on a left-right self-placement scale, by affiliation and attendance, 1997–2005**

	1997	2001	2005
Affiliation			
Anglican	5.49	5.53	5.83
Catholic	4.76	5.25	5.52
Other Christian	5.19	5.32	5.83
No religion	4.58	4.74	5.00
Attendance			
Frequent-attender	5.35	–	–
Infrequent-attender	5.18	–	–
Non-attender	4.88	–	–

Source: BES surveys.

1997 only). The scales ranged from 0 (most left-wing) through to 10 (most right-wing), with 5 as the mid-point. There is corroborating evidence for the EVS surveys, in that Anglicans are more likely to have right-wing orientations than Catholics and those with no religion. This is also the case relative to other Christians, with the exception of 2005, when the scores are identical (both at 5.83). The evidence for attendance is limited to the 1997 survey, but there is some link with frequency of participation. Those who attend frequently register the more right-wing score (5.35) compared to infrequent (5.18) and non-attenders (4.88).

Finally, the ESS is used to assess left-right orientations. The ESS has been running on a bi-annual basis since 2002, with the latest data available from the 2012 survey. Every survey in the series has featured a left-right self-placement scale ranging from 0 (most left-wing) and 10 (most-right-wing).[2] The question was worded as follows:

> In politics people sometimes talk of 'left' and 'right'. Using this card, where would you place yourself on this scale, where 0 means the left and 10 means the right?

As with the EVS, a wider range of religion measures can be used. As well as affiliation and attendance the ESS asks about frequency of prayer and how religious respondents are (note that usable measures of affiliation are not available for 2002–06). Both frequency of prayer and personal religiosity were divided into three categories for the purposes of the analysis undertaken here. Frequency of prayer is divided

Table 4.5   Mean scores on a left-right self-placement scale, by religious group, 2002–2012

	2002	2004	2006	2008	2010	2012
Affiliation						
Anglican	–	–	–	5.47	5.55	5.60
Catholic	–	–	–	4.90	5.28	5.20
Other Christian	–	–	–	4.77	5.02	5.22
No religion	–	–	–	4.84	4.82	4.77
Attendance						
Frequent-attender	5.47	5.16	5.39	5.05	5.19	5.28
Infrequent-attender	5.17	5.04	5.03	5.14	5.23	5.10
Non-attender	5.07	4.90	5.02	4.87	4.82	4.90
Prayer						
Once a week or more	5.23	5.11	5.31	5.09	5.20	5.20
Less often	5.26	4.93	5.08	5.27	5.21	5.32
Never	5.08	4.95	4.96	4.79	4.82	4.83
Religiosity						
Low	4.96	4.87	4.94	4.76	4.75	4.78
Medium	5.22	4.99	5.17	5.22	5.26	5.32
High religiosity	5.46	5.21	5.28	5.12	5.24	5.20

Source: ESS surveys.

between those who pray once a week or more, less often, or never pray. The religiosity scale, which ranges from 1 through to 10, is divided as follows: low religiosity: values 1–3; medium religiosity: values 4 to 7; high religiosity: values 8–10. The data from the ESS surveys are shown in Table 4.5. Looking first at affiliation (restricted to the 2008–12 surveys), again Anglicans are more likely to have a right-wing stance, on average, than other groups (Catholics, other Christians and those with no religion). In 2010 and 2012, those with no religion had the lowest scores on the self-placement scale.

The differences in group scores are narrower for attendance at religious services, though they are generally consistent in that those who do not attend register lower scores, on average, than frequent or infrequent attenders. Similarly, left-right scores are narrower based on frequency of prayer, but those who report they never pray tend to rank lower on the scale (that is, they show less right-wing orientations) in each survey. There is also a pattern evident based on personal religiosity. Those who report medium or high levels of religiosity show higher scores on the left-right scale in each survey, compared to those with low levels of religiosity. Taken together, across the EVS, BES and ESS surveys, those who are personally engaged with religion – whether through their sense of belonging, church attendance, or other beliefs and practices – are more likely to demonstrate right-wing orientations than those who have no religious affiliation, do not attend services, do not take part in other religious practices, are personally not particularly or at all religious and do not hold traditional religious beliefs. In other words, the left-right self-placement scales from the various survey series tend to reveal some degree of difference in ideological standing based on measures of belonging, behaving and believing, and these tend to be reasonably consistent across time.

Given the pattern that has arisen across surveys of Anglicans tending to have more right-wing orientations, based on the BSA ideological scales and the multi-survey self-placement measures, further multivariate analysis is conducted to assess the net effect of affiliation and other religious factors when accounting for the influence of sociological variables. The most recent EVS (2008) and ESS (2012) surveys are utilised, given the wide range of measures of religious engagement they offer. Given that the left-right self-placement scale is the dependent variable, linear regression is used for the multivariate analyses. The dependent variable is scored so that higher values represent more right-wing positions. The social variables included are sex, age, education, social class (except for the ESS), marital status and children in the household. The religious variables included for the EVS are affiliation, attendance, belonging to a religious organisation and belief in a personal God. The analysis of the ESS data includes frequency of prayer and personal religiosity, in addition to affiliation and attendance. Note that other Christians and members of non-Christian faiths have been combined into a single dummy category in the EVS due to sample size limitations. The results from the analyses are presented in Table 4.6 (EVS) and Table 4.7 (ESS).

Looking first at the analysis of the EVS data, being married and being in the highest occupational grade is associated with having a right-wing orientation, while completing education at an older age is negatively related to holding a right-wing stance. Interestingly, only religious affiliation has a statistically-significant effect in the analysis. In line with the earlier discussion, Anglicans are more likely to have right-wing orientations (Beta: .11) than those with no religion (the reference category) when accounting for other sociological factors, at least based on a self-placement scale. There are no other significant differences between religious groups and the reference category. Similar results are evident for the analysis based on the ESS survey data, where

Table 4.6   Linear regression of left-right self-placement scale, EVS 2008

Variable	B (SE)	Beta
Constant	5.08* (.28)	
Sex	.00 (.11)	.00
Age	.01 (.00)	.05
Marital status	.26* (.11)	.07
Children	.02 (.13)	.00
Finished education	−.03* (.01)	−.10
Occupation	.04 (.02)	.06
Anglican	.43* (.12)	.11
Catholic	−.16 (.19)	−.03
Other religion	.20 (.22)	.03
Attendance	.02 (.04)	.02
Member of religious organisation	−.03 (.20)	−.01
Personal God	.02 (.14)	.01
Weighted N	1,131	
Adjusted R Square	.03	

Note: *p<.05 or lower.
Reference category: no religion.
Source: EVS survey 2008.

Table 4.7   Linear regression of left-right self-placement scale, ESS 2012

Variable	B (SE)	Beta
Constant	5.05* (.24)	
Sex	−.01 (.09)	.00
Age	.00 (.00)	.02
Marital status	.10 (.10)	.03
Children	−.08 (.10)	−.02
Finished education	−.04* (.01)	−.07
Anglican	.66* (.13)	.15
Catholic	.20 (.17)	.03
Other Christian	.30 (.18)	.05
Other religion	−.21 (.21)	−.03
Attendance	.05 (.04)	.04
Prayer	−.02 (.03)	−.02
Religiosity	.04 (.02)	.06
Weighted N	1,728	
Adjusted R Square	.04	

Note: *p<.05 or lower.
Reference category: no religion.
Source: ESS survey 2012.

the only religion-based variable that has a significant effect is being an Anglican, which again shows a positive relationship with having more right-wing orientations (Beta: .15). None of the measures of religiousness (attendance, prayer or personal religiosity) has a significant net effect on left-right self-placement. The only social factor which is significantly associated with left-right self-placement is education (measured as the number of years of full-time education completed), where more years spent in education is negatively related to right-wing ideology.

Welfare ideology

It is also instructive to look at attitudes towards another long-running ideological scale which the BSA has carried since 1987. This relates to attitudes about welfare and therefore also taps into broader values and beliefs about social justice, redistribution and the role of government. Recent research, based on the BSA's 2009 survey which fielded a specialist battery of questions on these issues, found that 'clergy understand poverty very differently to their congregations, and that church attendance has little impact on people's underlying attitudes to these issues' (Church Urban Fund 2012: 4). Compared to the Church of England clergy, churchgoers underestimated the extent of poverty in Britain and only a minority thought it was due to injustice or structural reasons (Church Urban Fund 2012: 4). As already mentioned at the beginning of this chapter, recent research has found that religious factors – including belonging and behaving – shape public attitudes towards redistribution and welfare provision (VanHeuvelen 2014; Jordan, 2013; Stegmueller et al. 2012; Scheve and Stasavage 2006).

The BSA scale (also referred to as an individualist-welfarist scale) comprises eight separate questions, which are given below.

> How much do you agree or disagree that ... around here, most unemployed people could find a job if they really wanted one.
> How much do you agree or disagree that ... if welfare benefits weren't so generous, people would learn to stand on their own two feet.
> How much do you agree or disagree that ... many people who get social security don't really deserve any help.
> How much do you agree or disagree that ... most people on the dole are fiddling in one way or another.

How much do you agree or disagree that ... the government should spend more money on welfare benefits for the poor, even if it leads to higher taxes.

How much do you agree or disagree that ... the welfare state encourages people to stop helping each other.

How much do you agree or disagree that ... cutting welfare benefits would damage too many people's lives.

How much do you agree or disagree that ... the creation of the welfare state is one of Britain's proudest achievements.

As with the left-right scale, the response options take the form of Likert scales ranging again from 'strongly agree' through to 'strongly disagree'. The scale ranges from 1 (most pro-welfare) through to 5 (most anti-welfare), with a mid-point of 3. Note that five of these questions are worded in an anti-welfarist (or individualist) direction and three are worded in a pro-welfare (or collectivist) direction (listed in italics). Group mean scores over time are shown in Figure 4.3 (affiliation) and Figure 4.4 (attendance). In 1987, when the scale was first asked, Anglicans are slightly more anti-welfare (2.96) than the other groups (Catholics: 2.78; other Christian: 2.81; no religion: 2.84), a gap of 0.18 between the lowest and highest scores. In 2012,

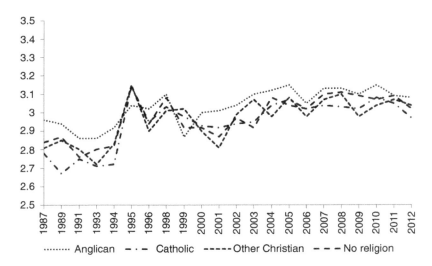

Figure 4.3 Mean scores on the welfare scale, by affiliation, 1987–2012
Source: BSA surveys.

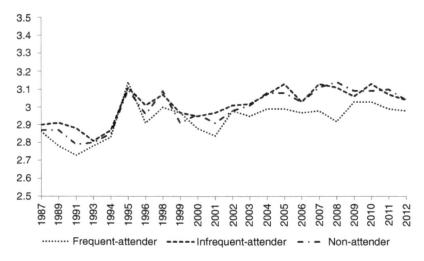

Figure 4.4　Mean scores on the welfare scale, by attendance, 1987–2012
Source: BSA surveys.

Anglicans rank highest at 3.08, followed by other Christians at 3.04 and those with no religion at 3.02. Catholics are the least individualist – or most pro-welfare of the groups – with a mean score of 2.97. When averaging the group scores over time, it is evident that they do not vary as much as do those produced for the BSA left-right scale. The overall average is 3.03 for Anglicans, 2.95 for Catholics, 2.96 for other Christians and 2.98 for those with no-religion.

Looking at mean scores on the welfare scale on the basis of attendance at religious services, in 1987 there is little to differentiate the three groups in the scale averages. There are scores of 2.86 for frequent-attenders, 2.90 for those attending less often and 2.87 for those who never attend (a gap of just 0.04). In 2012, again, the scores are clustered close together, at 3.04 for infrequent-attenders and non-attenders, and 2.98 for frequent-attenders. Averaged across time, the scores do not differ much, at 2.93 for frequent-attenders, 3.01 for infrequent-attenders and 2.99 for non-attenders.

Again, the underlying detail beneath the aggregated scale scores can be assessed by looking at levels of agreement with the eight items on welfare. Responses by affiliation and attendance are shown in Table 4.8. As with the responses to the items making up the left-right scale, there is no clear and consistent patterning here across the various questions. There are some differences in levels of agreement, where

Table 4.8 Welfare scale: Percent who agree, by affiliation and attendance

	Affiliation				Attendance		
	Anglican (%)	Catholic (%)	Other Christian (%)	No religion (%)	Frequent-attender (%)	Infrequent-attender (%)	Non-attender (%)
Stop helping	41.2	30.9	35.7	31.9	33.7	36.1	34.1
Spend more	35.1	37.9	31.7	34.0	38.9	31.7	34.4
Find a job	55.5	55.5	53.0	57.1	53.0	56.8	56.1
Don't deserve	39.9	34.3	36.9	36.0	32.5	33.8	37.9
Dole fiddling	38.6	38.1	32.4	39.2	32.7	33.5	40.3
Stand on own feet	61.4	46.9	55.6	50.4	55.2	56.9	52.8
Damage lives	42.3	51.0	44.0	48.9	49.4	45.8	47.9
Proudest achievements	60.9	60.2	56.3	50.7	63.6	56.0	53.1

Source: BSA 2012 survey.
Note: Combines 'strongly agree' and 'agree'.

Anglicans are more likely to offer individualist – that is, less pro-welfare – responses. Specifically, Anglicans are most likely to agree that the welfare state encourages people to stop helping each other (41.2 percent) and that if benefits were less generous more people would be self-sufficient (61.4 percent). These differences are most pronounced when Anglicans are compared to Catholics and those with no religion. One other difference of view occurs on the 'proud of the welfare state' question, with those with no religion least supportive of this statement (50.7 percent) and Anglicans and Catholics most likely to agree (60.9 percent and 60.2 percent respectively). Also, Catholics are more likely than Anglicans to agree that the welfare state damages lives: 51.0 percent and 42.3 percent, respectively.

There are few notable differences in pro-welfare or anti-welfare orientations evident on the basis of attendance at religious services. Those who attend services frequently are more likely to express agreement (63.6 percent) with the welfare state being one of the country's proudest achievements, compared to those who never attend (53.1 percent). On the question of dole fiddling by welfare recipients, those who never attend services are more likely to agree (40.3 percent) compared to regular attenders (32.7 percent) and irregular attenders (33.5 percent).

The more right-wing and anti-welfarist orientations of Anglicans resonate with findings from a contemporary survey of religion and popular attitudes in Britain. Based on the second Westminster Faith Debates survey of British adults, conducted in June 2013, it was reported that:

> But even when you control for age, more Anglicans fall at the 'free market' than the 'social welfare' end of the scale – and they are more 'free market' than the population as a whole. For example, just under half of all Anglicans, whether churchgoing or not, think that Mrs Thatcher did more good for Britain than Tony Blair, compared with 38.0% of the general population ... And nearly 70% of Anglicans believe that the welfare system has created a culture of dependency, which is almost 10 percentage points more than the general population (Woodhead 2013c).

Moreover, this survey also found that Anglicans were more likely than other religious groups, including Catholics, to believe that welfare spending should be reduced rather than increased or maintained at present levels (Bingham 2014).

Table 4.9   Linear regression of the welfare scale, BSA 2012

Variable	B (SE)	Beta
Constant	3.19* (.05)	
Sex	−.03 (.03)	−.02
Age	.00* (.00)	−.12
Marital status	.12* (.03)	.09
Children in household	.01 (.03)	.01
Degree qualification	−.19* (.04)	−.12
Salariat	−.08* (.03)	−.06
Owner-occupier	.11* (.03)	.08
Anglican	.10* (.04)	.06
Catholic	.00 (.05)	.00
Other Christian	.08* (.04)	.04
Other religion	−.07 (.06)	−.02
Attendance	−.01 (.01)	−.03
Weighted N	2,710	
Adjusted R Square	.04	

Note: *$p<.05$ or lower.
Reference category: no religion.
Source: BSA 2012 survey.

As a next step, multivariate analysis is undertaken of attitudes on the welfare scale, in order to see if religious affiliation and attendance have any net effects when accounting for a range of other social background characteristics. The other social factors included are the same as in Table 4.2 for the left-right scale. To reiterate, higher values on the scale used as the dependent variable indicate more individualist or anti-welfare orientations.

In keeping with their left-right beliefs, Anglicans are more individualist in their welfare orientations, compared to those with no religion (Beta: .06). This is also the case for other Christians (Beta: .04). Again, there are no significant differences for Catholics or members of non-Christian faiths, and attendance has no impact net of affiliation. The lack of distinctive beliefs for Catholics in Britain on welfare is interesting given that, as a religious tradition, it has stressed 'lessons of compassion and collective responsibility', with Catholics expected to be more supportive of social protection than Protestants (VanHeuvelen 2014: 271). The overall picture is somewhat different from that produced by existing cross-national research (Stegmueller et al. 2012), which has emphasised the role played by both belonging and behaviour, in that only religious affiliation appears to be consequential for general attitudes towards welfare provision in Britain. Again, it is Anglicans who stand out as more anti-welfarist, less in favour of collective provision and perhaps more supportive of individual self-reliance, in keeping with their more right-wing economic beliefs discussed earlier on. However, this finding for ordinary adherents stands somewhat in contrast to the tenor of announcements made by religious elites – including, leading clergy in the Church of England – concerning government policies on welfare provision in recent years.

Libertarian-authoritarian ideology

Earlier research into public opinion and voting behaviour in Britain found that attitudes were also structured along a second, non-economic dimension, primarily centring on social issues such as the death penalty, which tapped into liberal or authoritarian beliefs (Heath et al. 1991). The BSA surveys have asked an identical battery of six questions from 1986 onwards, which together comprise a libertarian-authoritarian scale, a reliable and valid multi-item measure (Park et al. 2012: 163). The six questions are worded as follows:

> Young people today don't have enough respect for traditional British values.
> People who break the law should be given stiffer sentences.
> For some crimes, the death penalty is the most appropriate sentence.
> Schools should teach children to obey authority.
> The law should always be obeyed, even if a particular law is wrong.
> Censorship of films and magazines is necessary to uphold moral standards.

As with the left-right and welfarism scales, Likert-style response options are used, which range from 'strongly agree' through to 'strongly disagree'. The questions are consistently worded so that agreement denotes support for more authoritarian opinions. Group mean scores on the libertarian-authoritarian scale are charted on the basis of affiliation and attendance. These mean scores are shown in Figure 4.5 (for affiliation) and Figure 4.6 (for attendance). What is immediately obvious is that the lines track each other closely over time, although there is evidence of slightly more variation in group scores on the basis of affiliation.

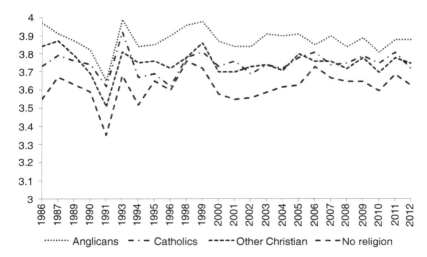

Figure 4.5   Mean scores on the libertarian-authoritarian scale, by affiliation, 1986–2012
Source: BSA surveys.

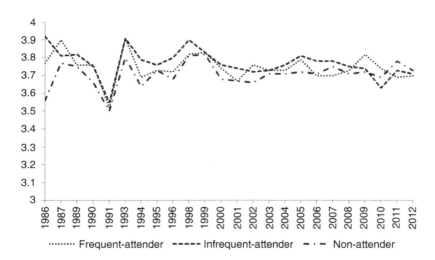

Figure 4.6   Mean scores on the libertarian-authoritarian scale, by attendance, 1986–2012
Source: BSA surveys.

Looking in more detail at the group scores over time (which again can range from 1 to 5 with 3 as the mid-point), Anglicans tend, on the whole, to have slightly more authoritarian views. In 1986, the mean score for Anglicans was 3.97 compared to 3.73 for Catholics and 3.55 for those with no religious affiliation. Other Christians had an average of 3.84, below that of Anglicans but higher than Catholics. In 2012, Anglicans (3.88) ranked above the other groups in their more authoritarian orientations. Catholics had a mean score of 3.72, while that of other Christians was 3.75. Those with no religion again had the lowest mean score, at 3.63. This ranking applies when averaging each group's mean scores across the entire period from 1986 to 2012. The average scores are as follows: Anglicans: 3.88; Catholics: 3.75; other Christian: 3.75; no religion: 3.62. Looking more broadly, it is clear that all groups are more authoritarian in their orientations over time than they are right-wing or anti-welfare. In fact, no individual reading on the libertarian-authoritarian scale registers at 3.50 or below between 1986 and 2012.

Next, libertarian-authoritarian orientations are examined on the basis of attendance at religious services. Is greater religious involvement associated with greater political conservatism (here, socially-authoritarian beliefs)? In 1986, those who attended services infrequently registered the highest mean score, at 3.96, compared to 3.77 for frequent-attenders and 3.56 for non-attenders (a gap of 0.40 between the highest and lowest scores, the largest differential for any of the BSA scales). In 2012, the differences were much narrower, with non-attenders registering the highest mean score (at 3.73), followed by 3.71 for infrequent-attenders and 3.70 for frequent-attenders. When scores are averaged over the 1986–2012 period, the differences in overall mean scores are narrower than those evident for affiliation: frequently-attending: 3.75; infrequently-attending; 3.77; never attends: 3.71. Again, the broad characterisation of public opinion being more socially-authoritarian than either right-wing or welfarist in socio-economic terms applies to each group when classified by attendance.

As was shown already in relation to the left-right and welfarism scales, there may be group differences on particular items which comprise the scales but which are not evident when aggregated into a multi-item attitudinal measure. Table 4.10 therefore shows responses based on religious affiliation and attendance for each of the six items comprising the libertarian-authoritarian scale. It presents the proportions who express agreement with each statement – that is, who give an authoritarian response. The more detailed assessment does show

Table 4.10   Libertarian-authoritarian scale: Percent who agree, by affiliation and attendance

	Traditional values (%)	Stiffer sentences (%)	Death penalty (%)	Obey authority (%)	Always obey law (%)	Censorship necessary (%)
Affiliation						
Anglican	77.0	87.6	60.7	88.4	43.9	76.9
Catholic	71.7	78.5	50.0	86.3	41.7	65.2
Other Christian	73.6	78.2	51.5	84.9	45.0	70.0
No religion	69.4	76.6	56.2	80.0	37.8	53.4
Attendance						
Frequent-attender	69.6	77.3	43.8	85.6	41.2	74.5
Infrequent-attender	70.4	79.6	53.4	82.5	40.0	67.8
Non-attender	73.5	80.0	58.9	83.0	41.2	59.0

Source: BSA 2012 survey.

some interesting differences of view, within the overall context of high levels of agreement across groups with many of the statements. It is evident that those with no religious affiliation are, for some measures, less socially-authoritarian than those belonging to a religious tradition. In response to the question on traditional values, those with no religion are somewhat less likely to express agreement than religious identifiers, as they are in response to the question on obeying authority. The largest difference, though, occurs in attitudes towards censorship, with just over half (53.4 percent) of those with no affiliation being in agreement, compared to around seven in ten or more of those belonging to the three religious groups (highest at 76.9 percent for Anglicans). This question, of course, refers to censorship in general, but – amongst those with a religious affiliation – it may elicit more specific concerns over material in the public domain which is offensive to religious traditions and beliefs. Differences are also evident for views on the death penalty, with Anglicans (60.7 percent in agreement) and those with no religion (56.2 percent) more in favour than Catholics (50.0 percent) and other Christians (51.5 percent). On the issues of stiffer sentences and traditional values, while agreement is generally very high, Anglicans are somewhat more authoritarian than the other groups.

Responses are also given for the three groups classified by attendance at religious services. Differences are again most evident for the questions on the death penalty and censorship, for which there is not a consistent group pattern of authoritarian responses. Those who attend services frequently are most likely to express agreement with censorship (at 74.5 percent) compared to those who attend infrequently (67.8 percent) or not at all (59.0 percent). However, they are least likely to register agreement with the question on the death penalty, with less than a majority in favour (43.8 percent), compared to over a half of infrequent attenders (53.4 percent) and about three-fifths of non-attenders (58.9 percent).

As for the left-right and welfare scales, a multivariate analysis is undertaken of the libertarian-authoritarian scale, using data from the BSA 2012 survey. The same model specification is used. Linear regression was used and the results are presented in Table 4.11. Controlling for a range of other sociological characteristics, including the socio-economic indicators, both affiliation and attendance have significant effects, although in opposite directions. First, *every* religious group – Christian and non-Christian – is more socially-authoritarian in their beliefs compared to those with no religion (Anglican – Beta: .14;

Table 4.11   Linear regression of the libertarian-authoritarian scale, BSA 2012

Variable	B (SE)	Beta
Constant	3.63* (.04)	
Sex	.03 (.02)	.02
Age	.00* (.00)	.08
Marital status	.04 (.03)	.03
Children in household	.08* (.03)	.06
Degree qualification	−.36* (.03)	−.22
Salariat	−.13* (.03)	−.09
Owner-occupier	−.07* (.03)	−.05
Anglican	.22* (.03)	.14
Catholic	.11* (.04)	.05
Other Christian	.17* (.05)	.10
Other religion	.24* (.06)	.08
Attendance	−.02* (.01)	−.06
Weighted N	2,747	
Adjusted R Square	.12	

Note: *p<.05 or lower.
Reference category: no religion.
Source: BSA 2012.

Catholic – Beta: .05; other Christian – Beta: .10; other religion – Beta: .08). There is more of a broader religious-secular divide in this area of ideology than was evident for left-right or welfare ideology, where Anglicans had distinctive beliefs compared to those with no religion. Second, net of affiliation, higher levels of attendance are negatively-related to authoritarian beliefs, which hints at attitudinal variation within religious traditions (note, also, that a greater proportion of the overall variance in the dependent variable is explained in this model: 12.0 percent compared to 6.0 percent for the left-right scale and just 4.0 percent for the welfare scale). In terms of the other variables, there is a stronger effect for education (measured by having a degree-level qualification) than for either the left-right or welfare scales, which, as previous research has noted, is particularly important for explaining liberal orientations (Heath et al. 1991: 173).

Attitudes towards the death penalty

The contemporary data presented for libertarian-authoritarian beliefs revealed some particularly clear differences in religious groups' contemporary beliefs about censorship and the death penalty. Existing research has shown that levels of authoritarianism vary by both religious belonging and behaving (Hetherington and Weiler 2009: 60). In this and the subsequent section, libertarian-authoritarian beliefs are 'unpacked', and separate analyses are conducted on religious groups' attitudes towards, respectively, capital punishment and censorship (both in general and the banning of offensive material on religious grounds).

Research into the effect of religion on attitudes towards the death penalty has shown significant differences on the basis of affiliation and other religious characteristics. Cross-national research – including Britain – into religion and attitudes on capital punishment showed that Protestants were more likely to be in favour (Hayes 1995). An extensive literature on religion and public opinion on capital punishment exists for US public opinion (Bader et al. 2010; Wozniak and Lewis 2010; Unnever and Cullen 2006; Unnever et al. 2005; Unnever et al. 2006). More specifically, research in the US has shown that 'Catholics have been consistently less supportive of the death penalty than white Protestants since the 1980s' (Hanley 2008: 122), with similar differences based on religious tradition documented in recent polling by Pew and Gallup (Pew 2012; Newport 2009). Other research has shown that the key difference in support for the death penalty in the US is between Christians – irrespective of their tradition – and those with no religion (Wozniak and Lewis 2010). These findings highlight the need for a contemporary analysis of the religious basis of views on capital punishment in Britain.

The issue of capital punishment is an archetypal example of the 'sanctity of life' issues for which, across the Christian traditions, the Catholic Church has strongly advocated a 'consistent life ethic'.

> Advanced most strongly by the Catholic Church, this ethic embraces the view that life should be preserved under all, or nearly all, circumstances. The consistent life ethic thus endorses the protection of human life through opposition to abortion, the death penalty, euthanasia, stem cell research, and war (Unnever et al. 2010).

However, little attention has been given to views of religious groups – whether Catholics or other traditions – in Britain in recent decades. Abolition was an important issue of social and political debate in the 1950s and 1960s and religious traditions and their leaders – including the Church of England bishops sitting in the House of Lords –

played a prominent role in public discourse. Historical research has examined the role and positions of Christian religious traditions in the debates regarding the campaign to abolish the death penalty in the early post-war decades (Twitchell 2012; McLeod 2004; Potter 1993), which was finally achieved through The Murder (Abolition of Death Penalty) Act 1965. This reform was one of several major, liberalising social reforms of the 1960s underpinned by support from across the main political parties (see Chapters 5 and 6 for analysis of two other areas of post-war legislative reform, abortion and homosexuality). As Machin notes, there was considerable diversity of view on the merits of abolition both between and within Christian traditions (1996: 367). In terms of the similarity of the views of religious leaders and ordinary adherents, Twitchell notes that 'one must distinguish between the hierarchy, the lower clergy and the ordinary member. Generally the lower down the ladder the more conservative the views were, on capital punishment and the issues' (2012: 155). Given this historical context, a detailed assessment of the opinions of religious groups towards capital punishment in the period since its abolition is overdue.

Opinion polls conducted in the early post-war years prior to abolition found some differences – though not always consistent – across categories of religious affiliation in levels of support for the suspension or abolition of the death penalty. A Gallup poll from 1947 found majorities across religious groups in favour of capital punishment: highest at 74.0 percent for the Church of England and 72.0 percent for Catholics, followed by 65.0 percent for Nonconformists. Support was lower for those with no religion and others (respectively, 55.0 percent and 58.0 percent) (Twitchell 2012: 157). Subsequently, polling was undertaken on the approval or disapproval of the suspension of hanging in surveys conducted in 1948 and 1956, which showed considerable change of opinion over time across religious groups. In 1948, only small minorities of Christian traditions wanted the suspension of hanging (10.0 percent for the Church of England, 15.0 percent for Catholics, 12.0 percent for the Church of Scotland and 17.0 percent for Nonconformists). In the 1956 survey, approval of suspension had risen to 45.0 percent for Catholics, 35.0 percent for Nonconformists, 32.0 percent for the Church of England, and 30.0 percent for the Church of Scotland (Twitchell 2012: 166). In the later survey, therefore, a plurality of Catholics – but still none of the other Christian groups – now approved of suspension of the death penalty. Those with no religious affiliation also registered a large increase in favour of suspension, from 16.0 percent to 26.0 percent. A Gallup poll undertaken in 1964 found that, concerning the abolition of the death penalty, Anglicans and Catholics were more in favour of retaining it (70.0 percent and 71.0 percent, respectively), than were members of the Free Churches (63.0 percent) (*Daily Telegraph* 1964).

Attitudes on the death penalty across time can be examined in detail using the BES and BSA surveys, allowing for a comparison of affiliation and attendance. Nearly every BES study has asked a question on this issue, although the wordings and response options have changed somewhat across surveys (a full list of question wordings is provided in the Appendix). Table 4.12 shows attitudes based on affiliation, showing responses to the various questions on the death penalty from 1963 to 2010 (none were asked in the two 1974 election surveys). In each case, Table 4.12 reports the proportion within each group with positive assessments of the death penalty.

Levels of pro-death penalty support vary over time, which will partly reflect the question wording and response options available in the different surveys. Generally, though, Catholics are least supportive of capital punishment, and Anglicans are most in favour. That is, in the earlier decades, Catholics were less likely to support keeping the death penalty or reinstating it; in the later decades, as well as again being less likely to favour its return, they were less likely to disagree with the

Table 4.12   Attitudes towards the death penalty, by affiliation, 1963–2010

		Anglican (%)	Catholic (%)	Other Christian (%)	No religion (%)
1963	Kept/kept for certain crimes	80.9	75.8	75.7	47.1
1966	Kept	82.3	83.3	84.5	59.1
1979	Very important or important it should be done	74.7	60.7	67.4	66.8
1983	Agree	60.7	50.2	52.5	54.8
1987	Agree	79.5	73.5	74.3	72.3
1992	Agree	49.9	40.4	42.2	43.6
1997	Agree	54.9	44.8	44.3	45.2
2001	Disagree	47.0	29.5	37.3	40.0
2005	Disagree	53.5	38.6	45.0	47.5
2010	Disagree	47.6	36.6	47.3	43.5

Source: BES surveys.

Table 4.13   Attitudes towards the death penalty, by attendance, 1963–2010

		Frequent-attender (%)	Infrequent-attender (%)	Non-attender (%)
1963	Kept/kept for certain crimes	73.4	81.0	80.7
1966	Kept	80.2	83.1	83.9
1979	Very important or important it should be done	61.8	71.6	67.6
1983	Agree	42.6	60.3	63.3
1987	Agree	65.7	81.2	76.8
1992	Agree	34.4	44.7	49.3
1997	Agree	42.5	46.9	51.3
2010	Disagree	41.5	47.4	44.9

Source: BES surveys.

proposition that the death penalty is never justified, even for very serious crimes. In some surveys, however, the gap between Anglicans and Catholics is less noticeable (1966 and 1987). Looking at the most recent BES surveys (for 2001–10), Anglicans are most likely to express opposition to the statements that the death penalty is never justified even for the most serious crimes (47.6 percent in 2010), and Catholics least likely (36.6 percent in 2010). Other Christians (47.3 percent in 2010) and those with no affiliation (43.5 percent) occupy positions, respectively, alongside or closer to Anglicans than Catholics.

Looking at attitudes on the basis of religious attendance, presented in Table 4.13, a pattern partly emerges from the BES surveys (data are not available for the 2001 and 2005 surveys). Although the levels of pro-death penalty sentiment vary over time, as has been noted for affiliation, in each survey those who attend services frequently are usually less likely to be pro-capital punishment compared to those who attend less often or not at all (albeit the differences were barely apparent in the 1966 survey). The most marked gaps occur in the 1983 to 1992 surveys. The levels of pro-death penalty sentiment expressed by infrequent and non-attenders are not too dissimilar across surveys.

Data from the BSA surveys cover the period from 1986–2012 and are reported in Figure 4.6 (for affiliation) and Figure 4.7 (attendance). First, however, it is worth noting that the 1986 BSA survey included a

question – not included on any subsequent survey – which asked the
following:

> How much do you agree or disagree that ... Britain should bring
> back the death penalty?

Reintroduction of the death penalty has been a periodic issue for parliamentary and public debate in the decades since abolition. It found
that levels of agreement with this proposition was highest amongst
Anglicans (77.5 percent), followed by those with no religion
(64.0 percent), and lowest amongst other Christians and Catholics
(respectively, 59.9 percent and 56.2 percent). There was also clear variation in levels of agreement based on religious attendance. Frequent-
attenders were much less likely to favour the reintroduction of the
death penalty (51.5 percent agreed) compared to those who never
attended (64.2 percent) and, especially, infrequent-attenders (highest
at 75.9 percent).

Are these differences sustained in the time-series data? Figures 4.7
and 4.8 show the BSA data for, respectively, affiliation and attendance,
covering the period from 1986 to 2012. Figures 4.7 and 4.8 chart the

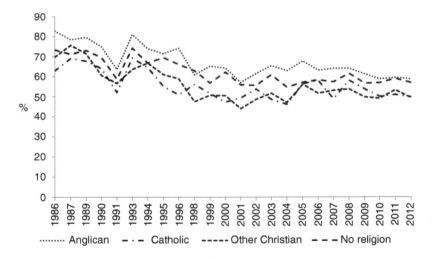

Figure 4.7   Percent agreeing with the death penalty, by affiliation, 1986–2012
Source: BSA surveys.
Note: Combines 'strongly agree' and 'agree' responses.

proportions that either strongly agree or agree with the following statement: 'for some crimes, the death penalty is the most appropriate sentence'. Levels of agreement were generally very high in the early BSA surveys but fall away over time, showing a weakening of authoritarian sentiment on this topic, particularly since the mid-late 1990s. Agreement is usually highest for Anglicans across surveys (nearing or over four-fifths on several occasions), followed by those with no religion. Agreement is consistently lower amongst other Christians and Catholics, who register lower support for the use of capital punishment. Over time, Anglicans have been more likely to take an authoritarian stance on the debate concerning the death penalty, with members of other Christian traditions more likely to be opposed or have reservations. This can be seen by averaged levels of agreement over time: Anglicans' level of agreement with the use of the death penalty is 67.3 percent, compared to 62.3 percent for those with no affiliation, and 55.7 percent and 55.9 percent, respectively, for Catholics and other Christians.

Figure 4.8 also shows that there have been clear differences in support for the use of the death penalty on the basis of religious attendance. Regular attenders have been consistently less likely to express

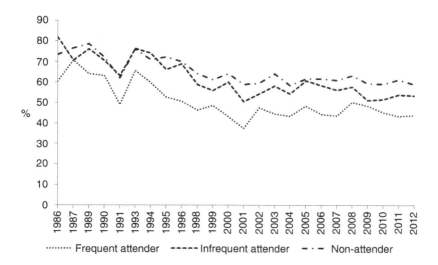

Figure 4.8   Percent agreeing with the death penalty, by attendance, 1986–2012
Source: BSA surveys.
Note: Combines 'strongly agree' and 'agree' responses.

agreement, with support nearly always falling below a majority since the late 1990s. Infrequent-attenders and non-attenders have been more likely to assent to capital punishment – nearly always expressing majority agreement – and have to some extent alternated across surveys as to who has expressed the highest level of agreement. As with affiliation, levels of authoritarian sentiment – across all groups – have decreased in recent years. Averaging levels of agreement over time, the figures are 50.6 percent for frequent-attenders, markedly lower than the 61.8 percent for infrequent-attenders and 65.4 percent for non-attenders.

The BSA surveys also enable some limited over-time comparison of attitudes based on religious beliefs. Specifically, the four measures of attitudes towards God used in Chapter 2 are employed here: two questions focusing on belief in God's existence, a question focusing on whether God is personally concerned with every human being, and a question asking whether life is meaningful only because God exists. To reiterate, these have been asked as part of the ISSP modules included in the 1991, 1998 and 2008 BSA surveys. Research into conceptions of God in the United States – beliefs about the forms and functions God is perceived to have (Froese and Bader 2007) – have shown that these are particularly consequential for public opinion towards the death penalty and punitive punishment for criminals (Bader et al. 2010; Unnever and Cullen 2006; Unnever et al. 2006; Unnever et al. 2005).

Data based on belief in and about God are available for the period 1991–2008, and are reported in Table 4.14. The differences in support for the death penalty across these measures of believing are generally not as consistent or as large as those found for the indicators of belonging and believing discussed already. The evidence does suggest, however, that those who do not believe in God, who disagree with God's concern for every human being and for whom God is not meaningful for daily life, are somewhat more likely to agree with capital punishment. Based on the most recent reading, the 2008 survey, the largest gap is evident for those who think that God concerns himself with all humans compared to those who disagree or who are neutral on this question. There is also a marked difference between those who have a firm belief in God compared to those who hold a more contingent view (with those who definitely do not believe positioned in between). The differences are narrower for the other belief question and that on whether life is only meaningful because God exists. Furthermore, attitudes can also be assessed by additional questions about God only included in the BSA 2008 survey (the data are reported

Table 4.14   Attitudes towards the death penalty, by belief, 1991–2008

Variable	Category	1991 (%)	1995 (%)	1998 (%)	2000 (%)	2008 (%)
Belief in God (1)	Believe in God	56.8	–	58.2	–	56.0
	Does not	60.4	–	62.1	–	60.4
Belief in God (2)	Believes in God	57.6	56.2	55.4	50.7	51.1
	Other response	59.7	71.6	62.1	63	61.3
	Does not believe in God	56.5	72.2	59.5	57.6	56.0
God concerns himself with every human being personally	Agree	55.7	–	55.4	–	49.6
	Neither	64.8	–	55.7	–	62.7
	Disagree	55.9	–	65.9	–	61.5
Life is only meaningful because God exists	Agree	55.0	–	49.6	–	56.6
	Neither	60.6	–	62.8	–	55.6
	Disagree	58.2	–	60.6	–	59.3

Source: BSA surveys.
Note: Combines 'strongly agree' and 'agree'.

in Appendix 3). These questions include measures tapping into the concepts of an *involved God* and an *angry God* (Froese and Bader 2007; Bader et al. 2010). Generally, there is little variation in levels of support for capital punishment, with the exception of the question asking about God and human sin. Even here, however, the difference is between those who do not believe in God (52.6 percent who agree) compared to those who take opposing positions on whether God is angered by human sin (yes: 61.9 percent; no: 58.3 percent). There is little difference in view based on whether individuals' believe God is directly involved in their affairs or not.

Finally, another set of questions on the death penalty were asked on the BSA surveys between 1983 and 1995. They refer to whether capital punishment should be used for murder in three sets of circumstances: for a terrorist act; for the killing of a policeman; and for other murders. The questions were worded as follows:

Are you in favour of or against the death penalty for ... murder in the course of a terrorist act?
Are you in favour of or against the death penalty for ... murder of a police officer?

Are you in favour of or against the death penalty for ... other murders?

Responses are provided in Table 4.15 (affiliation) and Table 4.16 (attendance), reporting the proportion in each group who said they were in favour of the use of the death penalty in each of the three scenarios. Across the board, support for the death penalty being applied is greatest in the cases of an act of terrorism or the killing of a police officer, and is slightly lower for unspecified, other murders. The results tend to underline the variation in attitudes evident in the BES and BSA data examined already. In terms of affiliation, Anglicans are usually more supportive of the use of the death penalty in each of the three sets of circumstances, with Catholics again being less in favour of its application. There is also some evidence of attitudes becoming less authoritarian over time, particularly for Anglicans and other Christians. Between 1983 and 1995 the proportion in favour changes little for those with no religion while opinion amongst Catholics hardens slightly. The differences between Anglicans and Catholics were narrower in 1995 than they were in 1983.

In terms of attendance, the evidence is in accordance with that examined already from the BES and BSA surveys. Regular attenders at religious services are somewhat less likely to be in favour of the death penalty, for all three questions. This group also shows a clear decline in pro-death penalty sentiment between 1983 and 1995, particularly for murder committed during the course of a terrorist act and for killing a police officer. Infrequent and non-attenders are more likely to support the application of the death penalty in each situation; while the former show a lessening of support for capital punishment over time, the latter does not. For regular and non-attenders, the gaps in death penalty support are roughly of a similar magnitude in 1995 as they were in 1983.

Taken together, the BES and BSA surveys tend to provide corroborating evidence – the former for different questions across surveys; the latter for a consistent question over time. Anglicans have been historically more in favour of capital punishment; Catholics, to some extent other Christians (including Nonconformists), and frequent-attenders have been less likely to show support for the death penalty. This association between Anglicans and more authoritarian views on capital punishment is generally robust across surveys using different question wordings and sets of response options. Concerns over the sanctity of human life may have been particularly salient for ordinary Catholics in

Table 4.15 Percent in favour of the death penalty, by affiliation, 1983–1995

	1983 (%)	1984 (%)	1985 (%)	1989 (%)	1990 (%)	1993 (%)	1994 (%)	1995 (%)
Murder in the course of a terrorist act								
Anglican	83.3	84.8	86.0	83.8	78.6	84.9	77.4	73.6
Catholic	63.0	68.1	66.7	72.9	67.0	69.7	60.9	67.7
Other Christian	75.7	74.4	71.1	77.7	59.9	67.5	73.5	66.5
No religion	76.1	79.1	82.1	77.8	72.1	75.9	69.9	72.7
Murder of a police officer								
Anglican	81.7	81.8	83.5	79.9	76.3	81.5	77.5	72.8
Catholic	60.7	66.3	62.6	67.2	62.4	73.1	59.3	61.3
Other Christian	74.6	71.5	65.4	73.1	57.8	64.3	67.8	65.9
No religion	71.2	71.1	74.6	72.6	67.9	69.2	65.7	70.6
Other murders								
Anglican	71.9	73.0	75.3	77.5	67.0	73.1	64.8	65.0
Catholic	52.4	59.5	55.7	69.7	60.0	65.8	44.2	57.7
Other Christian	65.4	62.7	55.5	65.2	50.0	56.3	61.9	57.8
No religion	62.6	66.5	69.3	71.7	63.5	65.9	58.7	63.8

Source: BSA surveys.

Table 4.16 Percent in favour of the death penalty, by attendance, 1983–1995

	1983 (%)	1984 (%)	1985 (%)	1989 (%)	1990 (%)	1993 (%)	1994 (%)	1995 (%)
Murder in the course of a terrorist act								
Frequent attender	70.4	69.5	67.8	69.9	65.5	68.9	66.2	58.1
Infrequent attender	80.9	83.2	84.0	81.4	71.8	80.3	78.9	68.6
Non-attender	79.4	81.4	82.4	82.8	75.4	79.0	72.9	76.9
Murder of a police officer								
Frequent attender	69.3	66.3	64.4	64.5	61.4	66.3	66.1	57.7
Infrequent attender	80.9	79.6	80.0	78.4	68.5	77.7	77.6	67.0
Non-attender	74.9	75.8	76.6	77.8	72.5	73.9	69.2	74.1
Other murders								
Frequent attender	56.6	58.9	53.1	61.4	52.2	59.1	50.7	49.2
Infrequent attender	70.2	70.1	70.6	73.7	63.1	69.3	67.4	59.3
Non-attender	66.9	70.2	71.8	77.0	66.1	68.3	61.9	68.0

Source: BSA surveys.

forming their views on this issue; even so, substantial proportions of Catholics have expressed support for use of the death penalty over time.

Attitudes towards censorship

Attitudes towards censorship or similar debates can be assessed in three respects. First, based on a BES question about whether the right to show nudity in films and magazines had gone too far, asked between 1974 and 1992 (as part of a wider set of questions gauging views on areas of social change). Second, by using the censorship item included as part of the BSA's composite libertarian-authoritarian index, for the period 1986 to 2012. Third, by looking at questions asking specifically about support for a law to ban books or films that offend those with strong religious beliefs, asked in the BSA surveys of 1990, 1991, 1994 and 2008.

The BES surveys asked the following question between 1974 and 1992 (which can be seen as something of a precursor for the BSA's own question on censorship):

About some changes that have been happening in Britain over the years. Do you think this has gone too far or not gone far enough ... The right to show nudity and sex in films and magazines?

The proportions who said that it had, to some extent, gone too far are reported in Table 4.17, which shows responses for affiliation and attendance. Looking at affiliation, there is relatively little change over time in the attitudes of Christians, but a somewhat larger decrease in the views of those with no religion (falling from 52.8 percent in 1974 to 43.2 percent in 1992). In all three surveys (1974, 1987 and 1992), those with no affiliation are clearly less likely to think that the right to show nudity had gone too far: around two-fifths in 1992 compared to large majorities of those with a religious affiliation. In each survey, the level of concern is highest amongst the other Christian category (at 71.2 percent in 1992). Data for attendance are only available for the 1987 and 1992 surveys, showing that there is clear variation based on frequency of attendance. Regular-attenders are much more likely to think that the right to show nudity has gone too far (or much too far). In 1992, 76.6 percent think this, compared to 60.6 percent of irregular-attenders and 52.3 percent of non-attenders. Infrequent-attenders show the largest absolute decrease, albeit over a five-year period.

Table 4.17   **Percent saying the right to show nudity in films and magazines has gone too far, by affiliation and attendance, 1974–1992**

	Anglican (%)	Catholic (%)	Other Christian (%)	No religion (%)
1974	65.6	67.3	75	52.8
1987	71.2	72.2	75	51
1992	63.4	63.6	71.2	43.2
	Frequent-attender (%)	Infrequent-attender (%)	Non-attender (%)	
1987	81.4	70.9	58.1	
1992	76.6	60.6	52.3	

Source: BES surveys.
Note: Combines 'gone much too far' and 'gone too far'.

The BSA time-series data for the general censorship question are shown in Figures 4.9 and 4.10 for, respectively, affiliation and attendance. They report the proportions either agreeing or strongly agreeing that censorship is necessary for the upholding of moral standards. It is evident from Figure 4.9 that the main difference is between those with and those without an affiliation. Usually around seven in ten of Anglicans, Catholics and other Christians express generic support for censorship to protect societal morality, with Anglicans and other Christians generally registering slightly higher levels of agreement. However, those with no affiliation evince much less support across surveys, often with only a small majority in favour of censorship.

Based on attendance at religious services, there is clear variation in levels of support for censorship. Support for censorship to uphold moral standards is highest amongst regular-attenders at worship services (often in the range of three-quarters to four-fifths of this group). Agreement is somewhat lower – but still generally very high – amongst irregular-attenders, and is lowest amongst those who do not attend religious services. Even so, support for such censorship often amounts to around six in ten of non-attenders. Figure 4.10 does not show any steady liberalisation of views over time, across all groups; indeed, support for censorship is higher for non-attenders in 2012 than it was in 1983. Averaged over the period, levels of agreement are 77.6 percent for frequent-attenders, 69.5 percent for infrequent-attenders, and 59.5 percent for non-attenders.

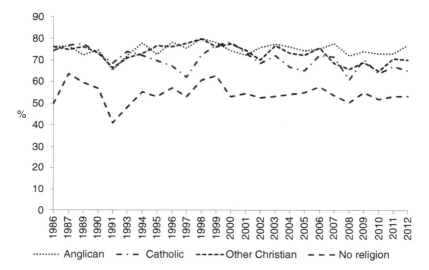

Figure 4.9 Percent agreeing with censorship, by affiliation, 1986–2012
Source: BSA surveys.
Note: Combines 'strongly agree' and 'agree' responses.

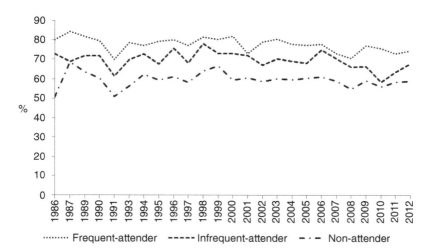

Figure 4.10 Percent agreeing with censorship, by attendance, 1986–2012
Source: BSA surveys.
Note: Combines 'strongly agree' and 'agree' responses.

As with the long-running BSA question on the death penalty, views on censorship can also be compared on the basis of the four questions about God asked between 1991 and 2008. The results are provided in Table 4.18. Overall, the data have a similar pattern to those for affiliation and attendance. Specifically, support for censorship to uphold moral standards is always higher amongst those who express a firm belief in the existence of God, who believe that God is concerned with all individuals and those for whom God is integral to their lives. These large differences are apparent in each survey, including the additional readings from 1995 and 2000 for one of the measures. The additional questions on God asked in the BSA 2008 survey show clear differences in attitudes towards the use of censorship for moral standards, for three of the four items (data are reported in Appendix 3). Support (expressed in levels of agreement) is noticeably higher among those who are sure they believe in God and those who think that God is directly involved in their affairs. For the last question on an angry God, those who think God is angered by human sin are most in favour of censorship (at 70.5 percent), followed by those who express the

Table 4.18   **Percent saying the right to show nudity in films and magazines has gone too far, by belief, 1991–2008**

Variable	Category	1991 (%)	1995 (%)	1998 (%)	2000 (%)	2008 (%)
Belief in God (1)	Believe in God	69.2	–	81.9	–	69.2
	Does not	48.2	–	56.1	–	48.2
Belief in God (1)	Believes in God	70.4	75.5	81.0	74.1	75.7
	Other response	56.2	63.8	72.4	68.1	59.9
	Does not believe in God	33.1	39.8	44.2	49.6	42.0
God concerns himself with every human being personally	Agree	69.0	–	83.7	–	71.4
	Neither	57.3	–	73.1	–	60.7
	Disagree	43.7	–	56.3	–	50.0
Life is only meaningful because God exists	Agree	75.8	–	87.1	–	76.0
	Neither	62.2	–	75.7	–	63.1
	Disagree	46.5	–	64.0	–	52.7

Source: BSA surveys.
Note: Combines 'gone much too far' and 'gone too far'.

opposite view (59.4 percent) and those who do not believe in God (at 35.7 percent). The differences are less pronounced based on the question about connecting with God, although those who say they do have their own way (beyond more formal religious settings) are somewhat more supportive of censorship. Overall, attitudes towards censorship for reasons of morality show clear differences between the religious and those less or non-religious, with the former consistently showing higher levels of support.

The second question is of especial interest here as it specifically refers to the proscribing of material (books or films) which offend people with strong religious beliefs. It was first asked in the 1990 survey, the year after the Satanic Verses controversy, which raised contentious issues regarding the claims of minority religious groups to the protection of their beliefs and identity in a free society, and asked in each of the surveys with the ISSP religion module (1991, 1998 and 2008). These issues have surfaced more recently: the protests by Sikhs over the content of a play being staged in a theatre in Birmingham in 2004; the demonstrations by Muslims in European countries – including Britain – against the publishing of cartoons depicting the prophet Muhammad; the passing of the Racial and Religious Hatred Act in 2006 and the debates it stoked regarding potential constraints on freedom of speech; and – particularly since 2001 – public debate concerning the presence of 'Islamophobia' in British society.

The question wording used has varied slightly, but the same set of response categories has been used across surveys. The specific wordings are as follows:

> 1990: Some books or films offend people in Britain who have strong religious beliefs. Do you think there should or should not be a law to ban such books or films?
> 1991 and 1994: Some books or films offend people who have strong religious beliefs. Should books and films that attack religions be prohibited by law or should they be allowed?
> 2008: Some books or films offend people who have strong religious beliefs. Should books and films that attack religions be banned by law or should they be allowed?

While the BSA question on censorship to protect moral standards generally showed clear majorities in support – albeit higher for those with an affiliation and who attend services often or less often, this question could perhaps be expected to show greater divergence in views

Table 4.19   Percent who think material offensive to those with strong religious beliefs should be banned, affiliation and attendance, 1991–2008

	Anglican (%)	Catholic (%)	Other Christian (%)	No religion (%)
1990	39.3	36.4	36.0	25.7
1991	30.5	33.6	35.4	15.2
1994	30.9	39.3	33.1	15.7
2008	30.9	28.9	31.4	19.7
	Frequent-attender (%)	Infrequent- (%)	Non-attender (%)	
1990	47.8	34.0	29.1	
1991	38.4	31.9	21.1	
1994	36.4	30.9	23.0	
2008	39.9	32.1	22.4	

Source: BSA surveys.
Note: Combines 'definitely should' and 'probably should'.

between these groups, given the specific subject matter. Table 4.19 shows responses for religious affiliation and attendance for the four BSA surveys, reporting the proportions who responded 'definitely should' or 'probably should' – that is, expressing support for censorship. The distributions of responses by religious affiliation show that, not unexpectedly, those with no religion are least likely to favour such a law (at levels of 15.0–25.0 percent). In terms of religious tradition, there are no major differences across Anglicans, Catholics and other Christians; support for such a law varies in the range of 30.0–40.0 percent, but by 2008 fell somewhat from 1991 levels. In 2008, support for this form of censorship is around three-tenths for Anglicans, Catholics and other Christians, compared to around a fifth for no religion (at 19.7 percent, falling from 25.7 percent in 1991).

Given the recent examples of protests mounted by members of minority religions in British society over the dissemination of material in the public domain which they perceive as offensive to their identity or beliefs, are they more likely to support such prohibition? Inspection of the data in 2008 for those who affiliate with non-Christian religions shows that support for censorship is considerably higher than for Christians, at 50.3 percent – just showing majority support – perhaps indicative of a perceived greater need for protection of their identities and beliefs as minority faiths in an increasingly secular society with a deep-rooted Christian heritage. A majority of non-Christians are also in favour in the 1990–94 surveys (at 57.6 percent in 1991 and 1994, and 62.9 percent in 1990 – the year after the Satanic Verses controversy of 1989), although these figures are based on much smaller numbers of respondents.

Based on attendance at services, those who attend most often are most likely to support such a law (highest at 47.8 percent in 1990, and standing at 39.9 percent in 2008). Those who attend services less often are positioned somewhat equidistantly between frequent and non-attenders, with the latter showing least support for such a law, at around a fifth in the 1991–2008 surveys. Amongst no group – whether defined by belonging or behaving – is there majority support for censorship to protect the beliefs and identity of religious groups.

Finally, attitudes on this question can be compared for the set of questions concerning beliefs and attitudes about God, for two surveys (1991 and 2008; different samples were asked the questions on banning offensive material and religious beliefs in the 1998 survey). The results are reported in Table 4.20. There is a similar pattern in both surveys, with those who express a firm belief in God, feel that God is concerned with all humans, and for whom God gives great meaning to their lives, tending to be much more supportive of the prohibition of

Table 4.20 Percent who think material offensive to those with strong religious beliefs should be banned, by belief, 1991–2008

Variable	Category	1991 (%)	2008 (%)
Belief in God (1)	Believe in God	35.5	35.4
	Does not	15.3	17.0
Belief in God (2)	Believes in God	42.1	44.3
	Other response	23.9	25.1
	Does not believe in God	9.7	15.7
God concerns himself with every human being personally	Agree	38.7	36.2
	Neither	26.7	27.2
	Disagree	14.2	17.9
Life is only meaningful because God exists	Agree	46.2	48.9
	Neither	26.7	33.6
	Disagree	18.2	18.2

Source: BSA surveys.
Note: Combines 'definitely should' and 'probably should'.

material that is offensive to those with strong religious beliefs. While no group registers majority support for banning such material in either survey, support in 2008 is highest for those for whom their life is meaningful because God exists (at 48.9 percent), followed by those who express a clear belief in God (have always or did not use to but do so now; at 44.3 percent). It is less than a fifth amongst those who do not believe in God on either measure and those who disagree with either of the other two statements. The data do not show any across-the-board increase or decrease in support for banning offensive material across nearly two decades.

Attitudes based on beliefs in or about God can be assessed further by using the questions included in the BSA 2008 survey (for which data are shown in Appendix 3). The pattern of responses for banning material offensive to those with strong religious beliefs is similar to that seen for attitudes towards censorship in general – whilst always a minority position, support is highest amongst those who believe that God is involved with their affairs (38.2 percent) and those who think that God is angered by human sin (39.6 percent). Support for censorship is also noticeably higher amongst those who declare that they have their own way of connecting with God outside of more formal religious settings (31.0 percent). Overall, across the measures of belonging, behaving and believing, those more religious are much more likely to support censorship on the grounds of material causing offence to those with strongly-held religious beliefs. Support is less evident amongst those who do not identify with a religion, who never or only occasionally attend worship services, and amongst those who do not believe in or are less personally engaged with, God.

As a final step, separate multivariate analyses were performed using the BSA death penalty and censorship items, using data from the BSA 2012 survey. The effects of belonging and behaving (but not believing) can be assessed. The models estimated included the same set of independent variables as included for the analysis of the general libertarian-authoritarian scale (reported in Table 4.11). However, in order to compare those who were in favour of the death penalty or censorship with those against or unsure, binary logistic regression estimation was used. The results are not reported in full (details are available on request), but some interesting differences in the effects of affiliation and attendance are worth noting. In terms of the contemporary religious basis of support for the death penalty, the only significant effect was for Anglicans (compared to those with no affiliation), who were more in favour of capital punishment. Accounting for affiliation, more frequent attendance at services had a negative relationship with support for the death penalty. For censorship, all religious groups (with the exception of Catholics) were significantly more likely to be in favour of censorship to protect moral standards. Additionally, more frequent attendance at worship services was significantly related to support for censorship. In sum, Anglicans show consistently authoritarian positions on both issues, while regular attenders show divergent associations: less punitive in their views on capital punishment, but stricter in their attitudes towards the need for censorship to uphold societal morality.

Conclusion

Building on the previous analysis of religion and party choice in postwar British politics, this chapter has provided a detailed assessment of the relationship of religion and core ideological beliefs, focusing on left-right, social welfare and libertarian-authoritarian orientations. What did it find in relation to the widely-held assumption, noted at the outset of this chapter, about the association of religion and political conservatism? There are interesting patterns concerning both economic and social issues. A clear and robust finding, evident across surveys and measures, appears to be that Anglicans are distinctly more likely to be the repository of political conservatism on socio-economic matters, as manifested in their more right-wing positions on the left-right self-placement scales, and the BSA left-right and welfarism scales. These findings stood up to controls for a range of other social factors, including standard indicators of individuals' socio-economic circumstances.

On the BSA libertarian-authoritarian scale, all religious groups were more authoritarian in their beliefs than the non-religious. Interestingly, when religious affiliation is accounted for, more frequent attendance had a negative association with authoritarian beliefs, which hints at variation within religious traditions based on levels of religiosity. In terms of specific social-authoritarianism beliefs, the religious – whether classified by belonging or behaviour – were less likely to be in favour of the death penalty but more likely to favour censorship, both in general terms and in support of a law banning material offensive to religious beliefs. Accounting for other sociological characteristics, Anglicans also proved to be the most authoritarian in their support for capital punishment; regular attenders were more in favour of censorship for moral standards but were less likely to adopt a stricter line on capital punishment. Overall, the greater ideological *conservatism* of

Anglicans, in their broad-based social and economic beliefs, shown in this chapter broadly fits with their traditional party-political *Conservatism* demonstrated in Chapter 3.

Appendix: BES questions on the death penalty

1963: Would you like to see the death penalty kept or abolished?

1966: Did you want to see the death penalty kept or abolished?

1979: Bringing back the death penalty?

1983: Please say whether you agree or disagree with each of these statements, or say if you are not sure either way ... Britain should bring back the death penalty?

1987: For some crimes, the death penalty is the most appropriate sentence?

1992 and 1997: Do you agree or disagree that ... Britain should bring back the death penalty?

2001, 2005 and 2010: Do you agree or disagree: The death penalty, even for very serious crimes, is never justified?

5
Religion and Abortion

This chapter provides a detailed assessment of trends in religious groups' attitudes towards abortion, an area which has historically seen staunch opposition from some religious traditions, particularly the Roman Catholic Church. As Jelen has observed: 'Given the relationship of the abortion issue to ultimate concerns of human life, and to questions of sexual morality, it is not surprising that much opposition to legal abortion has had a religious basis' (2009: 223–4). The landmark piece of legislation on this issue in post-war Britain was the Abortion Act 1967. Britain, along with other Protestant countries in Western Europe, generally established permissive legal frameworks governing abortion more quickly than did Catholic countries (Knill et al. 2014: 846).

Most of the Christian churches in Britain developed more pragmatic views towards abortion given the wider social reality of the issue in this period, however, 'the Roman Catholic Church was not prepared to compromise its view that abortion was tantamount to murder' (Yates 2010: 94). The Roman Catholic Church had been seen as a major opponent of the legislation (Hornsby-Smith 1989: 93). The legislation itself was supported by most MPs from Nonconformist traditions, divided MPs from an Anglican background and was vehemently opposed by many MPs with a Catholic affiliation from different political parties (Yates 2010: 95). Since the 1967 Act, 'there have been a series of unsuccessful attempts to put abortion back on the political agenda and thereby to restrict access' (Thorup Larsen et al. 2012: 121). Roman Catholics MPs, across party lines, have played a prominent role in various attempts made in parliament to amend the 1967 Act in subsequent decades and, more broadly, Catholics have been an important part of the membership base of the two main anti-abortion campaign organisations (Hornsby-Smith 1989: 93).

To examine the over-time attitudes of religious groups in Britain, this chapter examines a wide range of time-series data from the recurrent social surveys. It also utilises other polls and surveys which shed interesting historical and contemporary light on the views of religious groups. The aim here is to use different survey series as well as to examine different attitudinal indicators from these series, in order to provide as robust and detailed an account of trends in public opinion in recent decades as possible.

The chapter is divided into three main sections. The first section is based on analysis of historical opinion poll data, looking in particular at the attitudes of religious groups on the abortion issue in the period around the 1967 Abortion Act. The second section covers a much longer time-span, focusing on patterns and changes in group attitudes based on religious affiliation and attendance. It uses data from three long-running social surveys (BES, BSA and EVS). Given the historically distinctive stance of Roman Catholic teaching on the abortion issue, the third section looks more closely at attitudinal variation amongst Catholics in Britain, making detailed use of denomination-specific surveys undertaken recently and in earlier decades. While Catholics as a denomination have traditionally shown higher levels of opposition to abortion compared to other religious groups, it is instructive to examine which particular social groups within the Catholic community are more or less likely to have disapproved of abortion given the official strictures of their faith. The analyses contained in these three sections of the chapter build on and extend existing studies of public opinion towards legal abortion in Britain (Clements 2014d; Park and Rhead 2013; McAndrew 2010; Hayes 1995b; Francome 1989; Chapman 1986; Jowell and Airey 1984).

Attitudes towards abortion: Opinion polls

Before turning to the main analysis of recurrent social survey data (which enable analysis of attitudes from the mid-1970s onwards), attitudes towards abortion are analysed using public opinion data collected in the 1960s and early 1970s and – for some questions – in later decades. Several polls conducted in this period on the abortion issue provide data on attitudes by religious affiliation (but not attendance at services). These enable us to compare the attitudes of those who report adherence to different Christian traditions (Church of England,

Catholic, Nonconformist churches and Presbyterian or Church of Scotland; other groups are not reported due to the comparatively small numbers in the samples).

Gallup's post-war polling enables a comparison of religious groups' attitudes over time. First, attitudes are compared based on data from polls conducted by Gallup in 1966 and 1993. Responses here are shown for those belonging to four Christian traditions: the Church of England, Nonconformist churches, the Church of Scotland and Roman Catholics. Table 5.1 reports attitudes in relation to three different scenarios in which an abortion might be undertaken for the 1966 and 1993 polls. The questions asked were as follows:

Do you think abortion operations should or should not be legal in the following cases?
Where the health of the mother is in danger?
Where the child may be born deformed?
Where the family does not have enough money to support another child?

The response options were 'should be legal', 'should not' and 'don't know'. The proportions expressing opposition (saying 'should not') are reported in Table 5.1.

For the 1966 survey, considering the first scenario relating to the health of the mother, there is near-unanimous support for abortions being legal in such circumstances amongst nearly all groups (with opposition ranging from just 5.0–16.0 percent), with the exception of Catholics, for whom just over a quarter think it should not be legal (28.0 percent). The other two scenarios evince higher levels of 'should not' responses across all groups. Catholics and the Church of Scotland affiliates show higher opposition to abortion where a child may be born with a deformity (respectively, 36.0 percent and 26.0 percent) and, similarly, in relation to a family being unable to financially support another child (at 61.0 percent and 59.0 percent, respectively). For both of these scenarios, opposition is considerably lower amongst Church of England affiliates and Nonconformists. Across all groups, opinion is responsive to the particular circumstances surrounding each hypothetical abortion case. It is also apparent that, with the exception of circumstance of financial hardship, Catholic opposition to abortion clearly and consistently outranks every other Christian tradition, particularly Church of England affiliates and Nonconformists. Turning to the later survey from 1993, it is clear that, for two of the scenarios,

Table 5.1 Percent saying abortion should not be allowed, by affiliation, 1966 and 1993

	Church of England (%)	Church of Scotland (%)	Nonconformist (%)	Roman Catholic (%)
1966				
Health of mother is in danger	5.0	16.0	5.0	28.0
Child may be born deformed	8.0	26.0	9.0	36.0
Family cannot support another child	40.0	59.0	36.0	61.0
1993				
Health of mother is in danger	1.0	0.0	0.0	9.0
Child may be born deformed	10.0	3.0	13.0	22.0
Family cannot support another child	48.0	54.0	39.0	65.0

Source: Gallup. Data for 1966 compiled from Martin (1968: 185). The data for 1993 were kindly supplied by Dr Clive Field.

opposition has fallen quite markedly amongst Catholics: in the cases of health concerns for, respectively, mother and baby. Affiliates of the Church of Scotland also show clear decreases in opposition for these two scenarios. The picture is more mixed for those belonging to the Church of England and Nonconformists.

Table 5.2 shows the full set of responses to a question Gallup asked in 1973 and 1993. The question asked for respondents' views on the availability of abortion. In 1973 only very small proportions thought abortion should be available on demand (highest at 19.0 percent for those belonging to the Church of Scotland). With the exception of Catholics, in each case a majority believed that abortion should be available in particular circumstances. For Catholics 44.0 percent said it should be allowed on some grounds, but 40.0 percent said it should not be allowed at all – much higher than that recorded for the other groups. Two decades later, in 1993, all groups showed increases in the

Table 5.2   Attitudes towards abortion, by affiliation, 1973 and 1993

	Church of England (%)	Church of Scotland (%)	Free Church (%)	Roman Catholic (%)
1973				
Should be available on demand	18.0	19.0	8.0	11.0
Should only be allowed in particular circumstances	61.0	60.0	62.0	44.0
Should never be allowed in any circumstances	9.0	14.0	18.0	40.0
Don't know	11.0	7.0	13.0	5.0
1993				
Should be available on demand	31.0	29.0	30.0	18.0
Should only be allowed in certain circumstances	63.0	62.0	62.0	63.0
Should never be allowed in any circumstances	4.0	8.0	12.0	17.0
Don't know	3.0	2.0	6.0	3.0

Source: Gallup. Data kindly supplied by Dr Clive Field.

proportions who think that abortion should be available on demand or should be allowed in some circumstances (combined they comprise large majorities in each group). For Catholics, the proportion who said abortion should never be allowed fell to 17.0 percent.

In addition to evidence from the Gallup polls, data are analysed from a survey undertaken by National Opinion Polls (NOP) in March 1965. Responses are shown for the following categories: Church of England, Catholic, Nonconformist and Presbyterian or Church of Scotland. The opinion poll asked the following two questions:

Do you think that abortion should be legal in all cases, legal in some cases, or illegal in all cases?
Do you think that abortion should or should not be legally permitted in each of the following cases?

The first question was asked of all respondents but the second question was targeted at those who responded 'legal in some cases' or 'don't know' in response to the first question. Table 5.3 presents responses to both questions. Looking at responses to the first question, it is clear that while very few respondents think abortion should be legal in all cases (at 7.0 percent or lower), Catholics are less likely to say abortion should be 'legal in some cases' (53.0 percent) and slightly more likely to say it should be 'illegal in all cases' (36.0 percent). Those belonging to the Church of England are most likely to say abortion should be legal in some circumstances (69.0 percent) and least likely to favour a complete ban on abortion (21.0 percent). Similar to the Gallup surveys discussed already, the NOP poll asked an additional question about a series of eight different scenarios in which an abortion might occur. To reiterate, these scenarios were given only to those who responded 'legal in some cases' or 'don't know' for the first question. For each question, Catholics were consistently less likely to respond 'should be permitted' than are those affiliated with the Church of England. Generally, Nonconformists and those professing themselves as Presbyterian or Church of Scotland are less likely to think abortions should be permitted than are those belonging to the Church of England.

Taken together, the public opinion data show that, in the years proximate to the 1967 Abortion Act, there are clear differences on the basis of Christian affiliation. Despite the Catholic Church's prominent role in opposing reform of the abortion laws and the 1967 Act (Hornsby-Smith 1989: 91), ordinary Catholics are certainly not homogenous in their views in this period, with varying proportions supporting abortion rights in particular circumstances However, opposition to abortion tends to be higher on the part of Catholics compared to those who identify with other Christian traditions.

Religious groups' views on the 1967 Abortion Act itself – 'one of the most permissive abortion laws at the time' (Thorup Larsen et al. 2012: 114), which came into operation in 1968 – can be assessed by using evidence from a poll conducted by NOP in 1972. This also allows an examination of the opinions of different Christian traditions. The NOP poll was conducted in March 1972, several years after the acts came into effect, and asked several questions, which were worded as follows:

The Abortion Act, 1967, widened the grounds for legal abortion. Do you think the Act is right or wrong to allow legal abortion if the pregnancy may damage the pregnant woman's physical or mental health, taking account of her circumstances?
Do you think the Act is right or wrong to allow legal abortion if the pregnancy may damage the health of her existing family, taking account of her circumstances?

Table 5.3   Attitudes towards abortion, by affiliation, 1965

	Church of England (%)	Roman Catholic (%)	Nonconformist (%)	Presbyterian/ Church of Scotland (%)
Legal in all cases	6.0	7.0	5.0	4.0
Legal in some cases	69.0	53.0	63.0	61.0
Illegal in all cases	21.0	36.0	31.0	31.0
Don't know	4.0	4.0	2.0	4.0
Women's physical health may be seriously affected				
Should be permitted	68.0	48.0	58.0	61.0
Should not be permitted	3.0	5.0	2.0	2.0
Don't know	2.0	5.0	5.0	2.0
Women's mental health may be seriously affected				
Should be permitted	67.0	46.0	58.0	58.0
Should not be permitted	3.0	9.0	2.0	4.0
Don't know	3.0	3.0	5.0	3.0
Child may be born deformed				
Should be permitted	58.0	33.0	41.0	45.0
Should not be permitted	9.0	15.0	13.0	12.0
Don't know	7.0	8.0	11.0	8.0
Large family means another child would cause financial hardship and worry				
Should be permitted	35.0	16.0	22.0	25.0
Should not be permitted	33.0	37.0	34.0	36.0
Don't know	6.0	4.0	9.0	5.0
Child would be illegitimate				
Should be permitted	11.0	7.0	9.0	5.0
Should not be permitted	55.0	45.0	49.0	55.0
Don't know	7.0	5.0	7.0	6.0
Women is under 16 and unmarried				
Should be permitted	25.0	14.0	21.0	18.0
Should not be permitted	40.0	38.0	36.0	41.0
Don't know	8.0	5.0	9.0	6.0
Pregnancy results from rape				
Should be permitted	59.0	37.0	49.0	46.0
Should not be permitted	8.0	10.0	6.0	8.0
Don't know	6.0	10.0	10.0	5.0
Pregnancy results from incest				
Should be permitted	53.0	29.0	43.0	46.0
Should not be permitted	10.0	14.0	8.0	11.0
Don't know	10.0	13.0	15.0	8.0

Source: NOP, 25–29 March 1965. Data taken from Simms (1965–66: 51–2).

Do you think the Act is right or wrong to allow legal abortion if there is substantial risk that the child would be born seriously deformed?

The Abortion Act has been in operation since April 1968. Do you think the law should be left as it is, changed to make it easier to obtain legal abortion or changed to make it more difficult to obtain legal abortion?

In some areas it is difficult to obtain legal abortion because of the attitudes of local doctors. Do you think the National Health Service should make special arrangements in these areas or not?

For the first three questions the proportion in each religious group saying 'wrong' are reported; for question four, those who wanted the law changed to make abortion more difficult; and for question five, those who believed the NHS should not make special arrangements to make abortion more accessible. Therefore, the proportions opposed to abortion in different scenarios or in favour of restricting access to it are shown. Responses are shown in Table 5.4 for the following groups: the Church of England, Roman Catholic, the Presbyterian/Church of Scotland, Nonconformist and some other response (such as atheist, agnostic or refused).

Table 5.4   **Attitudes towards abortion, by affiliation, 1972**

	Church of England (%)	Roman Catholic (%)	Presbyterian/ Church of Scotland (%)	Nonconformist (%)	Other (%)
Damage woman's physical or mental health	18.0	39.0	24.0	19.0	21.0
Damage health of existing family	27.0	50.0	33.0	28.0	24.0
Child would be seriously deformed	13.0	32.0	12.0	12.0	15.0
Made more difficult to obtain abortion	42.0	61.0	44.0	51.0	29.0
Should not make special arrangements	19.0	40.0	29.0	23.0	16.0

Source: NOP, March 1972.

As with the surveys conducted before or around the time of the passing of the Abortion Act, the NOP survey reiterates the distinctive views of Catholics on this issue compared to other religious groups. Specifically, on each question, Catholics offer more restrictive views towards abortion. They are more likely to think that it is wrong to allow legal abortion for each set of circumstances, as permitted by the Abortion Act. Even so, the level of opposition expressed by Catholics does vary, being highest in situations where the pregnancy might damage the woman's family (50.0 percent) and lower for reasons of the woman's (39.0 percent) or unborn child's heath (32.0 percent). They are clearly more likely than all other groups to favour the Act being amended to make access to abortion more difficult (61.0 percent) and are more opposed to the NHS making arrangements in local areas where abortion is less accessible (40.0 percent). There is little apparent difference in levels of opposition amongst Church of England affiliates and Nonconformists (although the latter are more likely to think it should be made more difficult to obtain an abortion). Affiliates of the Church of Scotland or Presbyterians show somewhat higher opposition than Church of England adherents and Nonconformists for some questions. Those belonging to the varied 'other' category exhibit levels of opposition that are generally similar to those of Church of England affiliates, except in the case of making abortion more difficult, where they stand apart from all other groups (29.0 percent are in agreement).

Attitudes towards abortion: Recurrent social surveys

A detailed analysis of religious groups' attitudes in recent decades can be undertaken using long-running survey series. The analysis focuses on evidence from three long-running survey series: the BES (using data for the period 1974–97), BSA (using data for the period 1983–2012) and the EVS (covering the period 1981–2008). The first of the recurrent surveys used to examine public opinion towards abortion over time is the BES surveys, based on the standard post-election cross-section surveys conducted between 1974 (this refers to the October survey of that year) and 1997. The following question on abortion was asked in every BES survey during this period:

Has the availability of abortion on the National Health Service gone too far or not gone far enough?

The response options were: gone much too far, gone too far, about right, not gone far enough, not gone nearly far enough. For each survey the proportions responding 'gone much too far' or 'gone too far' were combined and attitudes are shown for both religious affiliation and attendance. The only change to the laws governing abortion during this period of time, indeed since the landmark 1967 Abortion Act, came in 1990 through the Human Fertilisation and Embryology Act, where the time limit was reduced to 24 weeks for most abortions.

Attitudes are displayed in Figure 5.1 (affiliation) and Figure 5.2 (attendance). Figure 5.1 shows that, across all religious groups, the proportion believing access to abortion on the NHS has gone too far has fallen across more than two decades of BES surveys. The relative ordering of the groups has not altered over time, however, with Catholics most likely to say it has gone too far in the 'bookend' surveys of 1974 (59.1 percent) and 1997 (47.8 percent). Those with no religion are the least likely to have thought – in each survey – that the availability of abortion had gone too far (falling from 34.6 percent in 1974 to 21.4 percent in 1997). Both Anglicans and other Christians (including Nonconformists) registered declines in concern over time about the

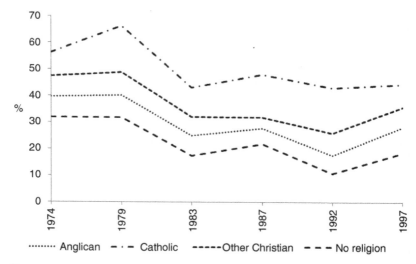

Figure 5.1   Percent saying the availability of abortion has gone too far, by affiliation, 1974–1997
Source: BES surveys.
Note: Combines 'gone much too far' and 'gone too far'.

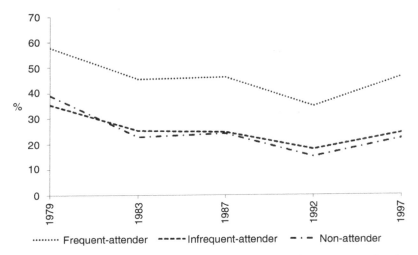

Figure 5.2 Percent saying the availability of abortion has gone too far, by attendance, 1979–1997
Source: BES surveys.
Note: Combines 'gone much too far' and 'gone too far'.

availability of abortion. The latter group consistently showed higher proportions saying gone too far than the former group, but lower than that expressed by Catholics.

Figure 5.2 shows equivalent data based on religious attendance (with the exception of the 1974 survey when a question on attendance was not asked).[1] Those who attended services often are the stand-out group, showing much higher levels of thinking it has gone too far compared to infrequent-attenders and non-attenders. This is the case in both 1979 and 1997. In 1974, the proportions are 57.8 percent for frequent-attenders compared to 35.4 percent for infrequent-attenders and 39.0 percent for non-attenders. In 1997, the proportions are 46.7 percent for frequent-attenders compared to 24.5 percent for infrequent-attenders and 22.4 percent for non-attenders. Overall, the BES data from the 1970s through to 1997 show that perceptions of abortion having gone too far fell across religious groups, based on both affiliation and attendance, including those most opposed at the outset of the time-series – Catholics and frequent-attenders.[2]

The most extensive set of questions on abortion have been asked in the annual BSA surveys, the second of the long-running survey series used here, which started in 1983. The BSA surveys can be used to analyse attitudes towards abortion undertaken under a variety of different circumstances, which tend to be categorised in existing research as *elective* (social) or *traumatic* (physical) reasons (Jelen and Wilcox 2003; Hoffman and Mills Johnson 2005). The BSA scale is based on a similar measuring instrument used to measure public attitudes towards abortion in the US General Social Survey, which began in the early 1970s (Greeley and Hout 2006). On 12 BSA surveys between 1983 and 2012, opinions towards seven different scenarios on abortion have been elicited, using binary response options of 'yes' and 'no'. The full question wording is as follows:

> Here are a number of circumstances in which a woman might consider an abortion. Please say whether or not you think the law should allow an abortion in each case.
> The woman decides on her own she does not wish to have the child.
> The couple agree they do not wish to have the child.
> The couple cannot afford any more children.
> There is a strong chance of a defect in the baby.
> The woman's health is seriously endangered by the pregnancy.
> The woman is not married and does not wish to marry the man.
> The woman became pregnant as a result of rape.

Previous research has shown that large majorities of public opinion in Britain and other countries are more likely to support abortions undertaken on traumatic grounds, while opinion is more divided over abortions carried out on elective grounds (Scott 1998). The traumatic grounds concern risks to physical health of the expectant mother, serious fetal defects, or the pregnancy being the result of rape or incest. The elective reasons cover personal and familial circumstances, such as a family being socio-economically disadvantaged and not being able to afford another child or a woman deciding on her own she does not want another child.

For the purposes of presentational clarity and based on the measurement strategy used by Adell Cook et al. (1992; see also Putnam and Campbell 2012), an additive index was constructed from data taken from BSA surveys conducted between 1983 and 2012. For each question, 'no' responses were scored as 0 while 'yes' responses were coded as 1 ('don't responses' were excluded from the construction of the index). Responses were then summed to create an index ranging from 0 (most anti-abortion) to 7 (most pro-abortion), with a midpoint of

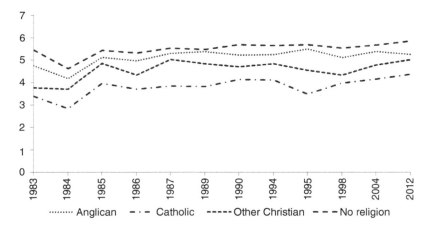

Figure 5.3   Mean scores on the abortion index, by affiliation, 1983–2012
Source: BSA surveys.

3.5. Higher scores therefore represent views more supportive of pro-abortion. The mean scores on the abortion index based on religious affiliation are shown in Figure 5.3.

In all cases, there is an upward trend in average scores, with all groups becoming more accepting of abortion over time. Catholics have the most restrictive attitudes in 1983, at 3.39, while those with no religion are the most supportive, at 5.45. Anglicans are closer to those with no religion than Catholics in their mean score (at 4.75), while other Christians are more proximate to Catholics (at 3.75). In 2012, the last survey for which the index can be constructed, those with no religion have shifted a little in a more pro-abortion direction – the mean score is now 5.84 (an increase of 0.39). The increases in mean scores over time are larger for the religious groups, particularly for Catholics and other Christians. In 2012, the averages are: Catholics: 4.36 (an increase of 0.97); Anglicans: 5.23 (0.48); other Christian: 5.0 (1.25). Anglicans are again closer to those with no affiliation, while other Christians are somewhat more positive than are Catholics. Notwithstanding clear changes over time in a more liberal direction, Catholics stand out as having the lowest scores on the index in both 1983 and 2012. The relative ordering of the groups, therefore, does not change in this period.

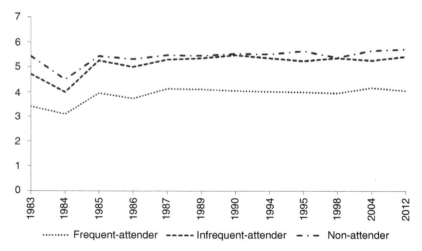

Figure 5.4   Mean scores on the abortion index, by attendance, 1983–2012
Source: BSA surveys.

Figure 5.4 charts the index scores between 1983 and 2012 for the three groups of frequent-attenders (once a month or more), infrequent-attenders (less than once a month), and those who never attend. The general trend – across the three groups – is for attitudes to liberalise across time, based on the summary index used here. Those who attend services frequently stand out as having the lowest scores on the abortion index in every survey, although the average score of this group increases somewhat from 3.41 (in 1983) to 4.05 (in 2012), an increase of 0.64. Those who attend infrequently or not at all also show a considerable increase in mean scores, from 4.72 to 5.42 (infrequent-attenders; a rise of 0.70) and 5.44 to 5.71 (non-attenders; a rise of 0.27). Based on the 1983 and 2012 surveys, the mean scores for infrequent-attenders are much closer to those of the non-attenders than they are for the frequent-attenders. Looking at both measures of religion, the largest increases between 1983 and 2012 are recorded based on affiliation (for Catholics and other Christians).

Summarising across abortion attitudes in order to compute index scores helps make overall sense of religious groups' attitudes, the data can also be examined in a different way, by looking at the positional distribution of opinion. In order to do this, respondents in each religious group were allocated to one of the following categories: consistently pro-abortion; pro-abortion in some but not all circumstances;

Table 5.5 Distribution of abortion positions, by affiliation, 1983–2012

	Anglican			Catholic			Other Christian			No religion		
	AA (%)	Sit. (%)	PC (%)	AA (%)	Sit. (%)	PC (%)	AA (%)	Sit. (%)	PC (%)	AA (%)	Sit. (%)	PC (%)
1983	1.6	72.6	25.8	12.0	72.9	15.0	5.9	83.6	10.5	0.2	55.5	44.3
1984	2.0	76.4	21.6	16.1	76.1	7.7	4.4	80.3	15.3	1.1	71.5	27.4
1985	0.2	63.1	36.7	9.2	67.6	23.2	4.8	57.9	37.3	0.8	52.9	46.3
1986	0.8	68.3	30.8	12.7	73.1	14.2	4.9	75.0	20.1	0.4	63.7	35.9
1987	1.0	59.7	39.4	11.4	69.3	19.3	1.4	59.9	38.6	0.5	52.0	47.5
1989	1.4	58.1	40.5	14.4	63.6	22.0	3.8	65.0	31.3	1.2	53.9	45.0
1990	2.3	55.3	42.4	13.3	62.2	24.4	2.2	67.2	30.7	1.0	47.8	51.2
1994	2.3	55.3	42.4	13.3	62.2	24.4	2.2	67.2	30.7	1.0	47.8	51.2
1995	1.0	58.2	40.9	13.2	66.2	20.6	6.3	67.2	26.6	1.2	50.0	48.8
1998	1.0	58.2	40.9	13.2	66.2	20.6	6.3	67.2	26.6	1.2	50.0	48.8
2004	1.2	56.3	42.5	13.0	51.9	35.2	8.4	52.3	39.3	1.0	47.4	51.7
2012	1.6	57.0	41.4	9.4	56.2	34.4	5.0	57.6	37.4	1.4	43.9	54.7
Change	0.0	-15.6	+15.6	-2.6	-16.7	+19.4	-0.9	-26.0	+26.9	+1.2	-11.6	+10.3

Source: BSA surveys
Note: AA=anti-abortion in all circumstances; Sit=situationalist; PC=pro-choice in all circumstances.

consistently anti-abortion. It is this middle group that previous research has labelled as holding 'situationalist' or qualified views on the issue of abortion. That is, respondents show a more conditional approach on the issue of abortion (Jelen 2003; Saad 2012a, 2012b), approving on some grounds and disapproving on others. Accordingly, Tables 5.6 and 5.7 show the proportions within each affiliation and attendance category, respectively, falling into each of these three categories in the BSA surveys from 1983 to 2012. The change over time in the proportion of each religious group falling within each category is reported in the final rows of Tables 5.6 and 5.7.

There are some interesting differences in the distribution of abortion positions based on religious affiliation, shown in Table 5.6. Catholics are more likely than the other groups to choose a strong anti-abortion position, disapproving of abortion on all grounds. Even so, the proportions within the category comprise small minorities of Catholics in each BSA survey (never rising above 15.0 percent in any survey, with the exception of 1984). In each survey, then, the overwhelming majority of Catholics adopt either a 'situationalist' or pro-choice position, although the former are much more numerous than the latter. Taking the most recent survey, 2012, over half of Catholics can be classified as 'situationalists' and around a third are consistently pro-choice. Very few Anglicans or those with no religion can be found in the anti-abortion category in each survey year (2.3 percent or lower for the former, 1.4 percent or lower for the latter). Those with no religion show a broadly even split between the 'situationalist' and pro-choice positions in recent surveys, although the latter is more prevalent in the 2004 and 2012 surveys. In recent surveys, round 55.0–60.0 percent of Anglicans adopt 'situationalist' positions with two-fifths in the pro-choice category. Other Christians differed in that they were somewhat more likely to hold 'situationalist' views compared to Anglicans and those with no religion, but not in relation to Anglicans in 2004 and 2012. The proportion of other Christians holding anti-abortion views is always lower than that registered for Catholics and in no survey is it above 9.0 percent.

Overall, all religious groups show a decrease over time in the proportions holding 'situationalist' views, Catholics included, with corresponding increases in those holding pro-choice positions. There has been less change over time in the views of those with no religious affiliation. These shifts add up to greater similarity in the distribution of abortion positions across groups in 2012 than was evident in the earlier surveys, although it should be reiterated that the 'situationalist

Table 5.6 Distribution of abortion positions, by attendance, 1983–2012

	Frequent attender			Infrequent attender			Non-attender		
	AA (%)	Sit. (%)	PC (%)	AA (%)	Sit. (%)	PC (%)	AA (%)	Sit. (%)	PC (%)
1983	10.1	78.4	11.5	1.5	73.6	24.8	0.2	55.5	44.3
1984	9.9	80.5	9.6	3.3	78.3	18.4	1.4	72.6	26.0
1985	8.0	70.2	21.8	1.2	59.5	39.3	0.6	55.1	44.2
1986	9.8	76.3	13.9	1.5	70.7	27.8	0.5	64.9	34.6
1987	6.1	71.4	22.5	2.0	56.5	41.5	0.6	54.2	45.2
1989	10.4	66.2	23.3	1.3	57.9	40.7	1.8	54.7	43.5
1990	12.0	62.2	25.8	1.3	53.1	45.6	1.4	48.7	49.9
1994	9.7	68.2	22.2	3.0	52.5	44.4	0.5	52.5	47.0
1995	9.9	61.3	28.7	1.0	52.5	46.5	1.6	46.6	51.8
1998	9.4	67.9	22.6	2.2	53.7	44.1	1.1	53.5	45.4
2004	10.5	62.9	26.6	2.5	50.0	47.5	1.5	49.6	48.9
2012	11.1	65.1	23.8	0.6	54.0	45.3	1.5	46.2	52.3
Change	+1.0	−13.3	+12.3	−0.9	−19.6	+20.5	+1.3	−9.3	+8.0

Source: BSA surveys.

Table 5.7 **Percent saying abortion is wrong, by affiliation, 1991–2010**

	1991 (%)	1998 (%)	2000 (%)	2008 (%)	2010 (%)
If there is a strong chance of a serious defect in the baby					
Anglican	9.7	6.7	9.7	9.4	9.4
Catholic	33.3	33.8	35.4	28.4	30.4
Other Christian	19.3	22.8	22.5	21.9	23.0
No religion	7.9	7.3	73	7.2	9.4
If the family has a very low income and cannot afford any more children					
Anglican	26.5	37.2	35.7	35.8	36.5
Catholic	56.5	54.0	58.5	50.6	60.9
Other Christian	38.8	45.9	49.0	46.7	44.3
No religion	22.5	33.1	30.3	29.3	28.5

Source: BSA surveys.
Note: Combines 'always wrong' and 'almost always wrong'.

group includes those with more or less restrictive views on when abortion should be allowed. Even so, those with no religion still stand out in 2012 as being more likely than all three Christian groups to take a consistently pro-choice stance on the issue.

Looking at the three groups for religious attendance (Table 5.6), frequent-attenders are most likely to adopt an anti-abortion stance over time, but this comprises a small minority in each survey (at 12.0 percent or lower). The large majority of frequent-attenders fall into the 'situationalist' category, in the range of 60.0–69.0 percent in recent years. Moreover, the proportions who support abortion under all circumstances has increased over time and, at around a fifth to a quarter in recent surveys, is usually more than double the proportion with an anti-abortion stance. The infrequent-attenders and non-attenders have a broadly similar distribution of positions based on the evidence presented in Table 5.6. In recent surveys, they have been split between the 'situationalist' and pro-choice positions, with very few in the 'anti-abortion' position, that is being against abortions on all medical and social grounds. The proportions of infrequent and non-attenders in the 'situationalist' category are lower than for frequent-attenders, but the former are around twice as likely to be in the pro-choice category as frequent-attenders, approving of abortion in all of the various circumstances asked about in the BSA surveys. In sum, all attendance groups have seen declines in the proportions registering 'situationalist' views and increases in pro-choice positions, although the magnitude of change is smaller for those not attending religious services. Across the three decades, there has been some convergence in positions on the abortion issue between infrequent-attenders and non-attenders, with the respective distributions more similar in 2012 compared to 1983.

The BSA surveys have asked other questions on abortion for which there are recurrent attitudinal data. These have involved gauging attitudes to similar scenarios to those discussed earlier, but using alternate question wordings with a different set of response options. The following questions have been asked on five surveys between 1991 and 2010:

Do you personally think it is wrong or not wrong for a woman to have an abortion ... if there is a strong chance of a serious defect in the baby?
Do you personally think it is wrong or not wrong for a woman to have an abortion ... if the family has a very low income and cannot afford any more children?

The response options were the following: 'always wrong', 'almost always wrong', 'wrong only sometimes' and 'not wrong at all'. For religious affiliation, Table 5.8 presents the proportions in each group saying an abortion would be 'always wrong' or 'almost always wrong'

Table 5.8   Percent saying abortion is wrong, by attendance, 1991–2010

	1991 (%)	1998 (%)	2000 (%)	2008 (%)	2010 (%)
If there is a strong chance of a serious defect in the baby					
Frequent-attender	28.8	33.3	32.1	33.8	32.7
Infrequent-attender	9.9	9.3	10.7	10.1	13.5
Non-attender	8.8	6.3	8.4	8.8	10.0
If the family has a very low income and cannot afford any more children					
Frequent-attender	45.5	56.8	60.9	55.0	55.5
Infrequent-attender	29.9	35.5	36.0	36.6	33.0
Non-attender	25.1	33.0	31.7	31.2	31.8

Source: BSA surveys.
Note: Combines 'always wrong' and 'almost always wrong'.

in each survey. Looking first at attitudes towards abortion in the case of there being a strong chance of a defect in the baby, Catholics are most likely to be opposed, highest at 35.4 percent in 2000. Other Christians register the second highest levels of opposition, peaking at 23.0 percent in 2010. Anglicans and those with no religion similarly show very low levels of opposition, with less than 10.0 percent in each group responding 'always wrong' or 'almost always wrong' across the surveys. Over time changes are generally minor across groups.

The second scenario concerns financial hardship and, as has been clear from the surveys already discussed, opposition is much higher across groups towards abortion in such circumstances. In each BSA survey, Catholics register the highest level of opposition, peaking at 60.9 percent in 2010. The lowest levels of opposition can again be found amongst Anglicans and those with no religion, although it is always higher amongst the latter than the former. Other Christians rank below Catholics in their opposition to abortion on these grounds. Interestingly, in contrast to the varied picture of change in opposition across most groups for the first question, opposition to abortion on these social grounds has increased across all groups over nearly two decades, particularly for Anglicans.

Next, responses to these two questions are assessed based on frequency of attendance at religious services. Table 5.8 shows responses for frequent-attenders, infrequent-attenders and non-attenders. There is a similar pattern of attitudes for both questions. Opposition is always higher across groups for abortion on the grounds of a family having a low income and not being able to afford to raise another child.

Frequent-attenders stand out for their much higher levels of opposition across surveys, and this opposition has increased over time for both questions, particularly so for the scenario concerning financial difficulties. Infrequent-attenders register levels of opposition which are much closer to those expressed by non-attenders, although they are generally slightly higher for the former group. Both of these groups also show some variation in their views over time. Non-attenders register a marginal increase in opposition for the serious defect scenario and a larger rise for the financial hardship scenario. Infrequent-attenders at religious services show a similar pattern of change: an increase in opposition towards abortion in the case of a serious defect and a rise on the grounds of financial hardship.

Data for these questions are also available for indicators of religious belief, specifically the four questions concerning God already used for analysis in Chapter 2. These data are reported in Table 5.9. Invariably, those who express a belief in God, agree that he is concerned with every human being, and think life is meaningful because of God's existence, are more likely to think that abortion, within either set of circumstances, is always or nearly always wrong. These groups also register increases in opposition over time, for both questions. Levels of opposition are again higher – for all groups – in the case of a family being unable to afford to bring up another child. Moreover, based on the additional questions about God (only included in the BSA 2008 survey), there are clear differences in view based on the items asking whether God is directly involved in an individual's affairs and whether God is angered by human sin but this is not so for the question on connecting with God (data are reported in Appendix 3). Specifically, those who believe that God has direct involvement in their affairs and those who think that God is angered by human sin are generally much more likely to disapprove of abortion in both sets of circumstances. There is little variation in disapproval based on whether respondents say they have their own way of connecting with God (beyond religious services and churches) or not.

The next step is to undertake multivariate analysis, using the BSA surveys, to assess the role played across time by religious affiliation and attendance in underpinning public opinion on abortion. Two sets of multivariate estimations are presented here, involving, respectively, the 1983 and 2012 and 1991 and 2010 surveys. An additive index, based on seven questions and constructed as described earlier in the chapter, is used to assess attitudes in the 1983 and 2012 surveys. It ranges from 0 to 7. Another additive index is constructed from the two

Table 5.9   Percent saying abortion is wrong, by belief, 1991–2008

Variable	Category	1991 (%)	1998 (%)	2000 (%)	2008 (%)
If there is a strong chance of a serious defect in the baby					
Belief in God	Believe in God	19.5	17.8	–	22.1
	Does not	7.6	4.5	–	5.1
Belief in God	Believes in God	26.3	31.2	31.2	35.0
	Other response	9.5	6.8	8.0	9.6
	Does not believe in God	8.2	6.2	11.8	5.8
God concerns himself with every human being personally	Agree	22.6	28.9	–	26.9
	Neither	9.7	3.5	–	9.4
	Disagree	6.9	5.1	–	5.5
Life is only meaningful because God exists	Agree	28.8	37.6	–	37.6
	Neither	10.8	12.2	–	12.0
	Disagree	8.1	5.3	–	6.2
If the family has a very low income and cannot afford any more children					
Belief in God	Believe in God	37.9	45.4	–	45.5
	Does not	21.9	36.3	–	26.7
Belief in God	Believes in God	45.7	56.3	59.0	58.2
	Other response	26.6	37.4	37.0	34.3
	Does not believe in God	23.5	35.6	33.3	24.0
God concerns himself with every human being personally	Agree	41.4	54.2	–	49.7
	Neither	26.6	32.9	–	32.3
	Disagree	23.1	38.7	–	30.5
Life is only meaningful because God exists	Agree	47.7	61.9	–	59.6
	Neither	27.8	37.3	–	36.8
	Disagree	26.5	37.9	–	30.7

Source: BSA surveys.
Note: Combines 'always wrong' and 'almost always wrong'.

questions on abortion (about defects and family income) asked in the 1991 and 2010 surveys, which ranges from 1 to 8. Higher values represent more pro-choice attitudes. Linear regression is used for both indices.

As well as affiliation and attendance, the models include variables measuring sex, age, education, social class and party support. To reiterate, some of these social factors – in particular, age and sex – may be correlates of religious belonging and behaviour as well as potentially having direct effects on attitudes towards abortion. Both social class and education are measured in different ways in the 1983 and 2012 surveys. In 1983, education is operationalised as a dummy variable measuring whether a respondent finished their full-time education aged 19 or over. In 2012, it is measured as a dummy variable capturing whether respondents have a degree-level qualification or higher. The religious affiliation variables are compared to the omitted reference category, those with no religion. The measure of social class in 1983 is a dummy variable recording whether a respondent is in a non-manual occupation or has a manual job (or other circumstances). The measure of social class in 2012 is similarly a dummy variable, differentiating between the salariat (those in managerial and professional occupations) and those in other occupations or with other circumstances. All other independent variables are measured the same way in 1983 and 2012.

Looking at the results in Table 5.10, there are significant effects on both religious belonging and behaving in both survey years. In 1983, being a Catholic is negatively-related to support for abortion (Beta: –.16), which is also the case for those belonging to another – Christian

Table 5.10   Linear regressions of the abortion index, BSA 1983 and 2012

Variable	BSA 1983 B (SE)		Beta	BSA 2012 B (SE)		Beta
Constant	5.84*	(.21)		6.08* (.23)		
Sex	–.13	(.10)	–.03	.01 (.13)		.00
Age	–.01*	(.00)	–.08	.00 (.00)		–.01
Nonmanual/Salariat	.24*	(.11)	.06	.22 (.14)		.06
TEA: aged 19 and over/Degree	.27	(.17)	.04	.51*(.17)		.11
Anglican	–.13	(.13)	–.03	–.19 (.18)		–.04
Catholic	–1.06*	(.21)	–.16	–.85*(.26)		–.11
Other tradition	–.89*	(.17)	–.17	–.32 (.19)		–.07
Attendance	–.23*	(.03)	–.25	–.25*(.04)		–.25
Conservative	.15	(.17)	.04	–.11 (.20)		–.03
Labour	.11	(.17)	.03	–.16 (.19)		–.04
Other party	.12	(.19)	.02	–.03 (.21)		–.01
Weighted N		1,330			870	
Adjusted R Square		.17			.11	

Note: *$p<.05$ or lower.
Reference categories: no religion; does not support a party.
Source: BSA 1983 and 2012 surveys.

or non-Christian – religious tradition (Beta: –.17). There is no significant difference between Anglicans and those with no affiliation. There is also a negative relationship for attendance at services; that is, those who attend more regularly are less supportive of abortion rights (Beta: –.25). This pattern for belonging and behaviour is partly repeated in 2012, controlling for other social characteristics and party support. Again, Catholics are less supportive of abortion compared to those with no religious affiliation (Beta: –.11), but there are no significant differences for Anglicans and those belonging to other religious traditions. There is also a negative relationship between attendance at religious services and support for abortion (Beta: –.25). Across three decades, the picture is more one of continuity than discontinuity in terms of the effects of religious belonging and behaving on support for abortion.

Analysis of the 1991 and 2010 BSA surveys is reported in Table 5.11. The results are in some respects similar to those seen in Table 5.10, with significant effects for belonging and behaving in both years. Being a Catholic has a strong impact on attitudes in both years (1983 – Beta: –.18; 2012 – Beta: –.16), with this group being much less likely to have

Table 5.11   Linear regressions of the abortion index, BSA 1991 and 2010

Variable	BSA 1991 B (SE)	Beta	BSA 2010 B (SE)	Beta
Constant	6.64* (.27)		6.6* (.25)	
Sex	–.01 (.11)	.00	–.18 (.13)	–.05
Age	.01 (.00)	.06	.00 (.00)	–.03
Degree	.31 (.20)	.05	.40* (.18)	.08
Salariat	.15 (.14)	.04	.24 (.15)	.06
Anglican	.09 (.15)	.02	.03 (.19)	.01
Catholic	–1.11* (.22)	–.18	–1.06* (.26)	–.16
Other tradition	–.32 (.18)	–.07	–.65* (.22)	–.13
Attendance	–.21* (.3)	–.24	–.22* (.04)	–.24
Conservative	.26 (.24)	.07	.35 (.21)	.08
Labour	.11 (.24)	.03	.13 (.21)	.03
Alliance/Lib Dem	.65* (.27)	.12	.38 (.25)	.07
Other party	–.45 (.35)	–.05	.20 (.26)	.03
Weighted N	966		734	
Adjusted R Square	0.13		0.16	

*Note: *p<.05 or lower.*
Reference categories: no religion; does not support a party.
Source: BSA 1991 and 2010 surveys.

pro-choice attitudes compared to those with no religious affiliation. There are no significant differences between Anglicans and the reference group in either year, while other religious traditions are less likely to hold pro-choice views in 2010 only (Beta: –.13). Attendance has consistent effects in both years, with more frequent attendance negatively related to pro-choice attitudes (1983 – Beta: –.24; 2012 – Beta: –.24). Based on the results from these respective analyses, anti-abortion attitudes in recent decades are most evident amongst Catholics and frequent-attenders, net of the influence of other social characteristics.

Trends in religious groups' attitudes on abortion can be further assessed by using the EVS surveys, all of which have asked a question on the justification of abortion. The question wording is as follows:

> Please tell me for each of the following statements whether you think it can always be justified, never be justified, or something in between. Abortion.

Respondents were asked to select their position on a scale ranging from 1 through to 10, where 1 denotes a stance that it is never justifiable and 10 denotes a position that abortion is always justifiable. Average scores are presented for a range of indicators of religion for each EVS survey, with higher scores representing greater approval of abortion. The data are reported in Table 5.12. The final column reports the change over time in the group mean scores.

The general picture is one of clear increases in group mean scores over time. That is, there has been an increase in the view that abortion is justified across various indicators of religious belonging, behaviour, and belief. Looking first at affiliation, those with no religion aside, all traditions show substantial increases from 1981 to 2008. The mean score for Catholics increased from 2.64 in 1981 to 3.92 in 2008, though it is still ranked lowest across the affiliation categories in the most recent survey, as it was in every prior survey. There have also been increases for the three attendance categories, though lowest for those who attend services on a regular basis. Those who attend infrequently rank in between frequent-attenders and non-attenders in the earliest and most recent surveys. For the other indicators of personal engagement with religion, the largest increases have occurred for those who are not a member of a religious organisation, who do not see themselves as a religious person, and those who do not believe in God and do not think there is a personal God. In no case has the ordering of the categories changed over time. That is, those who belong to an

Table 5.12 Mean scores of whether abortion is justified or not, by religious group, 1981–2008

	1981	1990	1999	2008	Change
Affiliation					
Anglican[a]	4.13	4.47	4.50	4.98	+0.85
Catholic	2.64	3.18	3.92	3.92	+1.28
Other Christian	3.67	2.86	4.76	4.94	+1.27
No religion	5.31	4.87	5.34	5.38	+0.07
Attendance					
Frequent-attender	3.21	3.80	3.46	3.48	+0.27
Infrequent-attender	4.01	4.41	4.80	4.83	+0.82
Non-attender	4.42	4.90	4.83	5.33	+0.91
Membership					
Member of a religious group	3.09	3.88	4.19	3.33	+0.24
Not a member	4.28	4.61	4.56	5.06	+0.78
Identity					
Is a religious person	3.52	4.03	3.96	4.09	+0.57
Is not a religious person/ is a convinced atheist	4.71	5.04	4.89	5.41	+0.70
Beliefs					
Believes in god	3.71	4.22	4.18	4.12	+0.41
Does not or other response	4.99	5.17	5.11	5.83	+0.84
There is a personal God	3.25	3.85	3.79	3.44	+0.19
There is not or other response	4.36	4.80	4.85	5.30	+0.94

Source: EVS surveys.
[a] Note that this category for the 1981 survey covers Protestant traditions apart from Nonconformists. For all subsequent surveys, Nonconformists and other Christian traditions fall within the 'other Christian' category.

organisation, see themselves as a religious person, and who express belief in God are less likely to believe abortion is justified in 2008, as they were in 1981.

As well as assessing mean scores on the justification of abortion scale, the EVS surveys have posed two identical questions on abortion between 1981 and 2008, relating to the social reasons for having an abortion. The question wordings are as follows:

Do you approve or disapprove of abortion under the following circumstances?
Where the married couple do not want to have more children?
Where the woman is not married?

Respondents were asked if they approved or disapproved, and the proportions responding 'disapprove' in the 'bookend' surveys, 1981 and 2008, are reported in Table 5.13. The percentage point changes in opinion for each question are again reported in separate columns. Looking first at responses by religious affiliation, Catholics are most likely to disapprove of abortion in the married couple scenario in 1981, but other Christians are more disapproving (for both questions) in the

Table 5.13   **Percent disapproving of abortion, by religious group, 1981–2008**

	Married couple			Unmarried woman		
	1981	2008	Change	1981	2008	Change
Affiliation						
Anglican[a]	61.7	46.6	−15.1	64.5	40.0	−24.5
Catholic	87.3	55.9	−31.4	87.3	58.6	−28.7
Other Christian	76.4	62.0	−14.4	88.2	64.5	−23.7
No religion	54.7	32.5	−22.2	55.7	29.8	−25.9
Attendance						
Frequent-attender	77.6	71.3	−6.3	77.6	60.4	−17.2
Infrequent-attender	62.5	44.6	−17.9	70.3	40.2	−30.1
Non-attender	60.6	34.9	−25.7	61.4	32.5	−28.9
Membership						
Member of a religious group	76.8	74.8	−2.0	76.7	75.7	−1.0
Not a member of a religious group	61.9	40.2	−21.7	65.3	36.7	−28.6
Identity						
Is a religious person	69.7	58.4	−11.3	74.2	55.8	−18.4
Is not a religious person/is a convinced atheist	58.8	33.6	−25.2	59.1	30.3	−28.8
Beliefs						
Believes in god	67.6	54.9	−12.7	72.2	51.7	−20.5
Does not or other response	57.0	30.2	−26.8	53.7	27.1	−26.6
There is a personal God	75.4	51.0	−24.4	77.2	47.6	−29.6
There is not or some other response	60.5	32.7	−27.8	63.5	29.3	−34.2

Source: EVS surveys.
[a] Note that this category for the 1981 survey covers Protestant traditions apart from Nonconformists. For all subsequent surveys, Nonconformists and other Christian traditions fall within the 'other Christian' category.

2008 survey. Those with no religion are least likely to disapprove in both surveys, followed by Anglicans. Around a third or fewer of those with no religion disapprove in the 2008 survey, while around two-fifths of Anglicans were opposed to abortions under either scenario. Despite these group differences, all four groups exhibit declining levels of disapproval over time, with the largest absolute declines for Catholics (at 31.4 and 28.7 percentage points, respectively).

Looking at the most recent survey, frequent-attenders are around twice as likely to disapprove as are non-attenders. Over time, the attitudinal gap has markedly widened between, on the one hand, those attending often and, on the other, those attending irregularly or not at all. In 1981, 77.6 percent of frequent-attenders disapproved of abortion when the woman is not married compared to 70.3 percent for infrequent-attenders and 61.4 percent for non-attenders. In 2008, however, while 60.4 percent of regular-attenders disapproved, only 40.2 percent and 32.5 percent of, respectively, infrequent-attenders and non-attenders did so. The decline in disapproval across time has been greatest for infrequent-attenders and non-attenders. Frequent-attenders register declines of 6.3 and 17.2 percentage points, respectively, for the two questions, which are considerably lower than those for the other two groups. In the recent survey, infrequent-attenders tend to express levels of disapproval closer to those registered by those who never attend. Based on the other measures of religion, including belief in God, the largest percentage point falls in disapproval from 1981 to 2008 are generally seen for those who do not hold traditional beliefs or who show less engagement with faith in other ways (are not a religious person or do not belong to a religious organisation). These are also the groups who registered lower levels of opposition to abortion in 1981 for both questions. However, all groups show lower disapproval in 2008 compared to 1981. The notable exception is that there is hardly any fall in disapproval for those who reported belonging to a church or religious organisation, while for those who are not members there are substantial percentage point falls. With the exception of membership of a religious group, all indicators show a liberalisation of opinion over time, albeit of varying magnitudes.[3]

Summarising across the evidence from the three recurrent surveys analysed here, multiple indicators of public opinion on abortion generally show that religious groups based on measurement of the three 'Bs' have become more liberal or accepting of abortion in recent decades. There are still robust differences between groups, of course, with Catholics and other Christians less accepting of abortion than

Anglicans and those with no religion; while regular-attenders at religious services are distinctive from irregular-attenders and non-attenders in showing higher levels of opposition. These findings are generally consistent across the BES, BSA and EVS surveys.[4]

The attitudes of the Catholic community

Historically, in relation to abortion it has been observed that 'There is, perhaps, no single moral issue to which official Catholicism is more strongly opposed' (Hornsby-Smith 1987: 162).[5] In wider society, the institutional Catholic Church, its clergy and many ordinary adherents traditionally held a distinctive stance on abortion, which set them apart from the wider population:

> ... the ferocity of the opposition of Catholic spokepersons on the matter of abortion is well known. While for many people abortion is often regarded as a type of contraception, in general Catholics see it as a distinct moral issue and one which they regard with particular abhorrence. Among Catholic lay leaders, the 1967 Abortion Act is generally considered to have been a political defeat of major proportions and lasting consequences. Catholics have been disproportionately active in the two main anti-abortion pressure groups in Britain ... In the public mind, therefore, Catholics in England and Wales were often defined in terms of the ferocity with which they opposed contraception, abortion and divorce, and propounded a sexual ethic manifestly at variance with the changing behavioural norms of British society (Hornsby-Smith 1987: 89–90).

More recent years have seen leaders of the Catholic Churches in Scotland, England and Wales continue to intervene in public debate and election contests, making controversial pronouncements on the issues of abortion or moral values in general (Jones 2005; Blake 2007; Carrell 2010). More recently in late 2013 the Catholic Church established its own initiative to survey adherents' attitudes on social-morality issues, asking national bishops' conference around the world to survey Catholics in their respective countries (McElwee 2013). A global survey of Catholics released in early 2014 underlined, cross-nationally, the depth of public disagreement with the church's official positions on social-moral issues such as abortion, divorce, contraception and same-sex marriage. The highest levels of attitudinal disagreement were found in Europe (unfortunately, Catholics in Britain were not sampled in the survey), North America and South America (Boorstein and Craighill 2014). Given this wider context, this section investigates the changing attitudes of Catholics on abortion, looking at which groups within the Catholic community hold more or less pro-choice views.

A survey of Catholics in Britain undertaken by Gallup in March 1967 asked whether abortion should be legal in three situations (where the health of the mother is in danger; where the child may be born with a deformity; and where the mother wants it). Overall, there was greater approval of abortion where the mother's health is endangered and where the child may be born with a deformity, with much less support for abortion when the mother chooses it (Martin 1968), as has been the case for the general population surveys analysed already. Differences on the basis of social background were evident. First, there were consistent differences in the views of men and women, with the latter less likely to say abortion should be legal in each situation (Martin 1968: 195). In terms of class, those in the lower social class were more in favour of legal abortion in each set of circumstances (Martin 1968: 195). However, the most marked differences occurred on the basis of attendance. Those attending often (at least 2 or 3 times a month) were much less likely to approve of abortion being legal in all three scenarios, most evidently when the baby may be born with a deformity (68.0 percent for those who attended rarely compared to 39.0 percent for those who went often) (Martin 1968: 195). Other survey-based research also shed some light on attitudes towards abortion, amongst Catholics living in England in the 1970s. It found that 'two-third of Catholics in England agreed with the statement "except where the life of the mother is at risk, abortion is wrong"' (Hornsby-Smith 1987: 110). When looking at group variation in attitudes, those more likely to disapprove of abortion were those who attended mass more frequently, and those aged 65 years and older, with little difference on the basis of social class (Hornsby-Smith and Lee 1979: 192).

To look more closely at attitudinal variation amongst Catholics in Britain, the BSA surveys are used to look at differences in abortion attitudes based on Catholics' attendance at religious services, divided into those who attend frequently and those who attend less often or not at all. The BSA surveys are preferable given the range of questions asked on this issue; their annual occurrence over the last few decades; and with each survey having collected data on both affiliation and attendance. The two sets of questions on abortion from the BSA series analysed above are used here. A note of caution is due at this point as Catholics have generally constituted about 10.0 percent of the samples in the BSA surveys (Field 2014b: 373) and so the unweighted bases for the two attendance categories will be rather small across the surveys (accordingly, the percentages have been rounded to the nearest whole number).

Therefore, based on the evidence presented, the broader picture over time is primarily of interest rather than specific figures for any particular survey. The attitudes of (i) regular-attenders and (ii) irregular-attenders or non-attenders amongst Catholics are examined over time, with the data presented in Table 5.14 and Table 5.15 (question wordings were provided earlier on). Table 5.14 reports data from the seven questions used to construct the abortion index used above (for the period 1983–2012). Here responses to each question are shown, specifically the proportions responding 'no' for each abortion scenario. The general pattern is consistent across the seven questions. Frequent-attenders are almost always more opposed to abortion, and often by large magnitudes. For both groups, disapproval is generally lower for circumstances involving the health of the mother being potentially at risk, where the health of the baby is at issue, and where the pregnancy is the result of rape.

Table 5.15 presents responses to two other questions asked in the BSA surveys between 1991–2010, reporting the proportions who said abortion was always wrong or nearly always wrong. Responses to these two questions – abortion in the case of the baby potentially having a serious defect and when a family cannot afford another child – show much higher levels of disapproval expressed by regular-attenders at religious services. In both groups, disapproval is always markedly higher in the scenario concerning a family with a low income unable to raise another child. In general terms, the evidence for attitudes based on attendance corroborates with that found for the preceding set of seven BSA questions on various abortion scenarios.

To provide a contemporary assessment of British Catholics' attitudes towards abortion, for a wide range of social characteristics – including attendance – data are utilised from a survey of Catholics conducted by YouGov in the run-up to the September 2010 papal visit (fieldwork for the poll was conducted between 31 August–2 September 2010, in England, Scotland and Wales, and the sample size comprised 1,636 adults aged 18 and over). The YouGov survey included three separate questions on abortion which were administered to the full sample. Two of these questions used binary response options, and the third employed a more graduated set of categories, which allowed respondents to express a 'situationalist' position (see the discussion of this

Table 5.14 Percent saying no to abortion, by attendance, Catholics, 1983–2012

		1983 (%)	1984 (%)	1985 (%)	1986 (%)	1987 (%)	1989 (%)	1990 (%)	1994 (%)	1995 (%)	1998 (%)	2004 (%)	2005 (%)	2007 (%)	2008 (%)	2012 (%)
The woman decides on her own she does not wish to have the child	Frequent-attender	80.0	85.0	68.0	80.0	79.0	72.0	74.0	70.0	66.0	64.0	67.0	62.0	53.0	59.0	75.0
	Infrequent or non-attender	56.0	70.0	31.0	50.0	49.0	53.0	47.0	45.0	49.0	38.0	28.0	37.0	27.0	28.0	37.0
The couple agree they do not wish to have the child.	Frequent-attender	75.0	85.0	65.0	75.0	73.0	67.0	70.0	65.0	77.0	57.0	65.0	–	–	–	54.0
	Infrequent or non-attender	55.0	74.0	31.0	34.0	44.0	42.0	52.0	17.0	47.0	43.0	30.0	–	–	–	25.0
The couple cannot afford any more children	Frequent-attender	78.0	75.0	59.0	77.0	73.0	69.0	63.0	62.0	69.0	68.0	53.0	64.0	71.0	59.0	75.0
	Infrequent or non-attender	44.0	68.0	31.0	44.0	44.0	47.0	42.0	33.0	49.0	41.0	22.0	43.0	28.0	44.0	35.0
The woman is not married and does not wish to marry the man	Frequent-attender	78.0	83.0	63.0	79.0	75.0	64.0	71.0	71.0	69.0	65.9	65.0	–	–	–	79.0
	Infrequent or non-attender	51.0	73.0	33.0	48.0	51.0	55.0	48.0	33.0	51.0	42.0	37.0	–	–	–	47.0
There is a strong chance of a defect in the baby	Frequent-attender	51.0	51.0	29.0	49.0	43.0	39.0	44.0	48.0	51.0	47.0	39.0	–	–	–	32.0
	Infrequent or non-attender	16.0	19.0	8.0	13.0	13.0	12.0	16.0	13.0	26.0	19.0	13.0	–	–	–	19.0
The woman's health is seriously endangered by the pregnancy	Frequent-attender	27.0	30.0	19.0	29.0	22.0	29.0	36.0	31.0	34.0	8.0	10.0	18.0	9.0	14.0	14.0
	Infrequent or non-attender	4.0	7.0	3.0	5.0	12.0	7.0	7.0	0.0	16.0	3.0	6.0	3.0	2.0	1.0	8.8
The woman became pregnant as a result of rape	Frequent-attender	24.0	36.0	21.0	29.0	24.0	27.0	36.0	29.0	29.0	30.0	19.0	–	–	–	29.0
	Infrequent or non-attender	6.0	10.0	8.0	9.0	10.0	14.0	3.0	0.0	21.0	11.0	9.0	–	–	–	6.0

Source: BSA surveys.

Table 5.15   Percent saying abortion is wrong, by attendance, Catholics, 1991–2010

	1991 (%)	1998 (%)	2000 (%)	2008 (%)	2010 (%)
If there is a strong chance of a serious defect in the baby					
Frequent-attender	48.0	53.0	55.0	45.0	32.0
Infrequent- or non-attender	17.0	17.0	17.0	18.0	28.0
If the family has a very low income and cannot afford any more children					
Frequent-attender	73.0	70.0	78.0	60.0	80.0
Infrequent- or non-attender	39.0	41.0	39.0	45.0	40.0

Source: BSA surveys.
Note: Combines 'always wrong' and 'almost always wrong'.

aspect in the previous section). The question wordings and response options were as follows:

> Generally speaking, do you think that women should or should not have the right to an abortion?
> 1. Women should have the right to an abortion.
> 2. Women should not have the right to an abortion.
> 3. Don't know.

> And do you think that women should or should not have the right to choose an abortion in the first three months of pregnancy?
> 1. Women should have the right to choose an abortion in the first three months of pregnancy.
> 2. Women should not have the right to choose an abortion in the first three months of pregnancy.
> 3. Don't know.

> Do you think a woman who is less than 20 weeks pregnant and wishes to have an abortion should:
> 1. Always be allowed to have an abortion.
> 2. Be allowed an abortion on grounds of rape, incest, severe disability to the child or as an indirect consequence of life-saving treatment for the mother.
> 3. Be allowed an abortion ONLY as an indirect consequence of life-saving treatment for the mother.
> 4. Never be allowed an abortion.
> 5. Don't know.

In order to provide a more robust picture of group variation, Table 5.16 shows the proportions holding more liberal or less restrictive views on abortion for each of these indicators. Specifically, it reports the proportions who (i) support a general right to abortion; (ii) who think women should have the right to choose an abortion in the first three months of pregnancy; and (iii) who favour women less than

Table 5.16   Attitudes towards abortion, by socio-demographic group, Catholics, 2010

		General right to an abortion (%)	Right to an abortion in first three months (%)	Always be allowed to have an abortion (%)	Situationalist (%)
Sex	Men	62.7	60.3	25.2	53.6
	Women	74.3	70.7	34.3	59.0
Ethnic group	White British	68.8	65.5	30.0	55.9
	Other ethnic group	71.0	69.4	33.4	55.4
Age group	18–24	60.0	54.3	25.3	65.3
	25–34	81.3	75.8	44.7	42.7
	35–44	78.0	77.9	36.3	52.4
	45–54	70.9	68.8	31.9	58.7
	55–64	67.2	64.4	25.9	57.5
	65–74	51.7	47.2	14.9	65.1
	75+	43.5	39.1	4.3	76.1
Aged completed full-time education	15 or under	59.3	57.0	19.3	63.3
	16	71.1	67.8	23.0	66.1
	17–19	73.2	68.3	34.0	51.9
	20 and over	70.7	67.4	34.4	50.9
	Still in education	63.8	60.7	31.0	57.8
Social grade	AB	64.7	63.7	29.7	55.9
	C1	72.6	68.9	35.6	50.1
	C2	73.9	69.6	32.6	56.0
	DE	68.9	64.1	23.8	62.1
Party support	Labour	74.9	70.5	34.4	55.8
	Conservative	60.2	58.8	23.1	60.2
	Liberal Democrat	72.4	69.8	32.9	52.4
	Other party	72.9	68.9	34.2	52.5
	None	71.5	67.5	32.4	51.8
Attendance	Frequent-attender	49.6	48.6	18.5	59.3
	Infrequent-attender	83.1	78.2	35.8	55.7
	Non-attender	85.7	81.3	44.0	50.1

Source: YouGov survey of adult Catholics in Britain, August–September 2010.

20 weeks into a pregnancy being allowed to have an abortion whatever the circumstances or who have a 'situationalist' view. Respondents were classified using the following set of variables: sex, ethnic group, age group, aged completed full-time education, social grade, the political party supported, and the frequency of attendance at religious services.

Looking first at demographic characteristics, it is clear that women are somewhat more supportive than men of abortion on each of the three indicators. There are large differences in the attitudes of Catholics when classified by age group. Those aged 75 and older are least likely to approve of abortion across each indicator, with just 4.3 percent saying women should always be allowed to have an abortion, albeit three-quarters take a 'situationalist' viewpoint on this question. They are followed by the 65–74 age group – 14.9 percent of whom think women should always be allowed to have an abortion. Generally, those most likely to approve of abortion are in the 25–34 and 35–44 age groups, followed by those aged 45–54 and 55–64. Interestingly, the youngest age group – 18–24 years – are somewhat less likely to be supportive of abortion than those in the cohorts spanning 25–64 years of age.

There are also clear differences by socio-economic background. In relation to education, those least in favour of abortion are those who completed their education at a younger age, either 15 or under or aged 16 years. Those who completed their education aged 17–19 years, aged 20 or over, as well as those still in some form of education, are more supportive of abortion rights. Based on social grade (for more details on this classification, see Chapter 2), the most liberal views are found amongst those in the C1 and C2 categories. Interestingly, the AB and DE categories – the most apart in terms of their socio-economic circumstances – evince lower levels of support for abortion.[5]

The largest differences across groups are found for frequency of religious attendance, which surpass the considerable differentials found between those in the younger and older age groups. Those who attend services frequently (defined as once a month or more) stand apart from those who attend less often (less than once a month) or not at all. Around half of regular-attenders support abortion rights on the basis of the first two questions. For the third question, just under a fifth think that abortion should always be allowed, with three-fifths taking a 'situationalist' position. In contrast, infrequent-attenders and non-attenders show overwhelming support for abortion rights on the basis of the first two indicators. The similarity of view expressed by infrequent and non-attenders is broadly in line with the attitudinal concordance shown by these groups in the general population earlier in this chapter. In response to the third question, they are about twice as likely as frequent-attenders to think that women should always be allowed an abortion, with majorities opting for the 'situationalist' position. If attendance is employed as a proxy for religious commitment or religiosity, it is clear that the most religious Catholics hold the most restrictive views in abortion. This was also the case for a survey of Catholics in England and Wales undertaken in the late 1970s (Hornsby-Smith and Lee 1979).

Finally, there are also some differences in view based on party affiliation (based on the long-standing BES question on party identification). Specifically, Conservative-supporting Catholics are less supportive of abortion rights, standing apart from the other partisan groups on each indicator. Those who affiliate with Labour, the Liberal Democrats, a minor party or who do not support any party show very similar levels of support across the three indicators. What is particularly notable for the third question is that, across all groups, the vast majority of respondents either support abortion in general or adopt a more or less restrictive 'situationalist' position. Only small or very small proportions think that abortion should never be allowed, which reflects the official teaching of their faith, highest at 12.1 percent for those attending church on a weekly basis, 11.4 percent for those aged 65–74 years, 9.3 percent for Conservative Party identifiers and 8.7 percent for those who left education aged 15 or under. Overall, just 6.4 percent of respondents in the YouGov 2010 survey support this strict interpretation of abortion, not too dissimilar to the 8.4 percent who hold this view based on self-identification as Catholics in the BSA 2012 survey.

Taken together the results for sex are different from those evident in the Gallup poll from the late-1960s discussed already, where women were somewhat less supportive of legal abortion, while the findings on the basis of mass attendance at services are broadly consistent. The evidence from the 2010 survey of Catholics in Britain therefore shows that, overall, considerable proportions of ordinary adherents deviate from official denominational teachings on abortion and that there is significant variation in opinion across some social groups.

Conclusion

This chapter has provided a detailed consideration of religious groups' attitudes on the abortion issue across time, focusing primarily on opinion based on religious affiliation and attendance. The first part of the chapter clearly demonstrated the liberalisation of opinion that has occurred on this issue since the 1970s and 1980s, evidence which was consistent across three different recurrent surveys. There has, therefore, been some convergence in view across religious groups, particularly as Catholics and those who attend services regularly, are more likely to have come to accept abortion, at least under certain circumstances. Even so, Catholics still stand out from Anglicans and those with no affiliation, as they tend to have more restrictive views on abortion.[6] There is also evidence that other Christians tend to express higher levels of opposition than Anglicans and those with no religion and, on some measures, exceed the level of disapproval registered by Catholics. This is also the case for those who attend services frequently, who are generally distinct from infrequent and non-attenders in showing greater opposition to abortion. Even so, when looking at the distributions of Catholics and frequent-attenders in terms of having anti-abortion, 'situationalist' or pro-choice positions, only very small minorities are found in the first category. The overwhelming majority of Catholics and regular-attenders either approve of abortion in some situations but not others, or do support abortion in all circumstances, at least based on the varying scenarios posed in the BSA surveys. More detailed multivariate analyses of attitudes towards abortion in the general population showed that the religious basis of opposition to abortion has showed considerable continuity across time, and has been most evident amongst Catholics and frequent-attenders. Religious factors in the form of belonging and behaving seem particularly important for undergirding opposition to abortion, while there are less clear and consistent effects for other social characteristics, such as sex, age and socio-economic status.

Detailed consideration of the contemporary attitudes of the Catholic community in Britain towards abortion showed interesting and some-times substantial variation across social group. Male Catholics, older Catholics, those who left school at an early age, and those who express support for the Conservative Party were less likely to hold liberal views on abortion rights. The most striking differences were apparent on the basis of church attendance, with the most regular church-goers most likely to uphold traditional religious teachings on abortion, compared to those attending less often or not at all (for more on this see, Clements 2014e). The empirical evidence presented here for Catholics in Britain speak to the broader debate over the decline of 'religious authority' (Chaves 1994), showing the growing disconnect between, on the one hand, the institutional church and its long-

standing strictures on abortion – and sanctity of life issues more generally – and, on the other, the liberalising trend evident in recent years
amongst ordinary Catholics, very few of whom adopt a consistent anti-
abortion position. Indeed, the data on abortion provide further insight
into the broader attitudinal trend noted by Hornsby-Smith for earlier
post-war decades, whereby Catholics were increasingly '"making up
their own minds" over an expanding area of issues' (1987: 90–1). This
has occurred in the context of the Catholic Church in particular and
Christian churches in general having suffered from a long-term loss
of public trust and respect (Field 2014c), as already discussed in
Chapter 2.

6
Religion, Homosexuality and Gay Rights

Building on the previous chapter's focus on religious groups' changing views on abortion, this chapter provides a detailed analysis of religious groups' attitudes towards homosexuality and related equality issues. There are obvious reasons for looking at religious groups' attitudes in this area across recent decades given that 'traditionally, sexual relationships and family life are areas which have been closely policed by religious organisations and religious teaching' (Francis et al. 2005: 45). Moreover, Hayes and Dowds' observe that ' ... some commentators go so far as to suggest that public disputes and related court battles over homosexual rights have now replaced abortion as the most significant and divisive moral issue within many contemporary western industrialized societies' (2013: 2). It is certainly the case that British society has seen major pieces of legislation enacted in recent years bringing greater social equality for same-sex individuals and relationships, which have often been opposed by religious traditions and organisations.

In Britain, homosexuality was decriminalised in the 1967 Sexual Offences Act, coming a decade after the publication of the report of the 1957 Wolfenden Committee on Homosexual Offences and Prostitution, which articulated a 'permissive principle' towards private lives and personal morality (Thorup Larsen et al. 2012: 128). The Wolfenden Report 'had won wide though by no means universal acquiescence among Christian leaders and Church assemblies' (Machin 1998: 192), although, as Machin observes:

> Such supporters of legalization, however, were by no means usually prepared to regard the homosexual orientation as equivalent to the heterosexual one. They were not, in many cases, prepared to abandon the traditional views that homosexuality was unnatural.

Consequently they did not as yet express an overt desire – such as has been expressed by some leading Christians since the 1970s – that homosexuals should enjoy the same freedom and rights as heterosexuals – for example, the right to live as a married couple after a church or civil wedding (1998: 192–3).

Several decades hence, the next legislative act on this subject was in a more restrictive direction, in the form of 'Section 28' from the 1988 Local Government Act, 'one of the few victories for the morally restrictive part of the Conservative party under Thatcher' (Thorup Larsen et al. 2012: 128). A series of major legislative advances for same-sex equality then followed under the Labour administrations in office from 1997–2010, including the repeal of 'Section 28'. Given the changing social, political and legislative context surrounding homosexual behaviour and same-sex equality issues in post-war decades, this chapter assesses both changes in the attitudes of religious groups on both same-sex relations in general and specific equality issues.

The chapter is therefore structured into two main sections. The first section looks at the general acceptability of homosexuality and same-sex relationships over time, using data from recurrent social surveys, which have included questions on this topic since their inception. The second section focuses on particular same-sex equality issues, such as adoption and marriage rights, both of which have been the subject of major pieces of legislation under recent governments, Labour between 1997–2010 and the Conservative-Liberal Democrat coalition since 2010. As with the previous chapter, evidence is sourced from separate recurrent social surveys, which offer different attitudinal indicators on this topic, in order to get as full a picture as possible of trends and patterns in attitudes amongst religious groups (for a fuller review of attitudinal trends in the general British population, see Clements and Field 2014). The analysis again builds on and contributes to the wider scholarly literature on public opinion towards homosexuality (Hayes 1995b; Evans 2002; Crockett and Voas 2003; Clements 2014b; Park and Rhead 2013; Heath et al. 2013a; Heath et al. 1993a), as well as denomination-specific studies of attitudes on this topic (Clements 2014e; Village and Francis 2008).

Attitudes towards homosexuality

This first section provides a detailed assessment of trends in general opinion on homosexuality, in terms of acceptance or approval across religious groups. The BSA series, which started undertaking yearly surveys in 1983, has gauged the general acceptance of same-sex relations by asking the following question in most surveys:

> About sexual relation between two adults of the same sex. Do you think it is always wrong, almost always wrong, wrong only sometimes, or not wrong at all?

Figure 6.1 charts attitudes towards sexual relations between same-sex adults over recent decades, based on affiliation. It uses the longest available time series on this issue, from the BSA cross-section surveys covering the period 1983 to 2012. It shows the proportions responding 'always wrong' or 'mostly wrong' (combined), for the following categories: Anglicans, Catholics, other Christian, and no religion. Overall, while the proportions with negative views rose slightly in the mid-1980s, it is clear that there has been a steady decline in disapproval of same-sex relations from the late 1980s onwards, with a consequent rise in those who do not really feel it is wrong.

Looking at the specific detail, there are large percentage point declines between 1983 and 2012 for all groups. The largest absolute decreases occurred for other Christians (−39.3) – who were the most

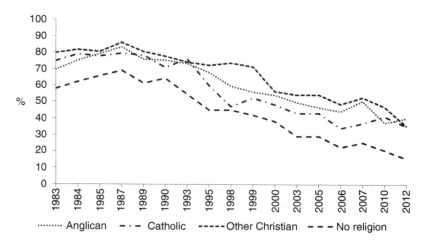

Figure 6.1   Percent saying same-sex sexual relations are wrong, by affiliation, 1983–2012
Source: BSA surveys.
Note: Combines 'always wrong' and 'almost always wrong'.

opposed in 1983 – and those with no religion (–39.0), with slightly smaller, but still substantial, declines for Catholics (–32.8) and Anglicans (–23.1). Catholics now rank below Anglicans in their level of negative sentiment, with the latter group more opposed in 2012, whereas they ranked slightly above them in 1983. Whereas the gap between those with no religion and the tradition (other Christians) with the highest level of negative opinion was 20.2 percentage points in 1983, the equivalent gap (this time, with Anglicans) is slightly higher in 2012 (24.6 percentage points).

What about changes in opinion based on attendance at religious services? Figure 6.2 charts attitudes for the three-way classification of religious attendance. It covers the period 1983–2012. All three groups have moved in the direction of becoming more accepting of same-sex relations, but the decline in opposition has been greater for those who attend infrequently or not at all than for those who go to services on a regular basis. In fact, over time, attitudes have clearly diverged on the basis of frequency of attendance, with infrequent-attenders now much closer to non-attenders in their opposition to same-sex relations, whereas this group was positioned in-between or closer to frequent-attenders in the earlier surveys. The decline in negative sentiment has been much higher for those who attend services infrequently

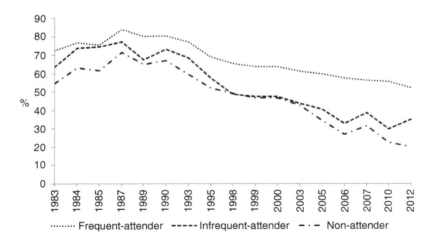

Figure 6.2   Percent saying same-sex sexual relations are wrong, by attendance, 1983–2012
Source: BSA surveys.
Note: Combines 'always wrong' and 'almost always wrong'.

(28.7 percentage points) or not at all (34.8 percentage points) compared to frequent-attenders, who still register a substantial decline (20.3 percentage points). The percentage point gap in negative opinion between frequent-attenders and non-attenders has significantly increased – nearly doubling, in fact – from 17.7 in 1983 to 32.2 in 2012.[1]

The changing association between attendance and attitudes on this question over time can be shown in another way (Chaves 2011; Chaves and Anderson 2012). Both can be measured as scales (with higher values representing more frequent attendance and greater opposition to same-sex relations) and bivariate correlation analysis undertaken for the 1983 and 2012 'bookend' surveys. The correlation statistics (which can range from 0 to 1 with higher values indicating a stronger association) show that the strength of association has increased over time, more than doubling from 0.14 in 1983 ($p=0.01$) to 0.32 ($p=0.01$) in 2012. This increasing strength of association, based on the same calculations for every survey between 1983 and 2012, is graphed in Figure 6.3.

Another way of examining patterns of change in religious groups' views over time is to divide the BSA time series data on same-sex relations into two periods which broadly differed in terms of the wider political and legislative context surrounding gay and lesbian equality issues. The two periods, reflecting the available survey time points, are

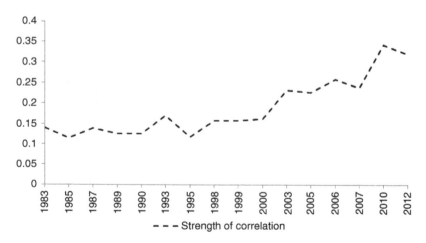

Figure 6.3   Bivariate correlations between attitudes towards same-sex sexual relations and attendance, 1983–2012
Source: BSA surveys.

1983–95 and 1998–2007. As Hayes and Moran-Ellis note in relation to the 1980s:

> The threatened stability of British society and the continuity of its moral regime were directly linked by the Conservatives to the perceived breakdown in traditional family values and practices. Subsequently, the designation and public curtailment of homosexuality was regarded as central to the moral rejuvenation of British society (Hayes and Moran-Ellis 1997: 24–5).

Whilst in the second period (from 1997 onwards) there were several major legislative reforms enacted by the Labour governments. These were (Stonewall 2012: 4):

- Adoption and Children Act 2002: Allows same-sex couples to adopt children.
- Employment Equality (Sexual Orientation) Regulations 2003 (now Equality Act 2010): Protection from discrimination and harassment for lesbian, gay and bisexual employees.
- Civil Partnership Act 2004: Grants partnership rights for same-sex couples which are the same as marriage.
- The Equality Act (Sexual Orientation) Regulations 2007 (now Equality Act 2010): Makes it unlawful to refuse people services, such as healthcare, on the grounds of their sexual orientation.
- Criminal Justice and Immigration Act 2008: Outlaws the stirring-up of hatred on the grounds of sexual orientation.

As an additional reform, gays and lesbians were allowed to serve openly in the British armed forces from 2000 onwards, which repealed a long-standing ban – maintained by the Ministry of Defence – on same-sex individuals being allowed to join the military. Under the Conservative-Liberal Democrat coalition government, in office since May 2010, legislation was passed legalising same-sex marriage, known as the Marriage (Same Sex Couples) Act 2013. This is only applicable to England and Wales, though with similar legislation having recently been enacted in Scotland.

   To compare public disapproval of same-sex relations in these two periods, the proportion in each religious group saying 'always wrong' or 'almost always wrong' is averaged across surveys. These calculations produce the figures shown in Table 6.1. The averages are much higher in the period covering most of the Conservative Party's unbroken

Table 6.1 **Percent saying same-sex sexual relations are wrong, by affiliation and attendance, average across time periods**

	Anglican (%)	Catholic (%)	Other Christian (%)	No religion (%)
1983–95	75.0	74.6	79.1	60.0
1998–2007	51.6	43.7	58.8	33.1

	Frequent-attender (%)	Infrequent-attender (%)	Non-attender (%)
1983–95	77.0	69.6	61.9
1998–2007	61.2	42.8	39.8

Source: BSA surveys.
Note: Combines 'always wrong' and 'almost always wrong'.

period in office (1979–97) than for the period corresponding to much of the Labour Party's time in government (1997–2009; the 2010 figures are excluded from the calculations for the second period as, even though this includes the final few months of Labour in office, the Conservative-Liberal Democrat coalition administration was in place from early May onwards). While Anglicans and Catholics showed almost identical levels of disapproval in the earlier period, Catholics registered lower levels of negative sentiment than Anglicans in the later period (declining from 74.6 percent to 43.7 percent). Moreover, the average for those with no religion is almost halved when comparing the two periods (from 60.0 percent to 33.1 percent). When looking at average levels of disapproval by attendance at services, between 1983–95 those who attended services irregularly (69.6 percent) were positioned equidistant between frequent-attenders (77.0 percent) and non-attenders (61.9 percent), whereas in the later period the mean level of opposition for infrequent-attenders (42.8 percent) more closely approximates that given for non-attenders (39.8 percent).

These figures are also supported by other questions on same-sex relations asked periodically in the BSA surveys. These have used variant wordings and response options relative to the BSA question used already. Two of the questions have been asked on more than one occasion. They are worded as follows:

About sexual relations between two adults of the same sex? Is it always wrong OR not wrong at all? How much do you agree or disagree that ... homosexual relations are always wrong?

For further comparison, responses are shown for the following question asked only in the BSA 2008 survey, which refers to 'morality or immorality':

People often disagree on the morality or immorality of certain behaviours. For each of the following types of behaviour, please indicate whether you consider the behaviour to be always wrong, sometimes wrong, or never wrong. Homosexual acts.

Responses to these questions are shown in Table 6.2 (affiliation) and Table 6.3 (attendance). The first question used response options ranging from 'strongly agree' through to 'strongly disagree'. Tables 6.2 and 6.3 report the proportions who (i) 'strongly agree' or 'agree'; (ii) those responding 'always wrong' or 'almost always wrong'; and (iii) those saying 'always wrong'. The questions asked on two surveys broadly coincide with the period of the recent Labour governments (1998–2008, 1996–2006), so it could be expected, based on the trends shown already, for these indicators to similarly show liberalisation of attitudes based on affiliation and attendance. This is indeed the case. The proportions who respond 'always wrong' or 'almost always wrong' falls across all religious groups between 1998 and 2008. Similarly, the proportions agreeing that homosexual relations are always wrong declined between 1996 and 2006, again for every group. Those with no religion register the lowest level of negative sentiment in every year. Moving to views on the basis of attendance at services, the declines have been more substantial for irregular-attenders and non-attenders

Table 6.2   Other indicators of attitudes towards same-sex sexual relations, by affiliation

	Anglican (%)	Catholic (%)	Other Christian (%)	No religion (%)
'Always wrong' or 'almost always wrong'				
1998	55.3	36.6	64.7	35.9
2008	43.3	31.4	49.2	22.4
'Strongly agree' or 'agree'				
1996	27.4	28.3	39.9	16.7
2006	18.0	20.1	30.3	12.7
'Always wrong'				
2008	38.0	26.3	44.6	23.7

Source: BSA surveys.

Table 6.3   Other indicators of attitudes towards same-sex sexual relations, by attendance

	Frequent-attender (%)	Infrequent-attender (%)	Non-attender (%)
'Always wrong' or *'almost always wrong'*			
1998	63.1	47.6	39.9
2008	57.5	34.9	28.3
'Strongly agree' or *'agree'*			
1996	37.9	24.5	20.9
2006	36.1	12.9	14.5
'Always wrong'			
2008	56.6	27.9	28.2

Source: BSA surveys.

for both over time indicators. Those who attend services on a regular basis register much smaller falls in disapproval over the decade covered by each indicator (from 63.1 percent to 57.5 percent and from 37.9 percent to 36.1 percent).

Returning to the data in Figures 6.2 and 6.3, all three attendance-based groups have registered substantial decreases in disapproval, but this liberalisation was faster and deeper for those who attended services less often or not at all, and thus slower and less marked for those who attend services on a regular basis. Comparing attitudes in 1983 and 2012, those who attend services infrequently have come to resemble more closely those who never attend services, whereas in 1983 their level of opposition to same-sex relations more closely mirrored that of frequent-attenders. These changes have led to a tighter association between level of attendance and attitudes towards homosexuality over time. Heath et al. also find a similar trend in their longitudinal analysis of BSA surveys, concluding that: 'the relationship between liberal attitudes and religiosity has, if anything, got stronger over time, especially with respect to the acceptability of same-sex relationships' (2013b: 184). A similar trend has also been evident amongst church-goers in the US based on survey data covering recent decades. As Chaves observes:

When it comes to attitudes about homosexuality, both frequent and infrequent attendees have become more liberal, but the most religious people are liberalizing more slowly than others. In the 1970s, 85 percent of weekly attendees said that homosexuality is always wrong compared to 67 percent of infrequent attendees, while since 2000 the comparable numbers are 79 percent and 48 percent. Both the religious and the nonreligious have liberalized on this issue, but the less religious people have liberalized faster (2011: 100; see also, Chaves and Anderson 2012: 227–9).

In Britain, too, the less religious, as measured by attendance, have liberalised faster since the early 1980s.

While there is comparatively little over-time evidence for attitudes towards homosexuality based on measures of religious beliefs in the BSA surveys, some indications can be gleaned from the data presented in Table 6.4. This shows attitudes towards same-sex relations for the four questions about God used in earlier chapters, for the period 1998–2008. Even though the time scale is much more limited, it is clear that, to some extent, a similar liberalisation of opinion has occurred for these indicators of believing. Across all groups, disapproval has fallen over the decade in question, although the differences in levels of disapproval are still evident in 2008. That is, those who believe in God, who believe that God concerns himself personally with every individual, and for whom life is meaningful only because God exists, are more likely to say that homosexuality is always wrong or nearly always wrong in both surveys. Based on those questions probing beliefs in and about god asked only in the BSA 2008 survey (data are

Table 6.4 Percent saying same-sex sexual relations are wrong, by belief, 1998–2008

Variable	Category	1998 (%)	2008 (%)
Belief in God (1)	Believe in God	56.6	46.1
	Does not	32.2	23.1
Belief in God (2)	Believes in God	67.4	62.5
	Other response	40.1	30.4
	Does not believe in God	35.8	20.9
God concerns	Agree	67.0	50.4
himself with every	Neither	37.6	30.6
human being	Disagree	34.4	24.7
personally			
Life is only	Agree	73.9	70.5
meaningful because	Neither	55.0	33.5
God exists	Disagree	32.0	23.6

Source: BSA surveys.
Note: Combines 'always wrong' and 'nearly always wrong'.

reported in Appendix 3), it is clear that those who believe God is directly involved in their affairs, and who believe that God is angered by human sin, are clearly less likely to approve of same-sex sexual relations. There is little difference in view, however, based on responses to the question about connecting with God outside of religious services and churches.

The role played across time by religious factors in underpinning opinion towards homosexuality is investigated in more depth by undertaking multivariate analyses of the 1983 and 2012 BSA surveys. In essence, is there a similar set of effects for religious belonging and behaving when examining attitudes at two time-points spanning three decades? The same model specification is adopted for both surveys, as was used for the analysis of abortion attitudes from the 1983 and 2012 surveys in Chapter 5. In order to provide a comparison of those for and against homosexual relations, a binary dependent variable was constructed. Those whose view was that same-sex relations was wrong to any degree (always wrong, nearly always wrong, sometimes wrong, rarely wrong, or it depends) are coded as 1, while those who said – unequivocally – that homosexual relations are never wrong were coded as 0. Results are shown in Table 6.5.

Table 6.5   Binary logistic regressions of attitudes towards same-sex sexual relations, BSA 1983 and 2012

Variable	BSA 1983		BSA 2012	
	B (SE)	Odds ratio	B (SE)	Odds ratio
Sex	.27 (.14)	1.31	.51* (.14)	1.66
Age	.03* (.00)	1.03	.02* (.00)	1.02
Nonmanual/Salariat	−.53* (.15)	.59	−.74* (.16)	.48
TEA/Degree	−.80* (.21)	.45	−.32 (.20)	.73
Anglican	.00 (.18)	1.00	.73* (.20)	2.07
Catholic	.36 (.32)	1.43	.51 (.28)	1.67
Other tradition	.44 (.25)	1.55	.86* (.20)	2.37
Attendance	.16* (.05)	1.17	.23* (.04)	1.26
Conservative	−.71* (.27)	.49	.23 (.22)	1.26
Labour	−.85* (.27)	.43	−.07 (.20)	.93
Other party	−1.02* (.29)	.36	−.21 (.22)	.81
Constant	.77* (.31)	2.15	−1.82* (.25)	.16
Weighted N	1,605		1,055	
Nagelkerke R Square	.14		0.25	

Note: *p<.05 or lower.
Reference categories: no religion; does not support a party.
Source: BSA 1983 and 2012 survey

Generally, religious belonging and behaving have more of an impact in 2012 than in 1983. In 1983, only attendance has a significant effect on attitudes towards homosexuality, with more frequent attendance associated with opposition towards same-sex relations. There are no significant differences between those groups with and the group without, a religious affiliation. In 2012, however, religion appears to be a more potent differentiator of attitudes on this topic. As well as the same pattern evident for attendance at services, there are also significant differences between, on the one hand, Anglicans (odds ratio: 2.07) and adherents of other traditions (odds ratio: 2.37) and, on the other, those with no affiliation. Catholics do not significantly differ from those with no religious affiliation in 2012. Overall, the model performs better in 2012 than in 1983 (as shown in the Nagelkerke R Square statistics).

Corroborating evidence of this overall shift in a more liberal direction from the BSA surveys can be seen in data from the EVS. In relation to same-sex relations, the EVS surveys have asked the following question:

> Please tell me for each of the following statements whether you think it can always be justified, never be justified, or something in between. Homosexuality.

This asks respondents to place themselves on a scale ranging from 1 to 10, whereby 1 means that homosexuality can never be justified and 10 means it can always be justified (for a cross-national analysis of public attitudes based on this question see Gerhards 2010). Mean scores can be examined over time using indicators of personal religion which appear in each EVS survey. Specifically, respondents are classified on the basis of: religious affiliation (again excluding the small numbers belonging to non-Christian traditions); frequency of attendance at services; whether a member of a religious group or not, whether a religious person or not, whether they believe in God or not and whether they think there is a personal God or not. The mean scores are reported in Table 6.6.

Looking in broad terms, there has been a shift in a liberal direction across *all indicators of religion* in the period 1981–2008. No group, whatever the classification, has a lower score in 2008 than they had in 1981. Overall, and in keeping with the evidence from the BSA surveys for the 1980s, there is not much upward movement in the mean scores between 1981 and 1990. The main upward shifts come between 1990

Table 6.6   Mean scores for whether homosexuality is justified or not, by religious group, 1981–2008

	1981	1990	1999	2008	Change
Affiliation					
Anglican[a]	3.32	3.44	4.76	5.44	+2.12
Catholic	3.61	3.27	5.25	5.74	+2.13
Other Christian	2.75	2.86	4.97	4.94	+2.19
No religion	4.45	3.87	5.29	5.82	+1.37
Attendance					
Frequent-attender	3.16	2.92	4.11	4.70	+1.54
Infrequent-attender	3.26	3.50	5.24	5.53	+2.27
Non-attender	3.62	3.86	5.04	5.76	+2.14
Membership					
Member of a religious group	2.99	3.23	4.49	4.87	+1.88
Not a member of a religious group	3.52	3.59	4.91	5.59	+2.07
Identity					
Is a religious person	2.94	3.00	4.55	5.03	+2.09
Is not a religious person/ is a convinced atheist	4.04	4.15	5.09	5.85	+1.81
Beliefs					
Believes in God	3.17	3.20	4.68	4.94	+1.77
Other response	4.22	4.34	5.22	6.25	+2.03
There is a personal God	2.70	2.84	4.34	4.60	+1.90
Other response	3.72	3.86	5.11	5.79	+2.07

Source: EVS surveys.
[a] Note that this category for the 1981 survey covers Protestant traditions apart from Nonconformists. For all subsequent surveys, Nonconformists and other Christian traditions fall within the 'other Christian' category.

and 1999 and 1999 and 2008. In 2008, the lowest scores are registered by other Christians, those frequently attending services, members of religious groups, those who consider themselves to be a religious person, and those who either belief in God or who think there is a personal God.

Some other aspects of the data are worthy of note, where clearer comparisons can be made with the BSA time-series data. Amongst religious traditions, in 2008 Catholics (5.74) are closer to the non-religious (5.82) than to the other traditions (for, example, Anglicans, at 5.44 and other Christians, at 4.94). In 1981, Catholics were closer to Anglicans than the non-religious. Another way of looking at this is that in 1981 the gap in mean scores between Catholics and those with no religion was 0.84, but in 2008 this has narrowed considerably to just 0.08. There are also interesting shifts amongst groups classified by their religious attendance. In 2008, those infrequently attending services (5.53) are much closer to non-attenders (5.76) in their mean score, whereas in 1981 they (3.26) were closest to the frequent-attenders (3.16). The gap in mean scores between frequent-attenders and non-attenders in 1981 was 0.46, but this had widened to 1.06 in 2008. For attendance at services, there is a similar trend to that present in the BSA data, with all groups liberalising in their attitudes, but with the less religious liberalising more quickly than the more religious. For each indicator of religion shown in Table 6.5, it is important to note that the relative ordering of the mean scores across categories does not change between 1981 and 2008. In every case, then, those who are not engaged or less engaged with personal religion are still more liberal in their attitudes than the more religious in 2008.

The EVS surveys can be used to analyse tolerance towards homosexuality using a different type of question, carried in the 1990, 1999 and 2008 surveys. This is known as a 'social distance' measure, and was worded as follows:

> On this list are various groups of people. Could you please sort out any that you would not like to have as neighbours? Homosexuals.

Table 6.7 reports the proportions who mentioned they would not like to have 'homosexuals' as neighbours. Two general aspects are particularly worthy of note. Firstly, levels of disapproval of having homosexuals as neighbours are generally low, even at the earliest time point (1990), and never reaches 40.0 percent or higher (highest at 37.3 percent for other Christians and at 37.0 percent amongst those who believe in a personal God). Second, as with the indicator of disapproval of homosexuality shown in Table 6.6, there is an across-the-board decrease in negative sentiment over nearly two decades, with decreasing opposition evidence between both 1990 and 1999 and 1999 and 2008 (the final column reports the percentage point change over time). By 2008, indeed, the level of negative sentiment is generally around a tenth or lower in most groups. In fact, there is not much variation across categories within the different measures of personal faith (lowest at 7.4 percent for Catholic, 8.1 percent for those who do not believe in God or are not sure, and 8.4 percent for those who do not belong to a religious group).

Table 6.7   **Percent saying they would not like to have homosexuals as neighbours, by religious group, 1990–2008**

	1990 (%)	1999 (%)	2008 (%)	Change
Affiliation				
Anglican	31.8	27.6	10.5	–21.3
Catholic	33.9	15.9	7.4	–26.5
Other Christian	37.3	18.2	14.0	–23.3
No religion	29.0	21.5	10.2	–18.8
Attendance				
Frequent-attender	32.3	24.7	10.3	–22.0
Infrequent-attender	31.9	23.3	10.0	–21.9
Non-attender	30.2	24.6	10.2	–20.0
Membership				
Member of a religious group	27.2	30.6	10.6	–16.6
Not a member of a religious group	31.9	23.9	8.4	–23.5
Identity				
Is a religious person	33.8	24.5	11.2	–22.6
Is not a religious person/is a convinced atheist	28.1	24.2	9.7	–18.4
Beliefs				
Believes in god	31.9	23.8	11.9	–20.0
Does not or other response	29.2	25.3	8.1	–21.1
There is a personal God	37.0	26.6	13.5	–23.5
There is not or other response	28.3	23.5	9.2	–19.1

Source: EVS surveys.

Differences in religious groups' attitudes can be assessed using recent evidence, based on a question asked in every ESS survey between 2002 and 2012.

> Using this card, please say to what extent you agree or disagree with each of the following statements. Gay men and lesbians should be free to live their own life as they wish.

Response options were in the form of a Likert-scale, ranging from strongly agree through to strongly disagree. The options disagree and strongly disagree were combined and responses for four measures of religion (affiliation – available for 2008–12, frequency of attendance, frequency of prayer and personal religiosity) are presented in Table 6.8. Frequency of prayer and personal religiosity were collapsed into three

Table 6.8   Percent disagreeing that gay and lesbians should be free to live their lives as they wish, by religious group, 2002–2012

	2002 (%)	2004 (%)	2006 (%)	2008 (%)	2010 (%)	2012 (%)
Affiliation						
Anglican	–	–	–	6.4	6.9	6.3
Catholic	–	–	–	9.7	7.3	6.0
Other Christian	–	–	–	20.0	17.3	9.8
No religion	–	–	–	4.1	3.3	2.5
Attendance						
Frequent-attender	19.0	16.0	17.7	20.3	11.3	9.3
Infrequent-attender	12.0	7.4	8.0	6.0	5.5	4.7
Non-attender	8.9	6.6	5.9	4.7	4.0	3.1
Prayer						
Prays once a week or more	16.2	12.4	16.6	16.1	9.8	7.7
Prays less often	11.0	7.5	5.6	5.1	4.3	5.1
Never prays	9.1	6.6	5.2	4.2	4.0	3.1
Religiosity						
High religiosity (7–10)	12.0	12.8	18.0	17.1	11.4	8.6
Medium religiosity (4–6)	13.1	8.2	6.3	6.7	4.7	5.3
Low religiosity (0–3)	10.3	6.6	5.7	3.7	3.6	2.7

Source: ESS surveys.
Note: Combines 'strongly disagree' and disagree'.

categories for the purposes of the analysis undertaken here. Frequency of prayer is divided between those who pray once a week or more, less often, or never pray. The religiosity scale, which ranges from 1 through to 10, is divided as follows: low religiosity has the values of 1–3; medium religiosity has the values of 4–7; and high religiosity has the values of 8–10. Affiliation and attendance are measured as per the other social surveys utilised in this chapter.

Given the liberalisation of opinion in recent years shown already based on much longer-running survey series, it would be expected that levels of agreement would be high for this question, given that it covers the period 2002–12 (for cross-national analyses of public attitudes based on this question see: Hooghe and Meeusen 2013; Takács and Szalma 2011). This is indeed the case for each survey wave. In 2002, levels of disagreement were in no case higher than 20.0 percent (highest at 19.0 percent for frequent-attenders and 16.2 percent for those who prayed most often). Even so, across the decade disagreement fell for most groups, so that in 2012, the highest levels of negative sentiment were just 9.8 percent (other Christians), 9.3 percent (frequent-attenders) and 8.6 percent (those with high levels of personal religiosity). Amongst those with no religion and who showed less frequent or no personal engagement with faith (never attend, never pray, low religiosity), disagreement was almost non-existent in recent surveys.

The EVS survey data tend to corroborate the over-time evidence from the BSA surveys, both in documenting a clear liberalisation of attitudes across religious groups and in showing which particular groups are more or less liberal in their present-day views. Based on the wealth of over-time evidence from the BSA and EVS surveys, and consolidated by more recent data from the ESS, there has been a substantial shift in a liberal direction across religious groups in British society, which seems to have occurred during the 1990s and continued in the following decades.

Another important area of public opinion on this topic concerns specific evaluations of gay and lesbian people. The US General Social Survey series has often employed 'feeling thermometers' asking respondents to evaluate gay and lesbian people as well as a range of other societal groups. The thermometers are based on scales ranging from 0 to 100, whereby a score of 0 denotes a very cold feeling and a score of 100 a very warm feeling (Wilcox and Wolpert 2000: 411). Unfortunately, similar measuring instruments have not featured in British social surveys, but the BES 2010 in-person survey did ask respondents to rate five different groups, including gay and lesbian people (the others being based on ethnic background). The scale used range from 0 to 10, where 0 denoted 'very unfavourable' and 10 represented 'very favourable' (with a scale midpoint of 5.0). The question wording was as follows:

Now, using a scale that runs from 0 to 10, where 0 means feel very unfavourable and 10 means feel very favourable, how do you feel about gay and lesbian people?'

As well as having a measure of religious affiliation (based on the same categories employed in this chapter), the BES 2010 survey also asked two questions on the extent of religious involvement in the last 12 months, relating to group activity (service attendance or other communal acts) and personal practice (prayer, meditation or other forms of worship). As with the questions on attendance at services from the other social surveys, the responses to these latter two questions were classified into three groupings: frequently (at least once a month);

Table 6.9   Mean scores of feelings towards gays and lesbians, by affiliation and attendance

Affiliation	Anglican	Catholic	Other Christian	No religion
	5.75	6.49	5.19	6.57

Attendance	Frequent-attender	Infrequent-attender	Non-attender
Attendance	5.40	6.00	6.32
Personal activities	5.58	5.93	6.29

Source: BES 2010 in-person survey (post-election cross-section).

infrequently (only at festivals); and not at all. Albeit this provides only a limited snapshot of religious groups' evaluations of same-sex individuals, the mean scores on this scale are reported in Table 6.9.

Overall, the differences in group attitudes present a broadly similar pattern to that evident for views towards homosexual behaviour analysed already. Those with no religion and Catholics are most favourable in their evaluations of same-sex individuals, with scores of, respectively, 6.57 and 6.49. Other Christians show the least favourable views of gays and lesbians, with a mean rating of 5.19. Anglicans are positioned in-between, more favourable than other Christians but less positive than Catholics and those with no religion, with a scale average of 5.75. A similar pattern to that shown already in the survey data is also evident for religious involvement. That is, on both measures of group-related activity and personal practice, those involved frequently gave lower favourability ratings compared to those with infrequent involvement or those who do not take part in religious activities. Specifically, the mean scores for frequent involvement in group and personal religious activity are 5.40 and 5.58, respectively, compared to 6.32 and 6.29 for those who report no involvement (in the last year) in any form of religious activity. In sum, then, those groups who express higher levels of opposition towards homosexuality and same-sex relations also possess less favourable views when asked about their specific view of gay and lesbian people.

Attitudes towards gay rights issues

The first section of this chapter has analysed general views of homosexuality, in terms of approval or disapproval of same-sex relationships. This second section focuses on more specific issues of equality for same-sex couples, looking at three areas: roles and occupations, adoption rights, and legal recognition of same-sex relationships. The latter two areas have been the subject of major pieces of equalities legislation for same-sex individuals and couples by recent government, which have engendered opposition from the leaders of both Christian denominations and minority faiths. To some extent, these legislative reforms have both reflected and contributed to a 'clash between civil and ecclesiastical norms in Britain' (Village and Francis 2008: 4). The focus here is primarily on using data from the BSA surveys, supplemented by other sources where appropriate. The analysis focuses, in turn, on attitudes towards gays and lesbians holding certain roles and professions, adoption by same-sex couples, and same-sex marriage.

Attitudes towards same-sex individuals holding certain roles and occupations

The BSA surveys have asked on several occasions whether it is right for homosexuals to be involved in public life – holding responsible positions – or to be employed as teachers in different educational settings. The question wordings for these three items are as follows:

> Is it acceptable for a homosexual person ... to hold a responsible position in public life?
> Is it acceptable for a homosexual person ... to be a teacher in a college or university?
> Is it acceptable for a homosexual person ... to be a teacher in a school?

The response options were 'yes', 'no', as well as respondents being able to choose from several qualified answers. The percentage of 'no' responses are shown in Table 6.10. Overall, levels of opposition have always been highest towards homosexuals being allowed to teach in schools, intermediate for teaching in further and higher education settings and lowest for being allowed to hold positions in public life. This ordering has remained the same over the course of the surveys, but for all three measures the proportions against has declined between 1983 and 2012.

In 2012 there is very little opposition to homosexuals having a responsible position in public life, highest at just 11.2 percent amongst other Christians, and lowest at 2.7 percent amongst those with no religion. Opposition to homosexuals occupying teaching positions is also very low, and does not exceed 20.0 percent for any group. As expected,

Table 6.10   **Percent saying no towards homosexuals occupying roles and occupations, by affiliation, 1983–2012**

	Anglican (%)	Catholic (%)	Other Christian (%)	No religion (%)
To hold a responsible position in public life				
1983	45.2	44.2	47.9	35.7
2012	7.2	5.5	11.2	2.7
To be a teacher in a college or university				
1983	51.8	48.5	52.1	42.1
2012	15.3	11.8	13.3	5.4
To be a teacher in a school				
1983	56.5	56.1	59.6	44.9
2012	19.2	14.4	15.7	7.5

Source: BSA surveys.

those with no religion register almost negligible levels of opposition (at 5.4 percent for teaching in further/higher education and 7.5 percent for schools). Opposition is highest amongst Anglicans for both teaching in post-compulsory settings (15.3 percent) and in schools (19.2 percent). Taking a longer view, there have been substantial declines in negative sentiment across all groups over the course of three decades. In fact, this set of questions registers the lowest level of opposition from religious groups across any of the various topics from the BSA surveys examined in this chapter.

There have also been substantial liberalisation of views based on attendance at religious services, shown in Table 6.11. Across all three groups, there have been large decreases in the proportions against homosexuals holding positions in public life, teaching in colleges or universities or being school teachers. Even so, the overall pattern evident in the 1983 survey is still there in 2012, with frequent-attenders most likely to register socially-conservative views. Levels of opposition are highest in relation to teaching in schools and lowest – clearly so for infrequent-attenders and non-attenders – for homosexuals holding responsible positions in public life.

Attitudes towards gay people in teaching occupations can be further compared by looking at responses to a one-off question asked in the 2006 BSA survey. It asked:

How suitable are gay men and lesbians for the job of primary school teacher?

Table 6.11   **Percent saying no towards homosexuals occupying roles and occupations, by attendance, 1983–2012**

	Frequent-attender (%)	Infrequent-attender (%)	Non-attender (%)
To hold a responsible position in public life			
1983	45.3	45.6	36.4
2012	18.3	6.5	4.8
To be a teacher in a college or university			
1983	50.7	51.1	42.6
2012	19.4	13.6	8.9
To be a teacher in a school			
1983	57.5	56.5	45.6
2012	23.8	17.5	11.0

Source: BSA surveys.

Response options ranged from 'very suitable' through to 'very unsuitable', and responses by affiliation and attendance are shown in Table 6.12, using broader suitable and unsuitable categories. While, on the one hand, Catholics (46.3 percent) and those with no religion (49.7 percent) are much more likely to believe gay men and lesbians are suited to such an occupation; on the other, Anglicans (36.3 percent) and other Christians (32.1 percent) are less support-ive. In each group a sizeable minority adopts a neutral stance (neither suitable nor unsuitable), and around a fifth to one-quarter of the religious traditions think them to some degree unsuitable (compared to just 14.6 percent for those with no religion). Turning to religious attendance, it is clear that those who take part in ser-vices on a regular basis are more likely to think gay men and les-bians unsuitable for such a role. Amongst frequent-attenders 30.9 percent believe that homosexuals are unsuited to be primary school teachers, compared to 17.4 percent of infrequent-attenders and 17.8 percent of non-attenders. A plurality of infrequent-attenders (43.2 percent) and non-attenders (45.6 percent) think that they are to some degree suitable for such a role. Responses to this question provide further evidence that those who attend services less often resemble non-attenders much more closely in their attitudes than they do regular-attenders.

Table 6.12   Attitudes towards gay men and lesbians being primary school teachers, by affiliation and attendance

	Anglican (%)	Catholic (%)	Other Christian (%)	No religion (%)
Very suitable or suitable	36.3	46.3	32.1	49.7
Neither	29.0	26.2	31.0	28.6
Suitable or very unsuitable	25.1	20.2	25.8	14.6
Can't choose	9.6	7.3	11.1	7.1

	Frequent-attender (%)	Infrequent-attender (%)	Non-attender (%)
Very suitable or suitable	31.1	43.2	45.6
Neither	27.8	30.9	28.6
Suitable or very unsuitable	30.9	17.4	17.8
Can't choose	10.3	8.5	8.0

Source: BSA 2006.

Attitudes towards adoption by same-sex couples

One issue which proved controversial under the New Labour governments was that of same-sex couples being able to adopt children. Legislation proposed by the government met with strong opposition from some religious bodies, particularly the Catholic Church (Woodward and Bates 2007). An assessment of trends in attitudes towards adoption by same-sex couples can be made as the BSA surveys have asked several questions on adoption between 1983 and 2012. On a number of surveys, separate questions have probed views about adoption by lesbian couples and gay male couples:

Do you think female homosexual couples – that is, lesbians – should be allowed to adopt a baby under the same conditions as other couples?
Do you think male homosexual couples (gay men) should be allowed to adopt a baby under the same conditions as other couples?

The response options were 'yes', 'no', 'depends on the person' and 'other'. Attitudes for the first two questions are shown for religious affiliation and attendance in, respectively, Figures 6.4 and 6.5 and Figures 6.6 and 6.7, which chart opposition to adoption by lesbian and gay couples (showing the proportions saying 'no'). Overall, the time-series data show that, on the whole, there were only small reductions in opposition in the 1980s and early 1990s. The largest falls occurred after 1993 across all groups, whether classified by affiliation or attendance. Unfortunately, the question was then not repeated until 2007, so more precise conclusions as to the timing and nature of the decline cannot be made.

Looking in more detail, while opposition has decreased over two and a half decades, majorities still oppose adoption by lesbian couples (except for those with no religion) based on the 2007 survey data. Opposition is highest amongst Anglicans (62.3 percent) and other Christians (58.2 percent). Compared to these groups, it is somewhat lower amongst Catholics (55.9 percent) and much lower amongst those with no affiliation (43.7 percent). Majority opposition is higher still in the case of gay male couples adopting children, and leading the opposition are again Anglicans (69.1 percent) and other Christians (66.2 percent), with those of no religion registering a bare majority against (50.9 percent).

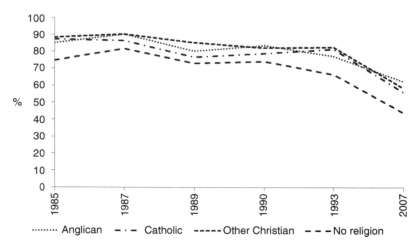

Figure 6.4 Percent saying no to adoption by lesbian couples, by affiliation, 1983–2007
Source: BSA surveys.

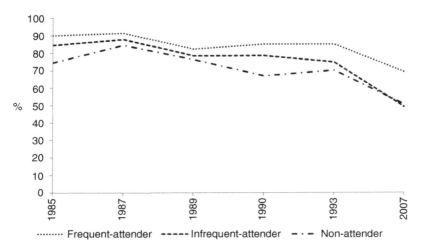

Figure 6.5   Percent saying no to adoption by lesbian couples, by attendance, 1983–2007
Source: BSA surveys.

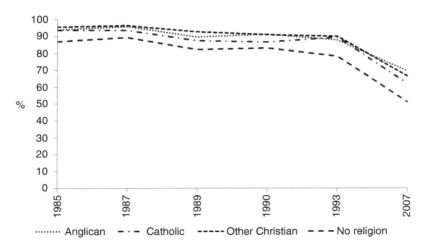

Figure 6.6   Percent saying no to adoption by gay male couples, by affiliation, 1983–2007
Source: BSA surveys.

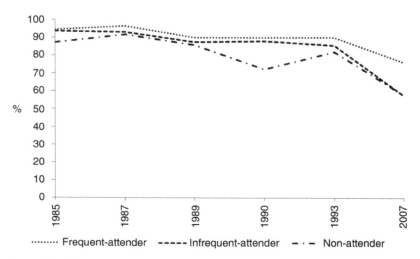

Figure 6.7   Percent saying no to adoption by gay male couples, by attendance, 1983–2007
Source: BSA surveys.

Catholics show a clear majority opposed to adoption by gay men (61.6 percent), but somewhat lower than that expressed by Anglicans and other Christians. Based on the classification of attendance, all groups have decreased their opposition to adoption rights for lesbians and gay male couples compared to the very high levels registered in 1983 (at 90.0 percent and 94.4 percent, respectively, for frequent-attenders). By 2007, frequent-attenders are still largely opposed to such adoptions occurring, but again infrequent-attenders' level of opposition more closely approximates that of non-attenders. In 1983, those infrequently-attending were nearer to frequent-attenders in their negative sentiment. More broadly, levels of opposition remain higher towards gay male couples adopting than towards lesbian couples.

Another BSA question, asked on only two occasions but over a longer time-span (1983 to 2012), refers in general to adoption by same-sex couples. It is worded as follows:

Do you think homosexual couples should be allowed to adopt a baby under the same conditions as other couples?

The response options were 'yes', 'no', 'other' and 'not male couples'. Levels of opposition expressed in the 1983 and 2012 surveys are

Table 6.13   Percent saying no to homosexual couples adopting children, by affiliation and attendance, 1983–2012

	Anglican (%)	Catholic (%)	Other Christian (%)	No religion (%)
1983	90.6	88.5	88.6	88.4
2012	59.9	50.2	55.6	33.8
Change	–30.7	–38.3	–33.0	–54.6

	Frequent attender (%)	Infrequent-attender (%)	Non-attender (%)
1983	88.9	89.8	84.4
2012	60.3	50.0	39.0
Change	–28.6	–39.8	–45.4

Source: BSA surveys.

reported in Table 6.13, for religious affiliation and attendance.[1] There have been large decreases in negative sentiment based on affiliation, with the largest decline being for those with no religion (falling from 88.4 percent to 33.8 percent), so that now just a third of this group are against homosexual couples adopting. Catholics register lower opposition in 2012 than do Anglicans or other Christian; but still a majority of each of these groups is against.

In 1983 similar and very high levels of opposition were registered by the three groups based on attendance, but this has clearly changed by the time of the 2012 survey, with much larger variation in levels of opposition. In 1983, 88.9 percent and 84.4 percent of, respectively, frequent-attenders and non-attenders were against adoption by same-sex couples, whereas their views had diverged markedly by 2012, even though the direction of travel was in a liberal direction. In 2012, 60.3 percent of regular-attenders were still opposed, compared to 39.0 percent of non-attenders; the infrequent-attenders were broadly equidistant in their level of opposition, at 50.0 percent.[2]

To investigate further the impact of religious factors – belonging and behaving – on attitudes towards gays and lesbians being in the teaching profession and adopting children, multivariate analyses were conducted using data from the BSA 1983 and 2012 surveys. Specifically, attitudes towards same-sex individuals being allowed to teach in schools and colleges (which elicited higher levels of opposition than working in universities or holding positions in public life) and same-sex adoption are assessed using binary logistic regression estimation. Previous analysis of the BSA 1989 survey found that Protestants and Roman Catholics were more likely to have conservative views on gay rights issues, including AIDS and homosexual adoptions, than those with no affiliation (Hayes 1995b: 471). There were also significant effects for church attendance in relation to attitudes towards AIDS victims, with regular-attenders more likely to hold conservative opinions (Hayes 1995b: 468).

For each of the model estimations concerning the BES surveys, those opposed to same-sex individuals being allowed to teach or adopting children were coded as 1 and those in favour coded as 0. The model specifications used are the same as those used for the multivariate analyses reported in Table 6.5. The results are reported in Table 6.14. First, looking at attitudes towards teaching in schools and colleges, it is clear that, in 1983, when overall opposition was very high, only religious affiliation had a significant impact. That is, those belonging to other religious traditions – not Anglicans or Catholics – were more likely to be opposed compared to those with no religion (odds ratio: 1.57). In 2012, however, both affiliation and attendance had significant effects. Again, members of other traditions are more likely to be opposed (odds ratio: 3.05), as are those who regularly attend religious services. Second, for attitudes towards adoption by same-sex couples, religious factors also have a more prominent role in 2012 than in 1983, when opposition was much higher in general. In 1983, the model performs very poorly overall. Of the religion variables, both belonging and behaving fail to have a significant impact on public opinion towards child adoption by gays and lesbians. In 2012 those belonging to other religious traditions are also more likely to be opposed to adoption by same-sex couples (odds ratio: 2.10). In 2012, also, Anglicans are significantly more likely to oppose adoption by same-sex couples (odds ratio: 1.54), though this is not the case for 1983. Religious factors – belonging and behaving – are therefore more potent differentiators of contemporary opinion on gay rights. Moreover, taking all the independent variables together, greater proportions of variance in the dependent variables are accounted for in the analyses of the 2012 data compared to the 1983 data (as reported in the Nagelkerke R Square statistics). This was also the case for the analyses undertaken in Table 6.5.

Attitudes towards same-sex marriage

The most recent debate over same-sex equality has involved the coalition government's plans for consulting over same-sex marriage, which

Table 6.14 Binary logistic regressions of attitudes towards gays and lesbians teaching in schools and colleges and adopting children, BSA 1983 and 2012

| | Teaching in schools and colleges | | | | Adoption | | | |
| | BSA 1983 | | BSA 2012 | | BSA 1983 | | BSA 2012 | |
Variable	B (SE)	Odds ratio	B (SE)	Odds ratio	B (SE)	Odds ratio	B (SE)	Odds ratio
Sex	.29* (.11)	1.33	.08 (.19)	1.09	.03 (.19)	1.03	.50* (.14)	1.65
Age	.03* (.00)	1.03	.04* (.01)	1.04	.01 (.01)	1.01	.04* (.00)	1.04
Nonmanual/Salariat	-.55* (.12)	.58	-1.27* (.26)	.28	-.29 (.20)	.75	-.30 (.16)	.74
TEA: 19 and over/Degree	-.63* (.20)	.53	-.49 (.34)	.61	-.23 (.30)	.79	-.58* (.20)	.56
Anglican	.14 (.15)	1.15	.46 (.27)	1.59	.31 (.24)	1.36	.43* (.21)	1.54
Catholic	.33 (.24)	1.39	.44 (.39)	1.56	.07 (.39)	1.07	.33 (.28)	1.40
Other tradition	.45* (.19)	1.57	1.11* (.27)	3.05	.11 (.31)	1.11	.74* (.21)	2.10
Attendance	.02 (.03)	1.02	.12* (.05)	1.13	.10 (.06)	1.11	.12 (.04)	1.13
Conservative	-.11 (.18)	.89	-.04 (.30)	.96	-.22 (.34)	.80	.12 (.23)	1.12
Labour	-.12 (.19)	.89	-.20 (.28)	.82	-.59 (.34)	.56	-.16 (.21)	.86
Other party	-.42* (.21)	.66	-.27 (.32)	.76	-.43 (.37)	.65	-.50* (.23)	.60
Constant	-.97* (.23)	.38	-3.95* (.39)	.02	2.12* (.40)	8.34	-2.55* (.27)	.08
Weighted N	1,526		1,053		1,561		1,019	
Nagelkerke R Square	.14		.23		.03		.26	

Note: *p<.05 or lower
Reference categories: no religion; does not support a party.
Source: BSA 1983 and 2012 surveys.

emerged in 2012. After a particularly divisive national debate over the proposals, the Marriage (Same Sex Couples) Act was enacted in 2013. As Kettell notes, 'the issue of same-sex marriage is a particularly incendiary one for religious groups' (2013: 2). Organised opposition to the proposals for same-sex marriage on the part of local and national clergy was evident in the national media. This included an article vehemently denouncing the proposals written by Cardinal Keith O'Brien, then leader of the Catholic Church in Scotland, in March 2012 (O'Brien 2012); a joint letter signed by over 1,000 Catholic priests in January 2013 (Bingham 2013a); a joint letter supported by leaders of mainly ethnic minority Christian churches in April 2013 (Bingham 2013b); and a letter in May 2013 signed by more than 500 imams from the Muslim faith representing mosques from across the country (Bingham 2013c). Letters from Catholic archbishops denouncing the proposals were read out at services at parish churches in England and Wales, and Scotland, respectively, in March and August 2012 (*The Guardian* 2012; McIver 2012). The principal campaign group opposed to the proposals, Coalition for Marriage, lists many serving and retired clergy, from both Christian denominations and non-Christian faiths, amongst the signatories of its petition. The issue also re-directed attention towards the internal difficulties of the Church of England, which has experienced a long-standing and debilitating divide on homosexuality and gay rights issues (Bates 2004).

It is particularly important, then, that an examination is provided of the attitudes of religious groups over time. The BSA has asked a question on same-sex marriage on three occasions: 1989, 2007 and 2012. The question wordings are as follows:

1989: Homosexual couples should have the right to marry one another.
2007/2012: Gay or lesbian couples should have the right to marry one another if they want to.

The response options ranged from strongly agree through to strongly disagree. The responses are shown in Table 6.15. For religious belonging, there has been substantial change on the issue of same-sex marriage over recent decades, with large declines in the proportions who disagree with such a measure. In 2012, none of the groups, based on affiliation, registers opposition greater than a third, which is lowest at 14.0 percent for the non-religious, followed by Catholics (at 25.5 percent). Opposition is slightly higher amongst Anglicans and

Table 6.15 Percent disagreeing with same-sex marriage, by affiliation and attendance, 1989–2012

	Anglican (%)	Catholic (%)	Other Christian (%)	No religion (%)
1989	71.2	72.7	80.5	54.4
2007	35.1	22.1	41.8	19.7
2012	32.5	25.5	31.8	14.0
Change	−38.7	−47.2	−48.7	−40.4

	Frequent-attender (%)	Infrequent-attender (%)	Non-attender (%)
1989	75.4	68.6	62.4
2007	48.5	24.2	24.6
2012	46.8	25.4	16.0
Change	−28.6	−43.2	−46.4

Source: BSA surveys.
Note: Combines 'strongly disagree' and 'disagree'.

other Christians (respectively, 32.5 percent and 31.8 percent). Based on attendance at services, there has also been a large fall in the proportion disagreeing across each group. Specifically, amongst frequent-attenders, the proportion opposed fell substantially from 75.4 percent to 46.8 percent. A similar pattern is evident for infrequent-attenders as was found with earlier BSA questions: they move from being equidistant in 1989 (at 68.6 percent) to more closely approximating non-attenders in their views in 2012 (25.4 percent compared to 16.0 percent for the latter group). Across time, the gap in the level of opposition has again widened across attendance groups: increasing from 13.0 percent in 1989 to 30.8 percent in 2012. In 2012, just 16.0 percent of non-attenders disagreed with marriage for same-sex couples.

Overall, then, religious groups' exhibited much higher levels of negative sentiment towards homosexuality and same-sex equality in the 1980s – the period of the Conservative governments' moral authoritarianism on social issues (Hayes and Moran-Ellis 1997) – which then fell substantially over the intervening two decades or so. In 1989, the obvious dividing line was between those with and without a religion, while, in 2007 and 2012, Anglicans and other Christians were more likely to be opposed than Catholics and the non-religious.

Given this changing bivariate association between attendance and same-sex marriage attitudes and as it has featured as the most recent subject of social and political debate over same-sex quality legislation, multivariate analysis was conducted to examine in finer detail the impact of religious affiliation and attendance in 1989, 2007 and 2012. Binary logistic regression estimation is used to analyse data from the three BSA surveys. For each survey, those opposed to same-sex marriage (either disagreed or strongly disagreed) were coded as 1 and those in favour (agreeing or strongly agreeing) or adopted a neutral position (neither agreed nor disagreed) were coded as 0. The focus here is in assessing which factors differentiate those who express outright opposition to same-sex marriage from those in favour or neutral. An identical model specification was employed for the BSA surveys to provide a similar comparison of the explanatory variables. As explanatory variables, the models include sex, age, education, social class, party support and left-right beliefs (not used in Tables 6.5 and 6.13 as the left-right scales was first included in the BSA 1986 survey). Results are shown in Table 6.16. First, looking at the results of the 1989 survey, there are strong effects for the affiliation variables: all groups –

Table 6.16   **Binary logistic regressions of attitudes towards same-sex marriage, 1989–2012**

Variable	BSA 1989 B (SE)	Odds ratio	BSA 2007 B (SE)	Odds ratio	BSA 2012 B (SE)	Odds ratio
Sex	.64* (.14)	1.89	1.27* (.19)	3.55	.66* (.18)	1.93
Age	.02* (.00)	1.02	.05* (.01)	1.05	.02* (.01)	1.02
Degree	–.67* (.25)	.51	–.48 (.25)	.62	–.86* (.27)	.42
Salariat	–.17 (.18)	.84	–.25 (.23)	.78	–.36 (.20)	.70
Anglican	.74* (.17)	2.09	.19 (.25)	1.21	.26 (.25)	1.30
Catholic	.66* (.27)	1.94	–.35 (.39)	.70	–.01 (.36)	.99
Other tradition	1.01* (.25)	2.75	.78* (.24)	2.19	.67* (.26)	1.95
Attendance	.02 (.04)	1.02	.19* (.05)	1.21	.27* (.05)	1.31
Conservative	.17 (.29)	1.18	.06 (.30)	1.06	.67* (.31)	1.94
Labour	–.06 (.28)	.94	–.06 (.28)	.94	.37 (.29)	1.45
Alliance/Lib Dem	.10 (.34)	1.11	–.12 (.39)	.89	.27 (.43)	1.32
Other party	.51 (.37)	1.67	–.15 (.34)	.86	.25 (.35)	1.29
Left-right	–.63 (.35)	.53	–.12 (.13)	.89	–.02 (.12)	.98
Constant	–.36 (.40)	.70	–4.25* (.50)	.01	–3.63* (.48)	.03
Weighted N	1,150		843		888	
Nagelkerke R Square	.14		.32		.22	

Note: *$p<.05$ or lower.
Reference categories: no religion; does not support a party.
Source: BSA surveys.

Anglicans, Catholics and other religions – are much more likely to oppose same-sex marriage compared to those of no religion. However, attendance does not have a significant impact. Interestingly, a different set of findings emerges when examining the results for the 2007 and 2012 surveys. Here, the variables for being Anglican or Catholic no longer have significant effects (though being a member of another tradition – Christian or non-Christian – still does). In these models, religious affiliation has a significant impact, with more frequent attendance related to greater opposition to same-sex marriage equality. For Anglicans and Catholics, it appears to be religious behaviour – and therefore religiosity – rather than merely belonging to a particular tradition which may underlie opposition to same-sex marriage. The stronger role for religious factors in underpinning views on gay marriage in 2007 and 2012 is in line with the similar findings (reported in Table 6.14) for the religious basis of contemporary views on adoption rights and working in the teaching profession. As was also the case for the analyses reported in Tables 6.5 and 6.14, higher proportions of variance in the dependent variables are accounted for in the analyses of the 2007 and 2012 surveys compared to the 1989 survey.

Conclusion

This chapter has provided a detailed analysis of the changing attitudes towards homosexuality and related equality issues amongst religious groups. Using a range of recurrent questions carried on several social survey series, it has been shown that there has been substantial liberalisation of attitudes towards same-sex relations, with much lower levels of disapproval across all groups in recent years. Therefore, Anglicans, Catholics, other Christians and those with no religion are much less likely in 2012 to believe that homosexuality is something to disapprove of than they were in the 1980s. Even so, those with no religion retain the more liberal stance that they held at the outset of the period examined here. A similar liberalising trend also occurred on the basis of attendance at religious services. All three groups (frequently-attending, infrequently-attending, does not attend) registered substantial decreases in disapproval, but this liberalisation was faster and deeper for those who attended services less often or not at all, and thus slower and less marked for those who attend services on a regular basis. Comparing attitudes in 1983 and 2012, those who attend services infrequently have come to resemble more closely those who never attend services, whereas in 1983 their level of opposition to same-sex relations more closely mirrored that of frequent-attenders. These changes have led to a tighter association between level of attendance and attitudes towards homosexuality over time.

On more specific issues, which have been the subject of socio-political debate, campaigns by religious institutions and civil society groups and major legislative reforms, such as adoption rights and legal recognition of same-sex couples, there is a similar trend of liberalisation in recent decades. Again, this trend has occurred across religious traditions and levels of attendance at services. There is also evidence to show that, in general and based on more recent survey evidence, Catholics are more supportive of gay rights than Anglicans. This provides a noteworthy contrast with the findings from the previous chapter, where, compared to Catholics, Anglicans have tended to show lower levels of negative sentiment towards abortion. That is, Catholics can appear more liberal in issues of gay rights than do Anglicans, whereas the former tend to be more socially-conservative on abortion issues than the latter. In terms of religious behaviour, infrequent-attenders tend to be positioned more closely to those who never attend services than they are to frequent-attenders, which was not necessarily the case in earlier surveys. As opinion has liberalised across British society on gay right issues in recent decades, clearer dividing lines have appeared between more religious people and those who are less religious or not religious at all, as manifested in belonging and behaving.

More detailed analyses of attitudes towards homosexuality in general, gays and lesbians being able to teach or adopt children, and same-sex marriage showed that religion was a more potent differentiator of contemporary opinion on these issues than it was for attitudes measured during the 1980s. As has been found for attitudes towards same-sex marriage elsewhere (Olson et al. 2006; Sheerkat et al. 2011), religious belonging and behaving are important sources of opposition to this most recent top-down reform in Britain to extend the rights of gays and lesbians. Even so, a wider set of social factors can be seen to influence public attitudes in Britain on gay rights issues. The broadly consistent empirical evidence for factors such as sex, age and socio-economic status (occupation and education) show that, as Hayes and Dowds have shown for opinion on these issues in Northern Ireland, 'attitudes towards same-sex issues are not solely determined by a religious framework' (2013: 17). Moreover, the effects for these other social factors are clearer and overall stronger when compared to those found for public opinion towards abortion in Chapter 5.

7
Religion and Foreign Policy

This chapter provides a detailed over-time analysis of religious groups' attitudes on foreign policy issues. The chapter looks at religious groups' attitudes on Britain's international role in terms of two broad issue areas: Britain's long-standing relations with the European integration process and the recent military interventions in Afghanistan and Iraq post-9/11. The intention here is not to provide comprehensive coverage of the multitude of long-running issues and short-run crises which have featured in Britain's post-war external relations. Indeed, even if this was the intention it would be severely hindered by the lack of a regular or periodic foreign policy attitudes survey of British public opinion in the post-war decades. The chapter does, however, provide some insight into the over-time attitudes of religious groups towards issues of *war* – recent military interventions – and *peace*, specifically, Britain's role in the European integration process. Policy-specific examples are therefore provided of the types of attitudinal measures which would fit into the broader opinion dimensions of 'militant internationalism' and 'cooperative internationalism' (Guth 2012). These two dimensions can be summarised as:

> Militant internationalism comprises a preference for security through military strength, national patriotism, and scepticism about international agreements. Cooperative internationalism, on the other hand, stresses the importance of diplomacy, multilateral agreements, and international cooperation on issues of world peace, world poverty, disease and environmental degradation (Guth 2012: 173).

Britain's military engagements in both Iraq and Afghanistan may have been perceived as part of a broader foreign policy strategy post-9/11 to combat terrorism and rogue states abroad in order to increase national security both externally and internally. Participation in the EU – the most advanced regional integration project around the globe – can be seen as the pooling of sovereignty for the purposes of economic and political cooperation between and beyond European states – in multiple policy domains – involving countries from the western and eastern sections of the continent. Indeed, openness towards Britain's relation with and role in the EU provides a key indicator of individuals being more broadly 'international' in outlook (Kiss and Park 2014: 11).

The chapter again makes extensive use of long-running surveys, BSA and BES, which provide multiple readings of public opinion for a limited set of foreign policy issues. It also utilises time-series data from the cross-national EB surveys of member states and prospective members, which have provided regular readings on the British public's mood towards their country's relations with the EU both before and since it joined in 1973. The chapter is structured as follows. It first reviews the extensive public opinion data bearing upon religion and the European integration process. It then looks at the recent military interventions in Iraq and Afghanistan in the context of Britain's role in the post-9/11 era. Taken together, the evidence presented and discussed here go some way towards examining where – and in what form – the religious dividing lines were and are in British foreign policy amongst the general public.

Attitudes towards European integration

This section provides a detailed analysis of religious groups' attitudes towards the European integration process in Britain, a country traditionally labelled a 'reluctant' or 'awkward' partner (George 1998; Geddes 2013). The 1990s witnessed the increasing involvement of Christian churches in the integration process and its existing role in formal and structured dialogue with EU institutions was given stronger backing in Article 17(3) of the Lisbon Treaty, ratified in 2009 (Mudrov 2014: 5). Accordingly, these recent developments and initiatives in the integration process have given greater prominence to the EU's 'spiritual dimension' (Hill 2009: 171), giving scholars cause to pay greater attention to the influence and status of religious actors in EU activities and policy-making and their role as interest groups (Leustean and Madeley 2013; Leustean 2012; Steven 2009), to dealineating the historical and contemporary positions of different denominations and national churches towards the integration process (Mudrov 2014; Hill 2009), and the relationship between denominations, 'confessional' parties and Euroscepticism in the member states (Minkenberg 2009, 2013).

Public opinion research, both cross-national and single-country, has similarly increased the attention given to religious factors in shaping public attitudes towards the integration process or particular aspects thereof. As Nelsen et al. observe: 'There are many historical, ideological, and institutional reasons to suspect that religious factors influence public attitudes toward integration' (2011: 2–3). Research has focused on the macro-level impact of countries that have a broad Protestant, Catholic or mixed confessional culture (or the level of secularisation) and the micro-level impact of religious identity and religiosity (Nelsen and Guth forthcoming; Nelsen et al. 2011; Nelsen and Guth 2003; Nelsen et al. 2001; Hobolt et al. 2011; Boomgaarden and Freire 2009; Hagevi 2000). One recent cross-national analysis concluded that:

> Being Protestant still means less support, but as some previous studies … found, the most devout Protestants now seem to break from the general scepticism of their confessional culture and join their Catholic brethren in supporting the EU. Being Orthodox also works to increase support for the EU, although somewhat more weakly than being a strong Catholic or Protestant. Being a Muslim tends to make one more skeptical of the EU, especially if one is devout, but the relationship is the weakest among European confessional cultures. And it seems clear that all these effects are influenced by a variety of contextual factors in each country group (Nelsen et al. 2011: 19).

Wariness or hostility towards the integration process has traditionally been higher in northern European countries where Protestantism has been the predominant – and, in some cases, the official state – religion, such as Britain, Denmark, Sweden and Norway (Vollard 2006: 276). Based on this existing cross-national public opinion research and Britain's long-standing reputation as one of the most Eurosceptic member states, there are two important areas of comparison – one national and one cross-national – on which this section focuses:

1. Historically and in the present day, have Catholics in Britain been *less likely* than Anglicans to hold Eurosceptic attitudes?

2. Historically and in the present day, have Catholics and Anglicans in Britain been *more likely* than Catholics and Protestants across member states to hold Eurosceptic attitudes?

Attitudes amongst religious groups in Britain are analysed first, followed by a detailed comparison of the views of Catholics and Anglicans in Britain with Catholics and Protestants across the EU as a whole.

Religious groups in Britain

Data are utilised from the BSA surveys to examine longitudinal British public opinion towards the EU. These relate to a simple withdraw-stay in question asked from 1983–91 and a question with a more differentiated set of response categories asked from 1993 through to 2012. The question wordings from the BSA surveys are as follows:

> Do you think Britain should continue to be a member of the European Union or should it withdraw? (1983–91)
> Do you think Britain's long-term policy should be ... to leave the European Union, to stay in the EU and try to reduce the EU's powers, to leave things as they are, to stay in the EU and try to increase the EU's powers, or to work for the formation of a single European government? (1993–2012)

For the second question, positions in favour of Britain leaving the EU or remaining and reducing its powers are treated as Eurosceptic responses here. These positions can be seen as approximately denoting 'hard' and 'soft' Eurosceptic positions, respectively (Szczerbiak and Taggart 2000). These are defined as follows:

> Hard Euroscepticism involves outright rejection of the entire project of European political and economic integration and opposition to their country joining or remaining members of the EU. Soft Euroscepticism, on the other hand, involves contingent or qualified opposition to European integration and can, in turn be further subdivided into 'policy' Euroscepticism and 'national-interest' Euroscepticism (Szczerbiak and Taggart 2000: 6).

Figure 7.1 presents the data for the 1983–91, based on support for withdrawal. It is clear that support for withdrawal fell steadily across all groups during the 1980s and that there is some oscillation in which group was more Eurosceptic. The second time-series reported in Table 7.2, taking in both 'soft' and 'hard' indicators of Euroscepticism shows a clearer pattern from the 1990s onwards, as usually – if not always – Anglicans displayed greater negative sentiment. Indeed, this is evident for the last decade or so of the period covered in Figure 7.2. Based on the figures from the most recent BSA survey (2012), 87.6 percent of Anglicans give a Eurosceptic response, compared to 63.7 percent of Catholics. In terms of the other groups, 77.3 percent of other Christians registered a Eurosceptic response, while negative views were somewhat less prevalent amongst those with no religion, at 67.3 percent. While negative sentiment has increased across the board in recent years, a sizeable gap remains between Anglicans and Catholics. Based on the BSA surveys, the ('hard' and 'soft') Eurosceptic 'gap' between these two groups has doubled from 11.2 percentage points in 1993 to 22.9 percentage points in 2012.

Of course, debates about the EU and country involvement involve much more than the question of staying or withdrawing. What about attitudes towards the single currency, one of the EU's flagship initiatives, a key part of political debate over Britain's EU relations from the 1990s onwards? The BSA surveys can again be used to examine

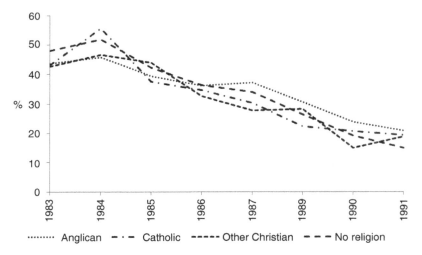

Figure 7.1 Percent wanting Britain to withdraw from the EC, by affiliation, 1983–1991
Source: BSA surveys.

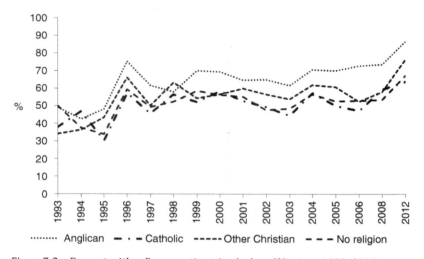

Figure 7.2   Percent with a Eurosceptic attitude, by affiliation, 1993–2012
Source: BSA surveys.
Note: Combines 'to leave the European Union' and 'to stay in the EU and try to reduce the EU's powers'.

attitudes towards the Euro, using data for the period 1993–2006. Again, the question used changed during the period covered here (with both versions administered in 1999). The wordings are as follows:

> About the future of the pound in the European Union. Which comes closest to your view? Replace the pound by a single currency OR use both the pound and a new European currency in Britain OR keep the pound as the only currency for Britain (1993–99).
> If there were a referendum on whether Britain should join the single European currency, the Euro, how do you think would you vote ... to join the Euro, or not to join the Euro? (1999–2006)

Data from these questions are shown in Figures 7.3 and 7.4, respectively. The levels of negative sentiment (in this case those who say 'keep the pound' or 'not join the Euro') amongst religious groups are reported. Over time, Anglicans are more likely to be opposed than Catholics, other Christians and those with no affiliation to Britain participating in the Euro, so there is a similar pattern for both general Eurosceptic sentiment and a policy-specific question. The last reading for this question was taken in 2006, and while 67.1 percent of

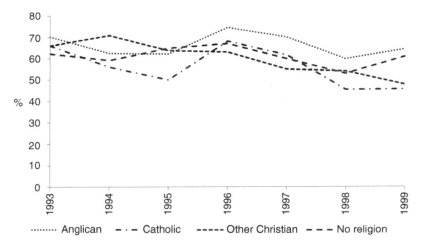

Figure 7.3 Percent opposed to a single currency, by affiliation, 1993–1999
Source: BSA surveys.

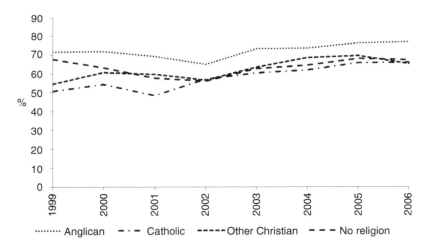

Figure 7.4 Percent opposed to a single currency, by affiliation, 1999–2006
Source: BSA surveys.

Catholics were against joining the Euro, the proportion was higher for Anglicans (at 77.1 percent). Levels of opposition for other Christians and those with no religion were very similar to that for Catholics (at 65.1 percent and 67.1 percent, respectively).

Evidence from the most recent BES surveys also underlines this picture from the BSA surveys of attitudinal variation based on religious belonging, principally between Catholics and Anglicans. Table 7.1 presents data from the 1987–2010 BES surveys, using differently-worded questions asking about approval of membership and participation in the single currency. The full question wordings (and survey years) are as follows:

Membership
Do you think Britain should continue to be a member of the European Community or should it withdraw? (1987–92)
Do you think Britain should continue to be a member of the European Union or should it withdraw? (1997)
Overall, do you approve or disapprove of Britain's membership in the European Union? (2001–10)

Single currency
Which one of these statements comes closest to your view about the future of the £ in the EC? (1992)
And here are three statements about the future of the pound in the European Union. Which one comes closest to your view? (1997)
Thinking of the Euro, which of the following statements on this card would come closest to your own view? (2001–10)

For clarity of presentation, Table 7.1 reports the percentages for each religious group giving Eurosceptic responses. For the 1987–97 surveys, this consists of those favouring Britain withdrawing and, for the 1992 and 1997 surveys those who wanted to keep the pound (as opposed to replacing the pound with a single currency, or having both coins in circulation). For the 2001–10 surveys this consists of those defined as those who 'strongly disapprove' or 'disapprove' of membership and those who would rule out 'on principle' Britain joining the Euro. The Euro question in the 2001–10 surveys did not have the option of both currencies in circulation.

In relation to general views on membership, the differences are rather muted in the earlier surveys (1987–97), with Anglicans slightly more likely than Catholics to favour Britain's withdrawal from the European Union – a clear indicator of 'hard' Euroscepticism. However, the Eurosceptic gap is more evident when measured by levels of disapproval of Britain's relations with the EU, which might be considered to be more akin to an indicator of 'soft' Euroscepticism. Catholics are less

Table 7.1   Percent with a Eurosceptic attitude, by affiliation, 1987–2010

	Anglicans (%)	Catholics (%)	Other Christian (%)	No religion (%)
Membership				
1987 – Withdraw	30.2	27.9	27.4	30.6
1992 – Withdraw	24.8	20.8	17.9	21.9
1997 – Withdraw	34.1	27.1	28.8	29.0
2001 – Strongly disapprove or disapprove	40.2	30.5	35.1	30.6
2005 – Strongly disapprove or disapprove	39.1	25.9	30.6	28.6
2010[a] – Strongly disapprove or disapprove	43.9	29.7	37.8	33.7
2010[b] – Strongly disapprove or disapprove	54.2	41.5	44.1	40.6
Single currency				
1992 – Keep the pound	58.2	51.6	49.6	50.3
1997 – Keep the pound	65.8	60.4	59.8	53.9
2001 – Rule out on principle	48.6	39.0	48.0	42.3
2005 – Rule out on principle	31.8	32.7	35.2	27.2
2010[a] – Rule out on principle	31.4	24.4	30.5	25.9

Source: BES surveys.
[a] In-person survey. [b] Campaign Internet Panel survey.

likely than Anglicans to express disapproval in the 2001–10 surveys. Most recently, disapproval registered at 41.5 percent for Catholics in the BES 2010 CIPS survey compared to over half for Anglicans (at 54.2 percent). Other Christians and those with no religion are nearer to Catholics in their levels of disapproval. Corroborating this, there is a similar finding with data from the BES 2010 in-person survey, with 43.9 percent of Anglicans disapproving compared to 29.7 percent of Catholics.

The differences between Anglicans and Catholics are less clear and consistent in relation to the single currency, with the gap in anti-Euro sentiment from 2001 narrowing in 2005, though widening again in the 2010 survey. In terms of the other groups, other Christians are closer to Anglicans in their level of anti-Euro sentiment, and the non-religious express a level similar to that of Catholics. The earlier data from the 1990s show that Anglicans are slightly more likely than Catholics to want to retain the pound; though Eurosceptic sentiment is somewhat higher across all groups in 1997.

As well as looking at Euroscepticism as manifested in opposition to membership or towards flagship EU policies, more affective attachment towards – or identification with the – EU or, more broadly, Europe, can be examined using data from the BSA series. Previous research has shown that members of particular churches (Church of England or Church of Scotland) were more likely to express a sense of British nationalism than those with no religion (Heath et al. 1999: 167). Other studies have shown that Anglicans were more likely to feel a sense of British patriotism (Tilley et al. 2005: 167) and more likely to hold an ethnic conception of identity and less likely to have an internationalist disposition (Kiss and Park 2014: 15–16). Research has also shown that Anglicans were more likely – and Catholics less likely – to think that it is important to be Christian in order to be considered as British (Storm 2011: 840). It is also instructive to look at the longer-term picture in Britain given both its engrained Euroscepticism and the broader finding from cross-national research that 'Protestant confessional culture reduces the number of "Europeans" in a member state and encourages exclusive national identity. Protestantism evidently makes national identity "sticker"' (Nelsen and Guth forthcoming: 566; for further studies see: Green 2007; Schnabel and Hjerm 2014).

BSA surveys have regularly asked about a series of territorial identities at different levels – supranational, national and sub-national (such as British, European, English, Scottish and Welsh) – using the following question:

> Please say which, if any, of the words on this card describes the way you think of yourself. Please choose as many or as few as apply.

Levels of European, British and English identity are charted, respectively, in Figures 7.5, 7.6 and 7.7, all covering the period 1996–2012.

Looking first at feeling European, what is evident is that only small proportions of each group see themselves as European and there is less variation in levels of identity compared to Eurosceptic sentiment discussed already. Even so, there is tendency over time for Catholics to be more likely than Anglicans to self-ascribe this identity, which is broadly in line with existing cross-national research on attitudes of EU member states (Green 2007; Nelsen and Guth, forthcoming). In 2012, the latest reading available, 17.0 percent of Catholics said they felt European compared to 12.6 percent of Anglicans, 13.7 percent for other Christians and 15.8 percent for those with no affiliation. A question in the BSA 2005 survey asked: 'In general, how much do you have

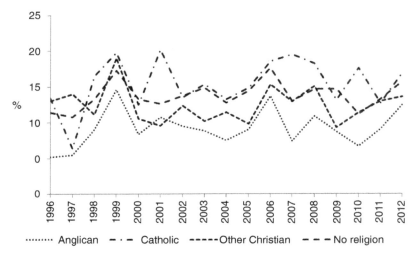

Figure 7.5 Percent who think of themselves as European, by affiliation, 1996–2012
Source: BSA surveys.

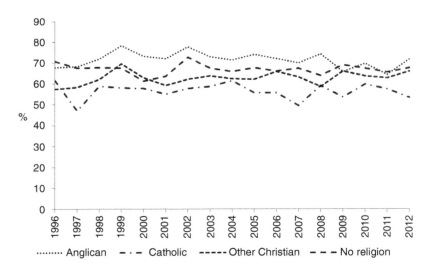

Figure 7.6 Percent who think of themselves as British, by affiliation, 1996–2012
Source: BSA surveys.

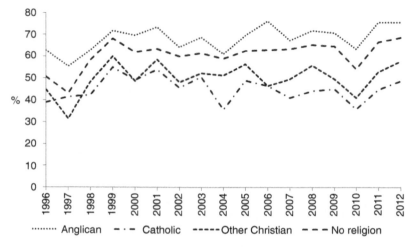

Figure 7.7 Percent who think of themselves as English, by affiliation, 1996–2012
Source: BSA surveys. Those living in England only.

in common with people who say they are European, compared with other people?' Catholics (24.2 percent) were more likely to say they had a lot or a little in common compared to Anglicans (13.4 percent), other Christians (18.4 percent) and those with no religion (17.1 percent).

The next sets of data (charted in Figures 7.6 and 7.7) show that levels of feeling British and English differ more markedly, in particular when comparing Anglicans with Catholics. Generally, Anglicans are most likely to report that they would describe themselves as British; with Catholics usually least likely to. In 2012, 71.9 percent of Anglicans felt British compared to just over half of Catholics (at 53.6 percent). Levels of feeling British are similar for other Christians and those with no affiliation (66.2 percent and 67.8 percent respectively), and markedly higher than that registered for Catholics.

The differences are even more pronounced between these two groups when it comes to self-identifying as English (here restricted to those living in England in the survey samples). In 2012 around three-quarters of Anglicans (75.6 percent) felt in some sense English compared to less than a half of Catholics (48.7 percent). Across the period 1996–2012, Anglicans were consistently most likely to think that feeling English applied to them; Catholics, usually if not always, were least likely to see themselves as English. Those with no religion were more likely than other Christians to see themselves as English in 2012 (at, respectively, 68.6 percent and 57.8 percent).[1]

As a final step, the influence of religious affiliation on attitudes towards Britain's relations with the EU and sense of identity is assessed by undertaking two sets of multivariate analysis. Firstly, using data from the BSA 2012 and BSA 2006 surveys, models are estimated to assess whether religious belonging shapes attitudes towards (i) EU membership and (ii) the Euro.[2] The response options for the membership and single currency questions are coded as 1 (Eurosceptic responses) and 0 (Europhile responses), to create a dichotomous dependent variable. First, for the membership question, those who replied 'to leave the European Union' or 'to stay in the EU and try to reduce the EU's powers' (therefore encompassing both 'hard' and 'soft' Eurosceptic positions) were coded as 1 while all other response options were coded as 0. Second, for the single currency item, those who did not want Britain to join were scored as 1 and those who did were scored as 0. Secondly, the impact of affiliation on sense of identity is assessed using the BSA 2012. Three separate binary logistic regression models are run here, assessing the factors associated with feeling European and – to provide a broader analysis – feeling British and English (for the latter, the analysis is limited to those living in England, who comprise 86.2 percent of the 2012 survey sample). Those who considered themselves to feel European, British or English were scored as 1 and those who did not were scored as 0.

Binary logistic regression was used to examine a range of sociological factors affecting EU-related attitudes and sense of identity. A range of social factors which previous research has shown to correlate with pro- or anti-EU opinion in Britain are accounted for, with Euroscepticism tending to be associated with being male, older, less well-educated or having lower socio-economic status and supporting the Conservative Party (Clements 2009). Aside from religion, the other independent variables are: sex, ethnic group, age, education, housing tenure, social class and party identification. Religious attendance is also included (measured as a scale with higher values denoting more frequent attendance at services) to provide more robust estimates for the affiliation variables. For the analysis of personal sense of feeling British and European, controls for region are also included (dummies for residing in Scotland, Wales or England). The reference categories are those with no religion and non-party identifiers (and lives in England). In the table, the 'Odds ratio' statistic indicates whether the impact of a particular explanatory variable increases or decreases the likelihood of giving a Eurosceptic response. A score higher than 1 indicates that an independent variable increases the odds of being Eurosceptic and a score lower than 1 indicates that it reduces the odds of being Eurosceptic.

The results for attitudes towards membership and the Euro are shown in Table 7.2. They demonstrate that, even when accounting for other socio-demographic characteristics and party attachments, there are some significant effects for the religion variables in relation to EU membership. Specifically, in relation to support for EU membership Anglicans are more than twice likely to hold ('soft' or 'hard') Eurosceptic views compared to those with no religion (odds ratio: 2.24). This finding for Anglicans provides further support for the exist- ing studies mentioned earlier on. There are no significant differences for Catholics when compared to those with no religion. Moreover,

Table 7.2   **Binary logistic regressions of Eurosceptic attitudes**

Variable	Membership: 2012 B (SE)	Odds ratio	Single Currency: 2006 B (SE)	Odds ratio
Sex	.52* (.15)	1.68	−.11 (.16)	.90
Ethnic group	−.12 (.29)	.89	−.53 (.36)	.59
Age	.02*(.00)	1.02	−.01 (.00)	.99
Degree qualification	−.29 (.20)	.75	−.86*(.19)	.42
Owner-occupier	.27 (.17)	1.30	−.38* (.18)	.68
Salariat	−.30 (.18)	.74	.01 (.21)	1.01
Anglican	.81*(.25)	2.24	.60*(.23)	1.83
Catholic	−.14 (.28)	.87	.26 (.28)	1.30
Other Christian	.49 (.26)	1.62	.20 (.25)	1.22
Other religion	−.58 (.38)	.56	−.35 (.46)	.70
Attendance	−.06 (.05)	.94	−.07 (.04)	.93
Conservative	.67*(.25)	1.96	.44 (.25)	1.55
Labour	−.38 (.21)	.69	−.64* (.21)	.53
Liberal Democrat	−.22 (.32)	.80	−.89* (.26)	.41
Other party	.09 (.27)	1.10	−.22 (.33)	.80
Constant	−.16 (.36)	.85	2.60* (.43)	13.44
Weighted N	1,011		965	
Nagelkerke R Square	.17		.13	

Note: *p<.05 or lower.
Reference categories: no religion; non-party identifier.
Source: BSA 2012 and BSA 2006 surveys.

while recent comparative research has found 'consistent evidence that religious, linguistic, foreign-born, and non-citizen minorities in the EU express higher levels of support for European integration than titular majorities' (Dowley and Silver 2011: 333), and other studies have shown that members of minority non-Christian religions are less Eurosceptic (Boomgaarden and Freire 2009; Hagevi 2002), there are no significant effects for the views of affiliates of non-Christian faiths in Britain. Turning to attitudes towards the single currency, once again Anglicans are significantly more likely to adopt a Eurosceptic viewpoint compared to those with no religion (odds ratio: 1.83). There are no significant differences for the other religious traditions. The model results show that attendance does not have a significant effect on attitudes towards the Euro.

What about religious belonging and a personal sense of feeling European, British or English? Does religious affiliation have significant effects net of other social and attitudinal predictors (including the nation where the respondent lives)? Results are presented in Table 7.3. Looking first at feeling European (which, it is worth noting, elicited much less positive reaction than did feeling British or English), there are no significant differences between any of the Christian groups and those with no religion. Interestingly, those who belong to a non-Christian faith are much less likely to adopt a sense of feeling European (odds ratio: 0.34), while frequent attendance at services is associated with a greater likelihood of feeling European. Catholics are much less likely to say they feel British (odds ratio: 0.44), but the opposite is the case for those who attend services on a regular basis. There are no significant differences for Anglicans, other Christians and those from non-Christian faiths, compared to those with no religion. With the sample restricted to those who reside in England, Catholics are also much less likely to say they feel English (odds ratio: 0.49) compared to those with no religion, as those who belong to a minority non-Christian faith (odds ratio: 0.45). Anglicans are somewhat more likely to feel English (odds ratio: 1.33).

This section has shown that Anglicans generally express higher levels of Eurosceptic sentiment than Catholics, and this stands over time and is robust when using different indicators from the two major British survey series. When accounting for a range of sociological factors and party-political attachments, Anglicans are significantly more likely to have Eurosceptic standpoints. Net of other factors Catholics are less likely to identity as British or English. Given these findings from the national context, the next section examines the attitudes of Anglicans

Table 7.3   **Binary logistic regressions of national identity**

Variable	European B (SE)		Odds ratio	British B (SE)		Odds ratio	English[a] B (SE)		Odds ratio
Sex	.68*	(.11)	1.98	−.16*	(.08)	.85	.04	(.09)	1.04
Ethnic group	.81*	(.24)	2.24	.47*	(.16)	1.60	1.50*	(.17)	4.46
Age	−.03*	(.00)	.97	−.01*	(.00)	.99	.00	(.00)	1.00
Degree qualification	.83*	(.13)	2.30	.11	(.12)	1.12	−.35*	(.12)	.71
Owner-occupier	.20	(.13)	1.22	.50*	(.09)	1.65	.28*	(.10)	1.33
Salariat	.38*	(.12)	1.46	.33*	(.09)	1.39	−.09	(.10)	.92
Anglican	−.02	(.16)	.98	.00	(.12)	1.00	.28*	(.13)	1.33
Catholic	.16	(.21)	1.17	−.82*	(.15)	.44	−.71*	(.16)	.49
Other Christian	−.14	(.17)	.87	−.20	(.12)	.82	−.24	(.14)	.79
Other religion	−1.08*	(.38)	.34	−.19	(.21)	.82	−.79*	(.24)	.45
Attendance	.07*	(.03)	1.08	.07*	(.02)	1.07	−.04	(.03)	.96
Conservative	.24	(.18)	1.28	.46*	(.12)	1.58	.28*	(.13)	1.32
Labour	.48*	(.16)	1.62	.48*	(.11)	1.61	.02	(.12)	1.02
Liberal Democrat	.56*	(.24)	1.76	.23	(.19)	1.26	.03	(.19)	1.03
Other party	−.07	(.22)	.93	−.14	(.13)	.87	−.10	(.15)	.91
Lives in Wales	−.84*	(.33)	.43	−.45*	(.17)	.64			
Lives in Scotland	−.35*	(.12)	.70	−.30*	(.07)	.74			
Constant	−2.60*	(.30)	.07	.12	(.20)	1.13	−.55*	(0.22)	.58
Weighted N	3,192			3,192			2,753		
Nagelkerke R Square	.15			.09			.17		

Note: *$p \leq$.05 or lower. [a] Based on those living in England only.
Reference categories: no religion; non-party identifier; lives in England.
Source: BSA 2012 survey.

and Catholics in Britain in comparison to their co-religionists across the EU.

Religious groups in Britain and the EU

Catholics have, over time, tended to be more pro-integration in their attitudes compared to Anglicans. What about the attitudes of Catholics in Britain and in the EU as a whole, given that the former reside in one of the traditionally most wary and reluctant member states in its approach to the integration process? The issue of European integration is an issue that immediately lends itself to cross-national comparisons of Britain and other member states, both for general populations as a whole and for particular societal groups. The long-running EB survey series can be utilised to assess levels of support for the integration process amongst Catholics in Britain compared to their co-religionists on mainland Europe. A similar analysis can be undertaken for

Anglicans in Britain and Protestants in the EU. It might be expected that Catholics in Britain, given their country's long-standing and distinctive public Euroscepticism, will be more Eurosceptic than their co-religionists in the EU as a whole.

First, data are employed from two European Communities Studies conducted in 1970, with separate but equivalent surveys undertaken for Britain and the existing six member states. Table 7.4 reports attitudinal data from identical questions fielded in both surveys, in order to compare public opinion in Britain and the member states as a whole. The questions concern support for Britain joining the EC, a United State of Europe, a European Parliament and a European government. Comparisons can be made of the attitudes of Catholics, Protestants (Anglicans) and those with no religion. First, across religious groups, there is much higher support for British membership in the existing member states compared to Britain itself! While opposition to accession is around 70.0 percent or higher amongst groups in Britain, those against British entry comprise very small proportions in the EC countries (ranging from just 10.0 percent to 15.7 percent).

There is a similar pattern for the other three questions concerning different goals of political integration. In all cases, Catholics, Protestants and those with no religion in the EC are much less likely to oppose a European government, Parliament and a United State of

Table 7.4   Percent with a Eurosceptic attitude, by affiliation, Britain and other member states

Britain	Anglican (%)	Catholic (%)	Other/no religion (%)
Against joining EC	78.3	69.9	69.2
Against United State of Europe	65.3	53.4	67.1
Against European Parliament	68.1	60.7	64.4
Not accept a European government	72.8	68.2	67.4

Member states	Protestants (%)	Catholics (%)	None (%)
Against Britain joining EC	10.0	14.1	15.7
Against United State of Europe	14.0	10.8	18.4
Against European Parliament	20.4	15.5	21
Not accept a European government	35.4	27.4	36.3

Sources: European Communities Study 1970: Member States; European Communities Study 1970: Great Britain.

Europe. Opposition is highest in relation to a European government (peaking at 36.3 percent for those with no religion). In contrast, for these three indicators in Britain, nowhere is opposition below 50.0 percent (lowest at 53.4 percent for Catholics concerning a United State of Europe). Within Britain and the EC, Catholics generally register lower levels of negative sentiment in 1970 compared to Protestants (Anglicans) and those with no religion. Overall, while there are differences *within* Britain and the EC member states on the basis of religious denomination – with Catholics tending to be more pro-integration in their views – there are much starker differences *between* religious groups in Britain and the member states.

Is a similar patterning of attitudes still in evidence in the present-day? A second survey is used to compare the contemporary views of religious groups in Britain and the EU as a whole. An extensive set of questions on the EU and its policies asked in the autumn 2006 EB study (number 67.1) is available, which also fielded a question on religious affiliation. Attitudes can be compared on a wider range of question than those available in the 1970 surveys (full question wordings are given in the Appendix). These relate to three areas of public opinion: (1) general dispositions towards the EU; (2) attitudes towards major policies; and (3) feelings of identity or citizenship. A more robust picture can be obtained from any group-related differences in attitudes by using multiple indicators of opinion. This more multifaceted picture also better reflects the growing complexity of the integration process – both economic and political – and the policy competences held at the EU level (with decisions in some policy areas made either exclusively or mainly by the EU or, in other domains, in conjunction with the member states). Table 7.5 and Table 7.6 compare the attitudes of, respectively, Catholics in Britain and the EU and Anglicans in Britain and Protestants in the EU. The EU data are based on the 25 actual member states when the survey was conducted. To simplify the presentation of the data, the tables report the levels of negative sentiment or Eurosceptic responses for each question.

Firstly, comparing the religious groups in Britain (using Tables 7.5 and 7.6), it can be seen that, across nearly all indicators, Anglicans express higher levels of Eurosceptic sentiment than do Catholics, although the magnitude of the difference varies. While similar proportions of both groups perceived their country not to have benefitted from membership (Catholics: 57.3 percent; Anglicans: 60.7 percent), there are larger differences across many other indicators, both for general support and policies. This is also the case for affective senti-

Table 7.5 Percent with a Eurosceptic attitude, Catholics in Britain and the EU

	Catholics – Britain (%)	Catholics – EU (%)	Difference
General support			
EU membership is a bad thing	33.9	13.9	+20.0
Country not benefitted from membership	57.3	42.0	+15.3
Overall negative image of EU	35.7	13.9	+21.8
EU – things are going in the wrong direction	52.1	34.1	+18.0
Tend not to trust the EU	68.6	41.7	+26.9
Against European political union	60.7	30.4	+30.3
Policies			
Against further enlargement	53.0	43.9	+9.1
Against Turkey joining	66.7	68.1	−1.4
Against EMU and single currency	64.8	31.7	+33.1
Against a Common Foreign Policy	44.1	20.2	+23.9
Against a Common Defence Policy	31.3	14.8	+16.5
Identity and citizenship			
Don't feel European	47.0	13.1	+33.9
European citizenship – never	67.2	41.3	+25.9

Source: EB 66.1 September–October 2006.
Note: The 'Difference' is calculated by subtracting the 'Catholics – EU' percentage figure from the 'Catholics – Britain' percentage figure.

ment, with Catholics less likely to report not feeling European and never having a sense of European citizenship. While just under half of Catholics do not feel European, the figure for Anglicans is well over half. Clearly, then, 'supranational' feelings are higher amongst Catholics than Anglicans (see Green 2007), which offers a similar picture to that gleaned from the BSA data shown already. Across the board, the lowest level of negative sentiment is expressed in relation to thinking membership is a bad thing, which arguably acts as an indicator of 'hard' Euroscepticism.

Next, attitudes are compared in Britain and the EU. The final column in both tables presents a net 'Difference' score which is calculated by subtracting each percentage in the 'Catholics – EU' or 'Protestants – EU' column for the corresponding figure in the 'Catholics – Britain' or 'Anglicans – Britain' column. So a positive net score denotes higher negative sentiment amongst that religious group in Britain and a negative net score *vice versa*. There is a consistent pattern to the data

Table 7.6   **Percent with a Eurosceptic attitude, Anglicans in Britain and Protestants in the EU**

	Anglicans – Britain (%)	Protestant – EU (%)	Difference
General support			
EU membership is a bad thing	41.8	21.8	+20.0
Country not benefitted from membership	60.7	46.9	+13.8
Overall negative image of EU	50.8	27.3	+23.5
EU – things are going in the wrong direction	65.0	46.9	+18.1
Tend not to trust the EU	79.2	60.5	+18.7
Against European political union	76.6	48.9	+27.7
Policies			
Against further enlargement	71.0	61.9	+9.1
Against Turkey joining	73.5	75.8	–2.3
Against EMU and single currency	73.2	43.0	+30.2
Against a Common Foreign Policy	50.5	30.4	+20.1
Against a Common Defence Policy	42.0	23.3	+18.7
Identity and citizenship			
Don't feel European	60.9	26.5	+34.4
European citizenship – never	78.0	51.5	+26.5

Source: EB 66.1 September–October 2006.
Note: The 'Difference' is calculated by subtracting the 'Protestants – EU percentage' from the 'Anglicans – Britain' percentage.

presented in both tables, as summarised in the 'Difference' columns. Across all indicators except one there are much lower levels of negative sentiment for both Catholics and Protestants across the EU. The exception is that of the opposition to Turkey – a country whose population is predominantly Muslim – joining the EU, where there are only minimal differences in opinion. That is, there are similar levels of opposition expressed by Catholics and Anglicans (Protestants) in Britain and across the EU as a whole. In any case, as Shakman Hurd, notes, 'Cultural and religious opposition to Turkey's accession is not only about defending the idea of a Christian Europe, though this is a significant consideration' (2006: 401).

The areas of clear attitudinal difference cover general support for the integration process, specific policy preferences and affective feelings. Catholics in Britain are twice as likely to be against the single currency and a common foreign policy than those in the EU as a whole; while

47.0 percent report they do not feel European compared to just 13.0 percent of their co-religionists across the EU. Anglicans are nearly twice as likely to be against an EU defence policy compared to Protestants in general; while they are more than twice as likely to say they do not feel European (60.9 percent compared to 26.5 percent). Differences are less marked for Catholics and Protestants concerning the general question on enlargement, where citizens in the EU may form a response through the prism of thinking about possible Turkish membership of the EU.

While around a third of Catholics in Britain think EU membership is a bad thing, this is just 14.0 percent for Catholics across the EU as a whole. Similarly, nearly two-thirds of British Catholics are against the Euro compared to less than a third of Catholics across the EU. There is a similar pattern for Protestants. For instance, around half of Anglicans have a negative image of the EU compared to just over a quarter of Protestants across the EU as a whole. Likewise, around half of Anglicans are opposed to a common foreign policy for the EU, while less than a third of Protestants hold this view. The only exception, as noted already, concerns attitudes towards Turkey joining the EU, with very high levels of opposition across all groups (albeit slightly lower for Catholics in Britain and the EU). When looking at the affective measures, once again Catholics and Anglicans in Britain are more likely to declare that they do not feel European and never feel a sense of European citizenship (as indicated by the 'difference' scores). Overall, then, while there are generally consistent within-country differences based on religious affiliation in Britain, there are also clear cross-national differences in Eurosceptic sentiment. Catholics in Britain, both historically and in the present day, tend to be more supportive of the EU and its flagship policies than Anglicans, but they exhibit higher levels of negative sentiment than their co-religionists on mainland Europe.

This brings us back to the importance of 'national contextual' factors in shaping the nature and extent of public Euroscepticism in EU member states, particularly in a country such as Britain where political parties, the media and other social institutions have adopted Eurosceptic stances at different points in time (Nelsen et al. 2001; Nelsen et al. 2011). Given the relevance of the Catholic Church to the origins and early development of the integration process and its supra-nationalist traditions as a faith, the differences in attitudes between Catholics in Britain and in the EU as a whole are noteworthy and can be examined further by looking at trend data from the EB surveys.

Does this gap in negative sentiment persist between the two 'bookend' surveys of 1970 and 2006?

The attitudinal measures from the EB surveys used tap into the distinction made in the public opinion literature on 'utilitarian' support, based upon 'an evaluation of the perceived benefits of integration', and 'affective' support, which is 'abstract and broad in nature, representing a general orientation towards integration' (Gabel 1998: 20). There is greater over time coverage of the former type of measure than the latter type in the EB surveys. The question used for eliciting 'utilitarian' support was worded as follows:

> Generally speaking, do you think that (your country's) membership of the European Community (Common Market) is ...? A good thing. A bad thing. Neither good nor bad.

The question used for tapping into 'affective' support is as follows:

> In general, are you for or against efforts being made to unify Western Europe? If 'for' are you very much for this, or only to some extent? If 'against' are you only to some extent against or very much against?

The level of sentiment is charted over time. For the 'utilitarian' measure, this consists of those saying membership is a 'bad thing'. For the 'affective' indicators, this involves those who are either 'against – to some extent' or 'against – very much' the unification process.

Figure 7.8 shows the proportion of Catholics saying their country's membership is a 'bad thing' and the proportion saying that they are 'against' unification. Over time there is a clear picture whereby negative views are more common amongst Catholics in Britain than their co-religionists in the other member states; and this gap is evident for both indicators of opinion. The divergence in negative sentiment on the 'bad thing' indicator is most stark in the 1970s and early 1980s. Subsequently, there is a sharp downward turn and negative sentiment remains lower for British Catholics during the remainder of the period, albeit consistently higher than that expressed by Catholics in member states as a whole. Although not shown here in visual form, a similar attitudinal trend is apparent for other longitudinal indicators of EU support. In response to other questions, over time Catholics in Britain are more likely to think than their co-religionists across the member states that their country has not benefitted from membership (for the period 1986–2006) and were more likely to express relief if the EU were ever to be dissolved (1973–98) (a full set of data are available on request).

Finally, this is repeated for Anglicans in Britain and Protestants in the EU, with data charted in Figure 7.9. A similar pattern is evident to that shown in Figure 7.8, albeit for a shorter time period (covering 1973–89).[3] There is a stark difference in the levels saying 'bad thing', with Euroscepticism much higher amongst Anglicans in Britain over time, although this difference does narrow in the later surveys. Similarly, Anglicans are more likely to say that they are against the unification process to some degree, but the difference is usually smaller than that seen for the indicator of 'utilitarian' attitudes. So for both Catholics and Anglicans in Britain, negative sentiment expressed through 'utilitarian' or 'affective' indicators has tended to be markedly higher over time than that expressed by Catholics and Protestants across the EU.

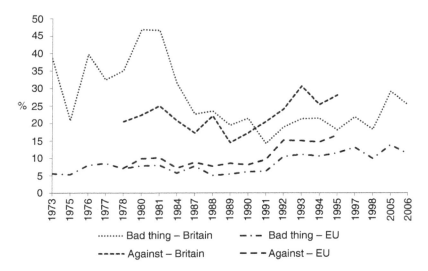

Figure 7.8   Percent who say membership is a bad thing and who are against the unification process, Catholics in Britain and the EU, 1973–2006
Source: EB surveys.

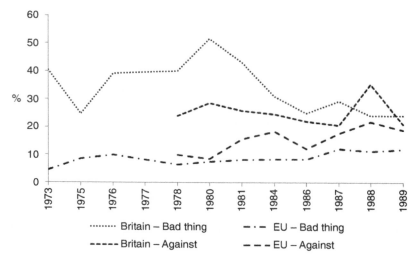

Figure 7.9   Percent who say membership is a bad thing and who are against the unification process, Anglicans in Britain and Protestants in the EU, 1973–1989
Source: EB surveys.

Attitudes towards military intervention

While looking at public opinion towards the EU can be seen as involving the peaceful transaction of regional inter-state politics and Britain's role within it, what about the issue of war and Britain's involvement in the use of military force, specifically overseas interventions? Have religious groups held distinct opinions on recent military interventions? What have been the views of those belonging to Christian traditions as well as minority faiths? Attitudes on these issues can be considered as indicators falling within the dimension of 'Militant internationalism' (Guth 2012). In the post-Cold War era, British foreign policy has been marked by involvement in a series of military interventions under Conservative and Labour governments. After the 1991 Gulf War, Britain participated in military and peacekeeping operations in Bosnia, Kosovo and Sierra Leone. After the terrorist attacks of 9/11 it took part in military action in Iraq and Afghanistan as part of the wider fight against terrorism. Britain's combat operations in Iraq officially ceased in April 2009 but it still has forces deployed in Afghanistan. Britain was also involved in United Nations-endorsed military action against the regime of Muammar Gaddafi in Libya in 2011. These interventions

have been politically controversial to varying degrees and public sentiment of course changes during the duration of military action. The
religious basis of support and opposition towards British involvement
in Iraq and Afghanistan is assessed.

Religious affiliation has been a prominent explanatory variable in
the literature on US public opinion towards the wars in Iraq and
Afghanistan and other policies in the post-9/11 era (Guth 2009).
Substantial differences have been documented based on religious
affiliation (Jones 2007) while one survey of US public opinion observed
that 'The relationship between religion and opinions about the war on
terror are powerful and universal', which included the relationship of
religious affiliation and attendance to support for the Iraq War (Baylor
2006: 36–7; see also Jones 2007).

In Britain, it was certainly the case that the leaders of and senior
bishops within the Anglican and Roman Catholics churches made clear
in public their doubts over the moral case for the war in Iraq, both in
the final run-up to the invasion and earlier on when it had become a
controversial proposal (Bates 2003; Alden 2002).[4] In late February
2003, The Church of England's General Synod had voted overwhelm-
ingly 'in favour of an emergency motion affirming that decisions about
how to secure the disarmament of Iraq within the framework of international law must be through the United Nations' (Gledhill 2003). One
YouGov poll showed that the public sided more with the leaders of the
Church of England and Catholic Church in thinking there was not a
moral case for war (50.0 percent) than with the Prime Minister, Tony
Blair, in thinking that there was a moral case for the conflict
(37.0 percent) (YouGov 2003a). While another showed that the public
was much more likely to agree with the Pope's view that the right
'moral' course was to avoid conflict (49.0 percent) than with Blair's
assertion that there was a 'moral case' for military action (27.0 percent)
(YouGov 2003b).

Religious groups in the general population

To examine religious groups' views on these military interventions,
data are utilised from the BES 2005 and 2010 surveys as well as the BSA
2011 survey. It is also worth noting at this point that all of the questions used here ask about attitudes post-intervention, in some cases
several years after the onset of military action. Unfortunately, no data
were available which would allow, based on religious affiliation, an
examination of *prospective* attitudes before the intervention in
Afghanistan in late 2001 and the invasion of Iraq in March 2003, or at

the outset of military action when there may be a 'rally round the flag effect' in the public mood.

Using evidence from the BES 2005 and 2010 surveys, a comparison can be made of attitudes towards the Iraq and Afghanistan conflicts based on religious groups in the general public. The question wordings are as follows:

> Please tell me whether you strongly approve, approve, disapprove, or strongly disapprove of Britain's involvement in Iraq (BES 2005)
> Please tell me whether you strongly approve, approve, disapprove, or strongly disapprove of Britain's involvement in the war against the Taliban in Afghanistan (BES 2010 in-person survey)
> Please indicate whether you strongly approve, approve, disapprove, or strongly disapprove of Britain's involvement in the war against the Taliban in Afghanistan? (BES 2010 CIPS)

For religious affiliation, Table 7.7 shows approval or disapproval of Britain's involvement in the Iraq and Afghanistan conflicts in response to identical questions administered in recent BES surveys (2005: Iraq; 2010: Afghanistan). Data are reported separately for Muslims and those belonging to other non-Christian traditions.

Table 7.7   Percent approving and disapproving of the wars in Iraq and Afghanistan, by affiliation

	Anglican (%)	Roman Catholic (%)	Other Christian (%)	Muslim (%)	Other religion (%)	No religion (%)
BES 2005 in-person survey: Iraq						
Approve	34.6	33.4	30.6	17.0	28.1	37.5
Disapprove	65.4	66.6	69.5	83.0	71.9	62.5
BES 2010 in-person survey: Afghanistan						
Approve	26.5	22.0	25.0	19.7	26.4	20.8
Neither	11.5	14.6	10.5	7.6	15.7	12.3
Disapprove	62.0	63.4	64.5	72.8	57.9	66.9
BES 2010 CIPS: Afghanistan						
Approve	35.7	31.8	36.1	16.5	30.3	31.6
Disapprove	64.3	68.2	63.9	83.5	69.7	68.4

Source: BES surveys.
Note: Combines 'strongly approve' and 'approve'; combines 'strongly disapprove' and 'disapprove'.

Table 7.8   Percent approving and disapproving of the war in Afghanistan, by attendance

	Frequent-attender (%)	Infrequent-attender (%)	Non-attender (%)
Approve	23.8	27.6	22.1
Neither	12.5	10.4	12.3
Disapprove	63.7	62.0	65.7

Source: BES 2010 in-person survey.
Note: Combines 'strongly approve' and 'approve'; combines 'strongly disapprove' and 'disapprove'.

For Iraq, disapproval was lowest amongst those with no religion, at 62.5 percent. In comparison, in the 2005 BES 83.0 percent of Muslims disapproved of the war in Iraq, with 71.9 percent of members of other religions also opposing. This compares to levels of disapproval of between 65.4–69.5 percent for members of different Christian traditions. Similarly for the two measures of attitudes towards Britain's role in Afghanistan (from the BES 2010 in-person and campaign internet panel surveys), Muslims again register the highest levels of disapproval, at 72.8 percent (in-person survey) and 83.5 percent (BES CIPS 2010). The levels of disapproval registered by the Christian groups are somewhat lower (in the range of 62.0 percent to 68.2 percent).

Attitudes towards the war in Afghanistan can be compared based on religious behaviour – attendance at religious services. The data are presented in Table 7.8. Religious attendance is based on three categories: frequent (at least once a month); infrequent attendance (less than once a month); does not attend. There is little variation across levels of attendance at religious worship; levels of disapproval range from 62.0 percent (infrequently attending) through to 65.7 percent (never attend).

Retrospective views of Britain's role in the Iraq and Afghanistan wars can also be assessed. Analysis of retrospective opinion in the US – whether the Iraq War was a mistake or not – showed substantial differences by religious factors:

> Americans' religious preference and frequency of church attendance are related to the belief that the war in Iraq was a mistake. Those who have a non-Christian religious identification or no religious

identification at all and those who seldom or never attend church are most likely to believe that the war was a mistake. Those who are Protestants or other Christians, and those who attend church frequently are least likely to believe that the war was a mistake (Newport 2006).

Two questions about retrospective judgements were asked in the BSA 2011 survey. They were worded as follows:

To what extent do you agree or disagree with the following statements: The UK was wrong to send its Armed Forces to Afghanistan? To what extent do you agree or disagree that ... The UK was wrong to go to war with Iraq in 2003?

Data are presented in Table 7.9. As was the case with Table 7.7, there is not much variation across religious groups in levels of agreement with the propositions that the UK was wrong to go to war with Iraq and dispatch military forces to Afghanistan. As was the case with disapproval of the Iraq War, there is higher agreement with Britain's role in Iraq being wrong compared to its participation in Afghanistan. Those with no affiliation expressed the lowest level of disagreement towards Britain going to war in Iraq, while Roman Catholics and other

Table 7.9   **Retrospective attitudes towards the wars in Iraq and Afghanistan, by affiliation**

	Anglican (%)	Roman Catholic (%)	Other Christian (%)	Non-Christian (%)	No religion (%)
Iraq					
Agree	58.6	63.4	60.0	59.9	55.1
Neither agree nor disagree	14.3	12.7	18.4	16.7	17.5
Disagree	25.8	20.8	20.1	14.5	25.8
Don't know	1.2	3.0	1.5	8.8	1.6
Afghanistan					
Agree	50.4	45.9	44.9	50.7	48.8
Neither agree nor disagree	19.4	20.7	18.7	18.0	20.9
Disagree	26.5	27.1	34.2	29.1	29.2
Don't know	3.7	6.3	2.1	2.3	1.1

Source: BSA 2011 survey.

Table 7.10   Retrospective attitudes towards the Iraq and Afghanistan wars, by attendance

	Frequent-attender (%)	Infrequent-attender (%)	Non-attender (%)
Iraq			
Agree	59.0	60.6	56.6
Neither agree nor disagree	17.7	12.9	16.9
Disagree	19.1	25.4	24.5
Don't know	4.2	1.1	2.0
Afghanistan			
Agree	39.9	50.2	50.2
Neither agree nor disagree	22.7	19.5	19.2
Disagree	31.8	28.8	28.5
Don't know	5.5	1.5	2.0

Source: BSA 2011 survey.

Christians did so for Britain's role in Afghanistan. If Muslims are separated from the 'other religion' category, it can be seen that they were most likely to agree that the UK was wrong to go to war with Iraq (at 60.8 percent, with just 9.8 percent disagreeing).

Table 7.10 next presents attitudinal data using the same three-way classification of attendance. Interestingly, there is some variation across religious behaviour. Specifically, for Britain's involvement in Afghanistan, agreement is noticeably lower for those who attend religious services frequently: at 39.9 percent compared to 50.2 percent for those who attend less often or not at all. This pattern is not evident for attitudes towards Britain's role in the war in Iraq.

As a final step in looking at attitudes in the general population, the BSA 2011 survey is used to robustly assess the influence of religion (both belonging and behaviour) on retrospective attitudes towards the Iraq War and the intervention in Afghanistan. As with the multivariate analyses conducted in earlier chapters, sociological model of attitudes was specified (controlling for demographic characteristics and socio-economic status), while also accounting for the impact of party loyalties. The impact of religious attendance (again employed as a scale) is also examined. Binary logistic regression is used to separately examine attitudes towards Iraq and Afghanistan. The dependent variables have been constructed so that those who either agree or strongly agree are coded as 1 and those who disagree to some extent or adopted a neutral position are coded as 0. The intention here is to ascertain which factors

Table 7.11   Binary logistic regressions of public attitudes towards the wars in Iraq and Afghanistan

Variable	Iraq B (SE)	Iraq Odds ratio	Afghanistan B (SE)	Afghanistan Odds ratio
Sex	−.15 (.11)	.86	−.26* (.11)	.77
Ethnic group	.31 (.23)	1.36	−.61* (.20)	.54
Age	.02* (.00)	1.02	.03* (.00)	1.03
Degree qualification	.36* (.15)	1.43	−.10 (.15)	.90
Owner-occupier	−.03 (.12)	.97	−.19 (.12)	.82
Salariat	.05 (.12)	1.05	−.05 (.12)	.95
Attendance	.00 (.03)	1.00	−.11* (.03)	.90
Anglican	−.23 (.15)	.80	−.14 (.16)	.87
Catholic	.41 (.22)	1.50	.04 (.22)	1.04
Other Christian	.07 (.17)	1.08	−.22 (.17)	.80
Other religion	.71* (.30)	2.03	.19 (.24)	1.21
Conservative	−.11 (.16)	.90	−.45* (.17)	.64
Labour	−.06 (.16)	.95	−.30* (.15)	.74
Liberal Democrat	.06 (.23)	1.06	−.39 (.23)	.68
Other party	.10 (.19)	1.11	−.22 (.18)	.80
Constant	−.91* (.30)	.40	.17 (.27)	1.18
Weighted N	1,585		1,573	
Nagelkerke R Square	.05		.07	

Note: *$p<.05$ or lower.
Reference categories: no religion; non-party identifier.
Source: BSA 2011 survey.

differentiate those with a negative view of the UK's role in each conflict from those who have a positive view or are broadly neutral. The results from the two binary logistic regressions are reported in Table 7.11.

The effects for the religion variables vary somewhat across the two models. First, in relation to public views of the Iraq War, those belonging to non-Christian faiths are more likely to agree (odds ratio: 2.03) than those with no religion that the UK was wrong to go to war. There is no impact for religious attendance. Second, for the Afghanistan intervention, the dummies based on religious tradition have no impact but there is a clear and significant effect for religious attendance. That is, accounting for a range of other social group characteristics, those who attend collective worship more regularly are less likely to agree that the UK's role in the Afghanistan conflict was wrong. It appears that religion in Britain clearly does not rival the importance of religious-based explanations for US public opinion towards post-9/11 military interventions and policies (Guth 2009; Smidt 2005; Barker et al. 2008; Baumgartner et al. 2008; Froese and Mencken 2009). Overall, the models do not explain much variance in the dependent variables (with Nagelkerke R Square statistics of, respectively, 0.05 and 0.07).

Religious groups in the ethnic minority population

As well as examining attitudes by religious belonging in the general population, which showed higher levels of disapproval amongst Muslims of the wars in Iraq and Afghanistan, a unique survey can be used to examine in greater detail attitudes based on the religious affiliations of ethnic minority groups in British society. Considering the opposition expressed amongst Muslims in Britain towards the invasion of Iraq in 2003, it is important to investigate whether there are differences by religious faith in attitudes towards the war in Afghanistan, particularly whether members of minority non-Christian religions are less supportive of Britain's involvement. Existing research has shown that, based on opinion poll data collected in recent years, Muslims in Britain are more likely to have negative views of the Iraq and Afghanistan conflicts and towards the broader war on terrorism (Field 2007, 2012). Recent polling of Muslims in Britain also found high levels of opposition to the United States and United Kingdom military operations in Afghanistan and Pakistan (77.0 percent were against), as well as opposition towards political intervention in those countries (BBC News 2009).

In the US, The Pew Research Center's (2007: 49) Muslim Americans survey, found that 75.0 percent of Muslims thought that invading Iraq was the wrong decision (compared to 47.0 percent of Americans in general). In both 2007 and 2011, 48.0 percent of Muslims thought the use of military force in Afghanistan was the 'wrong decision', compared to 29.0 percent (2007) and 35.0 percent (2011) of the general United States population (Pew Research Center 2011: 73). When asked if the United States-led war on terrorism was a sincere effort to reduce international terrorism, the majority of Muslims in the United States said it was not (55.0 percent) (Pew Research Center 2007: 49), though this fell to 41.0 percent in 2011. In a survey of Muslim-Americans, Patterson et al. (2011: 9) also found that few supported the war in Iraq. Moreover, when asked if the Iraq War was important for the security of the United States, more than 90.0 percent disagreed. Muslim-Americans were generally in agreement that their civil rights have suffered since the attacks of September 11 (Patterson et al. 2011: 9).

Table 7.12   Attitudes towards the war in Afghanistan, by affiliation, ethnic minority population

	No religion (%)	Christian (%)	Hindu (%)	Muslim (%)	Sikh (%)	Other (%)
Strongly approve or approve	17.8	21.8	26.5	7.6	26.5	12.9
Neither	22.3	19.0	16.0	14.0	15.1	19.4
Disapprove or strongly disapprove	51.9	46.5	37.8	63.1	49.5	54.8
Don't know/refused	8.0	12.7	19.8	15.3	9.0	12.9

Source: EMBES 2010.

Given this wider public context, a supplementary analysis is undertaken of the attitudes of minority groups in Britain by using the Ethnic Minority British Election Study 2010 (EMBES). This survey asked an identical set of questions about the war in Afghanistan to those administered in the main BES in-person 2010 survey. The focus here is again on levels of approval and disapproval for Britain's involvement in Afghanistan. The question asked in the EMBES was as follows:

Please indicate whether you strongly approve, approve, disapprove, or strongly disapprove of Britain's involvement in the war against the Taliban in Afghanistan.

Responses are initially examined by religious affiliation and then sub-divisions amongst Christians and Muslims. There are clear differences in levels of approval and disapproval of Britain's involvement in Afghanistan by religious affiliation, as shown in Table 7.12. Muslims are *least likely* to approve (7.6 percent), with Hindus and Sikhs showing the higher levels of support (26.5 percent for both groups). Muslims show the highest level of disapproval (at 63.1 percent) followed by those of no religion (at 51.9 percent).

Table 7.13, showing responses by Christian denomination, shows the highest levels of approval are expressed by Anglicans, members of Pentecostal churches and those in the 'other' Christian category (in the 25.0–29.0 percent range). The highest levels of disapproval reach around 60 percent, expressed by Orthodox Christians and (Seventh Day) Adventists. In Table 7.14, showing responses by Muslim tradition, Sunni Muslims and those who do not belong to a particular tradition

Table 7.13   Attitudes towards the war in Afghanistan, by Christian tradition, ethnic minority population[a]

	Strongly approve or approve (%)	Neither (%)	Strongly disapprove or disapprove (%)	Don't know/ refused (%)
Anglican	25.0	6.0	54.8	6.0
Baptist	12.2	18.4	49.0	18.4
Catholic	19.8	13.0	44.9	13.0
Methodist	14.7	11.8	44.1	11.8
Pentecostal	27.1	12.2	43.0	12.2
Orthodox	18.2	0.0	63.6	18.2
(Seventh Day) Adventist	10.0	25.0	60.0	5.0
Other	28.6	20.0	40.0	11.4
None in particular	19.4	11.1	55.6	13.9

Source: EMBES 2010.
[a]Excluding those who 'refused' or responded 'don't know' to the follow-up question.

Table 7.14   Attitudes towards the war in Afghanistan, by Muslim tradition, ethnic minority population[a]

	Sunni (%)	Shi'a (%)	Other (%)	None in particular
Strongly approve or approve	6.4	18.5	12.5	18.3
Neither	14.8	18.5	16.7	3.7
Disapprove or strongly disapprove	64.1	44.4	50.0	64.6
Don't know/refused	14.7	18.5	20.8	13.4

Source: EMBES 2010.
[a]Excluding those who 'refused' or responded 'don't know' to the follow-up question.

express the highest levels of disapproval (at 64.5 percent) compared to 44.4 percent for Shi'a Muslims and 50.0 percent for those belonging to other traditions. The vast majority of Muslims in Afghanistan practice Sunni Islam. Note that the Shi'a and 'other' categories are both based on relatively small numbers of respondents (in the EMBES survey, 83.4 percent of those who said they were Muslim reported belonging to the Sunni tradition in the follow-up question).

What about the role of religious affiliation and religiosity in shaping the attitudes of ethnic minority groups towards Britain's role in Afghanistan when accounting for other sociological and political variables? The author has undertaken a multivariate analysis of the EMBES survey in a separate study, concluding that:

> Importantly, ethnic background does not have any significant effects when religious-based variables are accounted for. The results for religious affiliation in Model 2 provide clear support for Hypothesis 1, as Sunni Muslims are much less likely to approve of the war compared to those of no religion (the reference category). The only other significant effect is for Hindus, who are more likely to approve of the war ... The findings for Sunni Muslims from this analysis nuance the evidence from opinion polls of Muslims' attitudes toward foreign policy issues ... Beyond the stand-alone impact of affiliation, the interactions between affiliation and religiosity are significant in the case of Sunni Muslims. Those Sunni Muslims for whom religion is particularly important in their lives and who take part in religious activities more often are less likely to approve of the war in Afghanistan (Clements 2013: 18).

Overall, then, and in addition to longer-standing debates over Britain's external relations, religion can also shape attitudes on newer issues and controversies which have appeared in British foreign policy in recent years.

Conclusion

This chapter has shown that there has been attitudinal variation in both long-standing and more recent issues central to Britain's foreign policy and its standing in the world. The chapter focused on two broad areas of international politics: *war* (recent overseas military interventions) and *peace* (Britain's involvement in European integration). These were taken as more specific indicators of policy attitudes within the broader dimensions of, respectively, militant internationalism and cooperative internationalism (Guth 2012).

In terms of Britain's long-standing relations with the European integration process, the extensive review of single-country and cross-national survey data from the 1970s onwards showed two findings. First, that across surveys and attitudinal indicators, Catholics have tended to be more supportive than Anglicans of Britain's relations with the EU. In other words, over time Anglicans have tended to register higher levels of Eurosceptic sentiment in relation to both EU membership and one of its flagship projects, the single currency. Anglicans certainly have demonstrated a greater affinity with seeing themselves as British or English than have Catholics. Recent evidence from a contemporary survey of faith and public life in Britain, undertaken in June 2013, also shows that Anglicans are more likely to be Eurosceptic than the general population (Woodhead 2013c). Multivariate analysis of contemporary attitudes also showed that, when accounting for a host of sociological factors correlated with Eurosceptic opinion, belonging to the Anglican tradition was significantly related to negative sentiment towards the EU.

Second, these within-country differences based on religious belonging are outweighed by the across-country difference in attitudes when comparing opinion in Britain and the EU as a whole. That is Catholics and Anglicans tend to have more in common with each other – in terms of their noticeably higher level of Eurosceptic sentiment – than with their co-religionists on mainland Europe.

The second area analysed here concerned more recent developments and controversies in British foreign policy: military interventions in Iraq and Afghanistan in the post-9/11 era. Overall, opposition was greater across religious groups to Britain's involvement in the Iraq War, which was highly controversial – both party-politically and across wider society – pre- and post-invasion in March 2003. Multivariate analysis of retrospective opinion of both conflicts showed a very limited impact for religious affiliation, although, interestingly, higher attendance at religious services was negatively related to opposition to Britain's role in Afghanistan. Separate investigation has shown that religion was an important source of attitudinal variation towards the war in Afghanistan amongst ethnic minority groups in Britain (Clements 2013). The results from this chapter have demonstrated that religion and sometimes religiosity can influence public attitudes on both long-standing foreign policy debates and issues which have emerged more recently.

Appendix

Question wordings from EB 67.1 2006

General support

'Generally speaking, do you think that (OUR COUNTRY)'s membership of the European Union is...?'
'Taking everything into account, would you say that (OUR COUNTRY) has on balance benefited or not from being a member of the European Union?'
'In general, does the European Union conjure up for you a very positive, fairly positive, neutral, fairly negative or very negative image?'

'I would like to ask you a question about how much trust you have in certain institutions. For each of the following institutions, please tell me if you tend to trust it or tend not to trust it. The European Union.'

'Are you, yourself, for or against the development towards a European political union?'

'At the present time, would you say that, in general, things are going in the right direction or in the wrong direction, in...? The European Union'

Policies

'What is your opinion on each of the following statements? Please tell me for each statement, whether you are for it or against it.'

'A European Monetary Union with one single currency, the euro.'

'A common foreign policy among the Member States of the European Union, towards other countries.'

'A common defence and security policy among European Union Member States.'

'For each of the following countries, would you be in favour or against it becoming part of the European Union in the future? Turkey.'

'What is your opinion on each of the following statements? Please tell me for each statement, whether you are for it or against it. Further enlargement of the European Union to include other countries in future years.'

Citizenship and identity

'Do you ever think of yourself as not only (NATIONALITY), but also European? Does this happen often, sometimes or never?'

'And would you say you are very proud, fairly proud, not very proud, not at all proud to be European?'

8
Conclusion

This book set out to assess how the attitudes of religious groups in Britain have changed or shown evidence of continuity across recent decades. It aimed to provide a detailed 'bottom-up' perspective to complement existing research which has often adopted a more 'top-down' focus on the historical and contemporary interconnections between religion and politics, studying the role of religion in shaping parties and the party system, the involvement of religious actors in the policy process and public debate, and relations between religious institutions and parties in office. In so doing, the study focused on a range of different aspects of public opinion – religious authority, party-political support, ideology, social-moral issues, abortion and homosexuality and foreign policy – in order to provide an extensive and wide-ranging analysis. Of course, no single monograph can provide a near-exhaustive treatment of the socio-political attitude and beliefs held by particular sectors of society or the general population as a whole. But given the wider historical backdrop of religious change in British society, the ongoing debates over the extent and nature of secularisation, and claims about the growing salience of religious issues and faith groups in politics in recent years, the book has tried to provide a reasonably comprehensive treatment of attitudinal change and continuity over time across religious groups. This width of topics contributes to the distinctiveness of this study, which makes a clear and important contribution to recent scholarly research on the historical and present-day connections of politics and religion in Britain (Steven 2011a, 2011b; Bruce 2012; Filby 2010). The research contained in the book also speaks to Steven's observation about religion being a 'neglected dimension' amongst scholars of British politics (2011a).

The book used a multifaceted approach to the micro-level analysis of religion, focusing on belonging, behaving and believing (Leege and Kellstedt 1993; Smidt et al. 2009); though, necessarily, it focused to a greater extent on the first two aspects. By doing this, and by also undertaking analysis of social survey series which between them provide multiple measures of particular attitudes and beliefs, a richer, robust and more rounded picture of trends and patterns in religion and public opinion has been provided. Overall, the empirical analyses contained in this book make an important contribution to the 'repurposing' (Field forthcoming) of micro-level data on religion available in social surveys and opinion polls.

More broadly, the research undertaken here makes a contribution to wider literatures in political science, the sociology of religion and – given the long-term perspective adopted in the study of attitudinal change and continuity – post-war British religious history. The findings presented in this study in relation to socio-political attitudes can be usefully set alongside the more extensive scholarly literature on religious change in Britain, which has assessed the nature and extent of the decline in the aspects of belonging, believing and behaving and related this to wider debates over secularisation (Davie 1994, 2015; Bruce 2013; Gill et al. 1998; Gill 2003; Voas and Crockett 2005). The methodological approach, breadth of topics and extensive survey data utilised have made a contribution to the systematic use of micro-level data – both social surveys and opinion polls – in order to examine popular religion and its social and political relevance or significance in post-war British society. More broadly, the extensive analyses and empirical findings contained in this study should also be of relevance to broader scholarly and societal debates concerning the presence and influence of religion in British society and politics and processes of secularisation, and to the challenges and issues faced by Christian religious denominations in retaining their grassroots adherents at a time when an increasing 'disconnect' has been evident between the latter, on the one hand, and religious leaders and institutions, on the other (Woodhead 2013b, 2013c).

The central part of this chapter is structured around the two broad themes set out at the beginning of this study, assessing the nature and extent of continuity and change in the socio-political attitudes of religious groups in longer-term perspective. The first section assesses the main chapter findings which relate to areas of continuity and the second section discusses the main chapter findings regarding attitudinal change. Finally, in the last section, the chapter offers some reflections on the limitations of the study and thereby suggests areas for future scholarly research.

Religion and areas of continuity in attitudes

The main areas of continuity documented in this chapter concern the analyses of party choice and ideological beliefs undertaken in Chapters 3 and 4, respectively, and the examination of Euroscepticism which formed part of the focus on foreign policy issues in Chapter 7. The detailed analysis of party choice certainly showed two key aspects of continuity in the associations between denominations and support for political parties. Firstly, the tendency for Anglicans to support the Conservative Party was shown both in relation to voting at post-war general elections and a broader measure of (inter-election) party support. Whilst the characterisation of the Church of England as the 'Conservative Party at prayer' has been less apt in recent times (Filby 2013), the evidence shows that there has been and still is, a greater propensity for Anglicans to support the Conservative Party. Second, a similar finding was evident for Catholics and support for the Labour Party over several decades. Moreover, when more detailed analysis of the sociological correlates of contemporary party choice was undertaken, religious belonging had the expected effect, net of socio-economic factors and other characteristics which have traditionally been related to electoral behaviour. Analysis of recent survey evidence confirmed some of these historical linkages when assessing broader sociological models of party support. The traditional linkages between parties and religious groups established by and which endured because of a 'frozen' religious cleavage in British society may still exercise influence over contemporary patterns of party support (Lipset and Rokkan 1967; Tilley 2014). However, while there was evidence of religious belonging having a clear impact in particular ways, there is little to support religious behaving (or practice) also underpinning party choice. There was little support for the finding from other countries whereby greater religiosity – often measured as frequency of attendance at services – is typically associated with support for centre-right parties (van der Brug et al. 2009).

Another area showing some degree of continuity, and which clearly links with the findings for party choice, is that of political ideology – the subject of Chapter 4 – with Anglicans showing greater social authoritarianism and economic *conservatism* in their orientations and beliefs, to go alongside their greater party-political Conservatism in post-war decades. This tendency towards political conservatism was evident for both abstract beliefs and more specific policy preferences (such as the death penalty), as well as self-defined ideological location. Taken together, the findings from Chapters 2 and 3 tend to support Heath et al.'s earlier conclusion that 'even in Britain, not a noticeably devout society, religion has some association with political behaviour and attitudes' (1993a: 66).

Another area of continuity, the subject of analysis in Chapter 7, is in the area of Britain's external relations, and pertaining specifically to attitudes towards the European integration process amongst Anglicans and Catholics. A consistent finding was that, compared to Catholics, Anglicans have tended to be more wary of and less supportive towards, their country's involvement in the EU (and its predecessor bodies – the Common Market, European Economic Community and European Community). More specifically, they have shown less support for British membership of the EU and have been more opposed to further engagement, in the form of national participation in the Euro. Other attitudinal indicators – such as support for other aspects of political and economic integration and evaluations of the EU, as well as affective orientations like feeling a sense of European identity – also show differences between Anglicans and Catholics, with the former group tending to be more Eurosceptic in their views. This Euroscepticism may be rooted in deeper values such as particular territorial identities or national attachment, but the evidence for this is somewhat more limited and is clearly an area for further research. This picture of differences in Eurosceptic sentiment between Anglicans and Catholics within Britain needs to be placed in the wider context of variation in levels of opposition to the integration process between religious groups in Britain and in the EU as a whole. Catholics across the EU were much more supportive of the integration process than their co-religionists in Britain, while Protestants in the member states were much less likely to be Eurosceptic than Anglicans in Britain. This difference in attitudes applied to various aspects of EU, including general support, key policies and a sense of attachment. This stresses the importance of 'national contextual' factors in shaping the nature and extent of popular Euroscepticism in EU member states, particularly in a country such as Britain where political parties, the print media and other groups – such as trade unions – have adopted Eurosceptic stances (Nelsen et al. 2001).

Religion and areas of change in attitudes

Chapter 2 examined data from the EVS and BSA surveys bearing upon public perceptions of religious authority in Britain, both of which showed some evidence of declining authority in these perceptions over recent decades. This change has occurred in two areas of public opinion towards religious institutions and religious leaders. First, the evidence from recent decades shows that there has been a modest decline in confidence in the church, albeit this is part of a wider pattern of changing perceptions of major societal institutions. Given this wider pattern, it is rather difficult to decisively attribute this changing perception of religious institutions to processes of secularisation as manifested in 'declining religious authority' (Chaves 1994; Hoffman 1998, 2013) in Britain. That said, though, detailed analysis of the micro-level correlates found that different religious factors largely explained contemporary public confidence (or lack thereof) in the church, but had much less impact – in relative terms, compared to social-structural factors or political orientations – when looking at the underpinnings of confidence in other national institutions.

While British public opinion seems to be somewhat less enamoured with religious institutions in general in recent decades – as manifested in declining confidence – attitudes have also shifted in relation to the exercise of religious influence and authority in the political process. Albeit this set of data only covered the most recent decades, it was still evident that, in this shorter timescale, public opinion has become less favourable to religious authority being exercised within day-to-day politics in relation to influencing both leaders and voters. The shifts in popular attitudes in relation to both confidence in religious institutions and their role in the political process from the 1980s and 1990s onwards, rather begs the question as to what shifts, if any, in public perceptions would have been documented in the earlier post-war decades, the 1950s and 1960s, which witnessed changes in popular religion (Field 2015). Taken together, the evidence and analyses contained in Chapter 2 speak, in general, to existing research and debate about secularisation and the 'decline of religious authority' in modern democracies and, in particular, the public presence of religion within British society (Bruce 2012).

The most prominent area of attitudinal change concerns the social-moral issues examined in depth in Chapters 5 and 6. They looked, respectively, at abortion as the archetypal 'life issue' and at homosexuality and gay rights – a core part of the recent equalities agenda in

British society, with liberalising legislation enacted initially in the 1960s, with several reforms eventually following under the recent Labour and Coalition governments. Taken together, the detailed treatment of religious groups' attitudes showed that, whether looking at religious belonging or behaviour, there had been significant liberalisation of opinion on both issues, particularly in the last couple of decades. The continuity evident here is that greater religiosity – whether evident in attendance or other indicators of commitment or involvement – still tends to correlate with more socially-conservative views towards abortion and same-sex relations and rights. Even so, the liberalisation of opinion was clear amongst the more religious in British society, however defined, but its impact has been slower or more sporadic compared to those who show less or no engagement with religion. Indeed, the changes in attitudes elucidated in Chapters 5 and 6 provide part of the important 'back-story' to contemporary debates over the lack of relevance and responsiveness of religion in wider society and the growing divides between grassroots adherents and the teachings and leadership of, in particular, the Anglican and Roman Catholic churches (Woodhead 2013b, 2013c).

The historical evidence presented here adds to scholarly understanding of the attitudes and beliefs of different religious groups, and provide a rich, longer-term perspective to major contemporary surveys of religion and popular opinion, in particular the Westminster Faith Debates surveys, from 2012 and 2013. In the broader socio-historical context, the shifts can also be seen in light of the religious change documented in the various micro-level indicators (relating to belonging, behaving and believing) discussed in Chapter 2. Changing attitudes on these two issues form part of a wider set of shifts in the broader climate of opinion on moral and social-equality issues; as religious groups have also increasingly adopted less traditionalist views on subjects such as personal relationships in recent decades (Park and Rhead 2013), and therefore have become more and more detached from and less influenced by, denominational teachings and beliefs. Even though there has been substantial change on the basis of religious belonging and behaving, some traditional lines of denominational difference remains on social issues – most obviously, and accounting for the historical liberalisation of opinion, Catholics still tend to hold more restrictive or traditionalist views on the question of abortion compared to Anglicans and those with no religion.

The weight of the empirical findings from Chapters 5–6 (attitudes towards abortion and homosexuality and gay rights), as well as from

Chapter 2 on religion in public life speak to Lee's recent conclusions about the implications of religious change in Britain:

> What does this decline mean for society and social policy more generally? On the one hand, we can expect to see a continued increase in liberal attitudes towards a range of issues such as abortion, homosexuality, same-sex marriage, and euthanasia, as the influence of considerations grounded in religion declines. Moreover, we may see an increased reluctance, particularly among the younger age groups, for matters of faith to enter the social and public spheres at all (Lee, L. 2012: 182–3).

More broadly, looking across areas of both change and continuity, the empirical findings from this study are also instructive in the context of Heath et al.'s study of declining social identities – class, party, religion and nation – which concluded that: 'While their members may have become ever fewer in number, religious organisations continue to act as powerful normative reference groups for those that remain' (2007: 28). When assessing the impact of religious orientations on socio-political attitudes in the chapters, they often had significant effects in the expected direction even when accounting for the impact of other demographic traits and social group characteristics.

Limitations of the study and areas for future research

While, overall, the findings make a distinct contribution and should be of interest to political scientists, sociologists of religion and historians of religion in post-war British society, any book-length study has its limitations, and these need to be acknowledged here. Firstly, while the recurrent social survey data used here has spanned several decades, most of these started in the 1970s (EB) or 1980s (EVS and BSA), with the exception of the BES, which commenced in the early 1960s. One clear lacuna in the study is the more patchy availability of data for some of the chapter topics in the early post-war period. Where available, national opinion polls or one-off social surveys have been used and discussed – for voting behaviour or abortion – but for other topics, such as same-sex relations and rights, or confidence in religious institutions, there is much less that can be said about change and continuity in religious groups' views for the 1950s and 1960s, given the relative lack of evidence. This is a pity given the lively scholarly debate over processes of religious change or decline in Britain – and the nature and extent of secularisation – in this period (Yates 2010; McLeod 2007; Brown 2006; Machin 1996, 1998). Second, a fuller set of social-morality issues could not be examined here. Two important areas of personal morality, abortion and same-sex relations, were looked at in detail but there was no consideration of other 'conscience' issues, such as euthanasia (or assisted dying), or areas of social equality, such as gender or racial, matters where religious adherents may have strong views shaped by beliefs and levels of commitment and where specific denominational traditions may have long-established teachings articulated by their leaders. A third constraint is that, invariably if not inevitably, the empirical analyses performed here relied on social surveys and opinion polls sampling the general adult population, from which the religious groups were constructed and analysed. Given this, the across survey examination of religious affiliation was not as finely-grained as it could have been, particularly the difficulties of disaggregating the 'other Christian category' for some surveys which encompasses different Nonconformist traditions and unaffiliated Christians. The exception to this general limitation was the denomination-specific survey of Catholics used to undertake a more focused analysis of attitudinal variation on the issue of abortion, one of particular historical significance for the Roman Catholic Church's social teaching. Therefore, while this study has made a major contribution to scholarly inquiry into change and continuity in the socio-political attitudes of religious groups in Britain across recent decades, as well as ascertaining the views of the general population towards religious authority, there is clearly a need for more focused empirical research examining the religious engagement, social attitudes and political involvement of specific faith communities.

Notes

Chapter 2   Religious Authority

1   The social grade scheme has commonly been used by market research organ-isations for opinion polling and has been employed in some academic-led social surveys. The detailed classification is as follows (grade; status; occupa-tion): *A*: upper middle class – higher managerial, administrative, or profes-sional; *B*: middle class – intermediate managerial, administrative, or professional; *C1*: lower middle class – supervisory or clerical, junior manage-rial, administrative, or professional; *C2*: skilled working class – skilled manual workers; *D*: working class – semi-skilled and unskilled manual workers; *E*: lowest level of subsistence – state pensioners or widows (no other earner), casual or lowest grade workers. The six categories are generally col-lapsed into four groupings for the purposes of analysis, AB, C1, C2 and DE, which is reflected in this and subsequent chapters.

2   Further analysis was undertaken of the EVS 2008 survey to examine the impact of religious factors on public confidence in each societal institution shown in Table 2.6. This involved estimating separate binary logistic regres-sions and, in each case, the model only included the religious factors. There was considerable variation in the explanatory impact of religious factors across institutions (as shown in the Nagelkerke R Square statistic for each model). They accounted for 42.0 percent of the variance in confidence in the church, but much lower for the other institutions – ranging from 1.0 percent (the education system) to 5.0 percent (the armed forces).

Chapter 3   Religion and Party Choice

1   For a detailed analysis of the political and electoral fortunes of Christian parties in Britain, see Bruce (2012: 122–38). While this chapter does not examine party support patterns for non-Christian religions, due to the gen-erally small sample sizes in the surveys analysed, there is an extensive body of work on the historical patterns of voting (and political attitudes) of the Jewish community in Britain (see, for example, Alderman 1995).

2   Parts of this chapter – specifically, some of the sections based on analysis of the BES surveys – draw on some of the material and analysis contained in the recent Theos report (2014), *Values and Voting in the UK: Does Religion Count?*, co-written by the author and Nick Spencer.

3   The author is very grateful to Dr Clive Field for supplying the relevant data tables from these two Mass Observation surveys.

4   Prior to this, local studies of political attitudes and voting behaviour shed some light on the variable connection between religion and political parties depending on the area studied. For example, Birch's study of the town of Glossop in north-west England found that amongst industrial workers,

Anglicans were much more likely to have voted for the Conservative Party in the 1951 general election compared to Catholics, Nonconformists and those with no religion (1959: 112).

5 The BSA surveys undertaken in 2001, 2005 and 2010 also asked respondents about voting behaviour at the relevant general election. Inspection of the data shows that Catholics were much more likely to vote for Labour compared to the Conservatives at each election. Anglicans were more likely to have voted for the Conservative Party, with the exception of 2001, where they reported a higher level of support for Labour. Ipsos MORI data on party support by religious affiliation at the 1992–2005 general elections also show Catholics' greater tendency to support Labour (Ipsos MORI 2005b).

6 The BES 2010 CIPS dataset was obtained from the main BES 2009–10 website at: http://bes2009-10.org/.

Chapter 4   Religion and Ideology

1 The proportion in each EVS survey sample with missing data for the left-right self-placement question is as follows: 1981: 17.1 percent; 1990: 8.3 percent; 1999: 18.8 percent; 2008: 20.5 percent. The proportion missing in each BES survey is as follows: 1997: 16.3 percent; 2001: not applicable; 2005: 16.6 percent.

2 The proportion of missing data for the left-right self-placement scale in each ESS survey is as follows: 2002: 10.1 percent; 2004: 9.9 percent; 2006: 11.5 percent; 2008: 9.9 percent; 2010: 16.2 percent; 2012: 17.2 percent.

Chapter 5   Religion and Abortion

1 The October 1974 BES survey did not ask directly about the frequency of attendance, but instead asked the following question to respondents who said they belonged to a religion: 'To what extent would you say you are now a practicing member: very much so, to some extent, or not really?' Those who said 'very much so' were much more likely to think that the availability of abortion had gone too far (62.5 percent), compared to those responding 'to some extent' (49.5 percent) or 'not really' (34.0 percent).

2 Data from polls conducted by MORI in 1980 and 1997 also show that Catholics became less opposed to abortion over time. Disagreement with the statement that 'abortion should be made legally available for all who want it' fell from 56.0 percent in 1980 to 38.0 percent in 1997, while agreement increased from 34.0 percent to 50.0 percent. The author is grateful to Dr Clive Field for supplying these data.

3 The EVS surveys asked about approval or disapproval regarding medical grounds for abortion, but only in 1981 and 1990 (question wording: 'Where it is likely that the child would be born physically handicapped' and 'Where the mother's health is at risk by the pregnancy'). Inspection of the responses based on the same set of religious factors used in Tables 5.12 and 5.13 shows a similar pattern of opposition. That is, Catholics and other Christians, as well as frequent-attenders, were most likely to disapprove of abortion under both sets of circumstances, as were members of a religious group, those who

saw themselves as a religious person, those who believed in God, and those who thought there is a personal God. In both surveys, levels of disapproval were generally lower for the question asking about the health of the mother.

4 These group differences are also evident from recent opinion polls which have asked about attitudes towards abortion. For example, a YouGov survey undertaken in November 2007 (n=1,983) of adults in Britain asked the following question: 'It should be legal for a woman to have an abortion when she has an unwanted pregnancy?' Protestants and those who did not profess a religious affiliation were more likely to express agreement with this statement (58.0 percent and 74.0 percent, respectively) than were Catholics (43.0 percent). Amongst Catholics, 27.0 percent disagreed compared to just 7.0 percent and 4.0 percent, respectively, of Protestants and those with no religious affiliation (YouGov 2007).

5 Thorup Larsen et al. note that: 'Since 1967, there have been a series of unsuccessful attempts to put abortion back on the political agenda and thereby to restrict access. Bills have regularly been submitted and occasionally debated in parliament, and more recently amendments to government bills have been offered; most of these provide for tightening the normal time limits allowed for abortions or for removing the statistical argument and thereby limiting the discretionary space of medical decisions' (2012: 121).

6 Similarly, compared to Anglicans and those with no religion, Catholics have tended to hold more restrictive views towards euthanasia or assisted suicide, as evidenced by historic polling (*New Humanist* 1976, 1979) and more recent surveys (Gledhill and Gibb 2013; YouGov 2013a). For further analysis of religion and attitudes on this topic, see Clery et al. (2007) and McAndrew (2010). For a study of Catholics' attitudes, see Clements (2014f).

Chapter 6   Religion, Homosexuality and Gay Rights

1 The BES series asked the following question about gay rights in the 1987, 1992 and 1997 surveys: 'Do you think Britain has gone too far or not gone far enough in attempts to give equal opportunities to homosexuals, that is, gays and lesbians?' Analysis of the responses based on affiliation and attendance shows that the proportions saying 'gone much too far' or 'gone too far' fell across-the-board over the decade. In each survey, those most likely to give this response are frequent-attenders and Anglicans and other Christians. For religious attendance, the gap in the levels of those responding 'gone too far' widened over time between, on the one hand, frequent-attenders and, on the other, infrequent- and non-attenders. Based on affiliation the gap also widened, particularly between, on the one hand, those with no religion and, on the other, Anglicans and other Christians. In each survey, Catholics were somewhat less likely than other Christian traditions to think that equal rights had gone too far.

2 The EVS 2008 survey also asked a similar question on this topic ('Homosexual couples should be able to adopt children'), with response options ranging from 'strongly agree' through to 'strongly disagree'. Analysis of the data shows a similar pattern to that obtained for the most recent BSA

survey. That is, in terms of attendance, disagreement is higher amongst frequent-attenders (54.1 percent) compared to infrequent-attenders (43.5 percent) and non-attenders (40.1 percent); and, for affiliation, highest amongst other Christians (60.7 percent), lower at 48.8 percent for Anglicans and 44.3 percent for Catholics; and lowest amongst those with no religion (at 35.1 percent).

Chapter 7   Religion and Foreign Policy

1 Based on combining responses to the BSA question discussed already and to a follow-up question, respondents can be classified according to which identity they think *best* describes themselves. Anglicans are much more likely to see being British or English as best describing themselves (42.7 percent and 50.1 percent, respectively) compared to Catholics (respectively, 30.7 percent and 30.3 percent). Catholics were more likely than Anglicans to see European as best describing themselves, albeit the proportions were very small (at 8.9 percent and 1.3 percent, respectively). Catholics were also more likely to choose national identities such as Scottish and Irish.

2 Unfortunately, due to changes over time in the country-specific categories applicable to Britain for the religious denomination variable in the EB surveys, separate data are not available after 1989 for those who report they belong to the Church of England (as this group has been coded as part of a broader 'Protestant' category).

3 For a detailed treatment of the responses of the Church of England to Britain's involvement in recent military conflicts, see Lee, P. (2012).

4 The questions on Iraq and Afghanistan were each administered to approximately half of the sample of the BSA 2011 survey: Iraq: n=1,673 (50.5 percent); Afghanistan: n=1,638 (49.5 percent); total n=3,311.

Appendix 1 Measures of Religion in the Recurrent Social Surveys

Survey	Years	Measure	Wording
BES	1963, 1964, 1966	Affiliation	'What is your religion?'
BES	October 1974	Affiliation	'Do you belong to any religious denomination?' If 'yes': 'Which denomination?'
BES	1979	Affiliation	'Do you belong to any church or religious group?' If 'yes': 'Which denomination?'
BES	1983, 1987, 1992, 1997	Affiliation	'Do you regard yourself as belonging to any particular religion?' If 'yes': 'Which one?'
BES	2001	Affiliation	'Do you regard yourself as belonging to any particular religion?' If 'yes': 'Which denomination?'
BES	2005	Affiliation	Do you regard yourself as belonging to any particular religion? If 'yes': 'Which denomination or religion?'
BES	2010	Affiliation	Do you regard yourself as belonging to any particular religion? If 'yes': 'Which religion or denomination?'
BES	1963, 1964, 1966	Attendance	'How often do you attend church (chapel) (synagogue)?'
BES	October 1974	Attendance	'To what extent would you say you are now a practising member'
BES	1979	Attendance	'How often do you attend church, chapel or other place of worship?'
BES	1983, 1987	Attendance	'Apart from special occasions, such as weddings, funerals, baptisms and so on, how often nowadays do you attend services or meetings connected with your religion?'
BES	1992, 1997	Attendance	'Apart from such special occasions as weddings, funerals, baptisms and so on, how often nowadays do you attend services or meetings connected with your religion?'

Survey	Years	Measure	Wording
BES	2010	Attendance	'In the past 12 months, how often did you participate in religious activities or attend religious services or meetings with other people, other than for events such as weddings and funerals?'
BSA	1983–2012	Affiliation	'Which religion or denomination do you consider yourself as belonging to?'
BSA	1983–2012	Attendance	'Apart from such special occasions as weddings, funerals and baptisms, how often nowadays do you attend services or meetings connected with your religion?
BSA	1991, 1998, 2008	Belief in God	'Which best describes your beliefs about God?'
BSA	1991, 1993, 1995, 1998, 2000, 2008	Belief in God	'Which statement comes closest to expressing what you believe about God?'
BSA	1991, 1998, 2008	Belief in God	'Do you agree or disagree that ... There is a God who concerns Himself with every human being personally?'
BSA	1991, 1998, 2008	Belief in God	'Do you agree or disagree that ... To me, life is meaningful only because God exists?'
BSA	2008	Belief in God	'Are you absolutely sure you believe in God, somewhat sure, not quite sure, not at all sure, or are you sure you do not believe in God?'
BSA	2008	Belief in God	'I have my own way of connecting with God without churches or religious services'
BSA	2008	Belief in God	'If you have religious beliefs, do you think that God is directly involved in your affairs?'
BSA	2008	Belief in God	'Do you think that God is angered by human sin?'
EVS	1981	Affiliation	'What is your religious denomination?'
EVS	1990, 1999, 2008	Affiliation	'Do you belong to a religious denomination?' If 'yes': 'Which one?'
EVS	1981, 1990, 1999, 2008	Identity	'Independently of whether you go to church or not, would you say you are ...'
EVS	1981, 1990, 1999, 2008	Attendance	'Apart from weddings, funerals and christenings, about how often do you attend religious services these days?'
EVS	1981, 1990, 1999, 2008	Belief in God	'Which, if any, of the following do you believe in? God.'

Survey	Years	Measure	Wording
EVS	1981, 1990, 1999, 2008	Belief in God	'Which of these statements comes closest to your beliefs?'
EVS	1981	Membership	'Which, if any, of the following do you belong to?' 'Religious or church organisations.'
EVS	1990, 1999, 2008	Membership	'Please look carefully at the following list of voluntary organisations and activities and say ... which, if any, do you belong to?'
ESS	2008, 2010, 2012	Affiliation	'Do you consider yourself as belonging to any particular religion or denomination?' If 'Yes': 'Which one?'
ESS	2002–2012	Attendance	'Apart from special occasions such as weddings and funerals, about how often do you attend religious services nowadays?'
ESS	2002–2012	Prayer	'Apart from when you are at religious services, how often, if at all, do you pray?'
ESS	2002–2012	Religiosity	'Regardless of whether you belong to a particular religion, how religious would you say you are?'
EB	1973	Affiliation	'Do you belong to some religious denomination?'
EB	1974–2006	Affiliation	'Do you regard (consider) yourself as belonging to a (particular) religion? If 'yes': 'Which of them?' 'Which one?'

Appendix 2 Measurement of Independent Variables Used in the Multivariate Analyses

This Appendix provides details on the measurement of the most commonly used independent variables employed in the multivariate analyses in Chapters 2–7. Where variable measurement differs because of the specific survey being used or other reasons, this is usually noted in the relevant chapter.

Sex: measured as a dichotomous variable (1 if male; 0 if female).

Age: measured as a continuous variable.

Marital status: measured as a dichotomous variable (1 if married; 0 if has some other status)

Children in household: measured as a dichotomous variable (1 if there are children in the household; 0 if there are none).

Education: measured as a dichotomous variable (1 if has a degree-level or higher-level qualification; 0 if has lower-level or no qualifications).

Social class: measured as a dichotomous variable (1 if a member of the salariat; 0 if other occupational grade).

Tenure: measured as a dummy variable (1 if an owner-occupier; 0 if in private rental sector or public rental sector – local authority or housing association).

Affiliation: measured as a series of dummy variables (Anglican, Catholic, other Christian, other religion, no religion). In some instances, the other Christian and other religion categories are combined.

Attendance: a scale ranging from 1=never attends through to 7=attends once a week or more.

Party support: measured as a series of dummy variables (Conservative, Labour, Liberal Democrat, other party, no party).

Additional religion variables used in analyses of the EVS and ESS surveys are as follows:

EVS

Membership (of a church or religious organisation): measured as a dichotomous variable (1 if a member; 0 if not)

Religious person: measured as a dichotomous variable (1 if is a religious person; 0 if some other response).

Believe in God: measured as a dichotomous variable (1 if believes in God; 0 if does not believe in God or some other response)

Personal God: measured as a dichotomous variable (1 if believes there is a personal God, 0 if believes there is not a personal God or some other response).

ESS

Prayer: measured as a scale (ranging from 1 if never prays through to 7 if prays several times a day).

Religiosity: measured as a scale (ranging from 1 if not at all religious through to 10 if very religious).

Appendix 3   Attitudes Based on Additional Questions Asking about God, BSA 2008

| Variable | Category | Chapter 2 | | Death penalty: Agree (%) | Chapter 4 | Censorship on religious grounds: Agree (%) | Abortion if strong chance of a serious defect: Disapprove (%) | Chapter 5 | Chapter 6 |
		Not influence voters: Agree (%)	Not influence government: Agree (%)		Censorship for moral standards: Agree (%)			Abortion if family cannot afford more children: Disapprove (%)	Same-sex relations: Wrong (%)
Belief in God	Absolutely sure do believe	–	–	60.1	70.5	–	–	–	–
	Other response	–	–	62.5	59.7	–	–	–	–
	Sure do not believe	–	–	60.0	48.1	–	–	–	–
God is directly involved in your affairs	Yes – definitely or probably	71.8	59.2	57.0	70.5	38.2	23.8	47.8	47.2
	No – probably or definitely not	77.0	70.3	61.7	50.6	23.2	7.9	29.6	29.5
	Don't believe in God	80.4	79.1	55.1	42.7	15.0	5.9	29.7	21.0
Have own way of connecting with God	Agree	77.7	69.3	60.9	65.7	31.0	12.8	37.4	36.9
	Neither	75.2	70.6	56.6	55.1	23.5	11.0	35.6	32.0
	Disagree	76.1	70.2	56.1	56.2	21.0	15.8	36.8	34.1

Variable	Category	Chapter 2 Not influence voters: Agree (%)	Chapter 2 Not influence government: Agree (%)	Death penalty: Agree (%)	Chapter 4 Censorship for moral standards: Agree (%)	Censorship on religious grounds: Agree (%)	Abortion if strong chance of a serious defect: Disapprove (%)	Chapter 5 Abortion if family cannot afford more children: Disapprove (%)	Chapter 6 Same-sex relations: Wrong (%)
God is angered by human sin	Yes – definitely or probably	72.8	61.4	61.9	70.5	39.6	22.8	49.2	46.0
	No – probably or definitely not	75.3	70.2	58.3	59.4	24.0	9.3	29.8	31.6
	Don't believe in God	92.9	75.4	52.6	35.7	11.1	7.0	35.2	26.8

Source: BSA 2008 survey.

List of Survey Datasets

British Election Study

Alt, J., Crewe, I. M. and Sarlvik, B., British Election Study, February 1974; Cross-Section Survey [computer file]. Colchester, Essex: UK Data Archive [distributor], 1976. SN: 359, http://dx.doi.org/10.5255/UKDA-SN-359-1.

Brand, J. A. and Mitchell, J. C., General Election in Scotland, 1992 [computer file]. Colchester, Essex: UK Data Archive [distributor], March 1994. SN: 3171, http://dx.doi.org/10.5255/UKDA-SN-3171-1.

Butler, D. and Stokes, D. E., Political Change in Britain, 1969–1970 [computer file]. Colchester, Essex: UK Data Archive [distributor], January 1980. SN: 1093, http://dx.doi.org/10.5255/UKDA-SN-1093-1.

Butler, D. and Stokes, D. E., Political Change in Britain, 1963–1970; Merged File [computer file]. Colchester, Essex: UK Data Archive [distributor], January 1974. SN: 44, http://dx.doi.org/10.5255/UKDA-SN-44-1.

Clarke, H. et al., British Election Study, 2005: Face-to-Face Survey [computer file]. Colchester, Essex: UK Data Archive [distributor], November 2006. SN: 5494, http://dx.doi.org/10.5255/UKDA-SN-5494-1.

Heath, A. et al., British Election Study Ethnic Minority Survey, 2010 [computer file]. Colchester, Essex: UK Data Archive [distributor], April 2012. SN: 6970.

Heath, A. et al., British General Election Study, 1997; Cross-Section Survey [computer file]. 2nd Edition. Colchester, Essex: UK Data Archive [distributor], May 1999. SN: 3887, http://dx.doi.org/10.5255/UKDA-SN-3887-1.

Heath, A. et al., British General Election Study, 1992; Cross-Section Survey [computer file]. Colchester, Essex: UK Data Archive [distributor], April 1993. SN: 2981, http://dx.doi.org/10.5255/UKDA-SN-2981-1.

Heath, A., Jowell, R. and Curtice, J. K., British General Election Study, 1983; Cross-Section Survey [computer file]. Colchester, Essex: UK Data Archive [distributor], 1983. SN: 2005, http://dx.doi.org/10.5255/UKDA-SN-2005-1.

Heath, A., Jowell, R. and Curtice, J. K., British General Election Study, 1987; Cross-Section Survey [computer file]. 2nd Edition. Colchester, Essex: UK Data Archive [distributor], April 1993. SN: 2568, http://dx.doi.org/10.5255/UKDA-SN-2568-1.

Clarke, H. et al., British General Election Study, 2001; Cross-Section Survey [computer file]. Colchester, Essex: UK Data Archive [distributor], March 2003. SN: 4619, http://dx.doi.org/10.5255/UKDA-SN-4619-1.

Crewe, I. M., Robertson, D. R. and Sarlvik, B., British Election Study, May 1979; Cross-Section Survey [computer file]. Colchester, Essex: UK Data Archive [distributor], 1981. SN: 1533, http://dx.doi.org/10.5255/UKDA-SN-1533-1.

Crewe, I. M., Robertson, D. R. and Sarlvik, B., British Election Study, October 1974; Cross-Section Survey [computer file]. Colchester, Essex: UK Data Archive [distributor], 1977. SN: 666, http://dx.doi.org/10.5255/UKDA-SN-666-1.

Crewe, I. M., Robertson, D. R. and Sarlvik, B., British Election Study, October 1974; Scottish Cross-Section Sample [computer file]. Colchester, Essex: UK Data Archive [distributor], 1977. SN: 681, http://dx.doi.org/10.5255/UKDA-SN-681-1.

McCrone, D. et al., Scottish Election Survey, 1997 [computer file]. 2nd Edition. Colchester, Essex: UK Data Archive [distributor], June 1999. SN: 3889, http://dx.doi.org/10.5255/UKDA-SN-3889-1.

Miller, W. L. and Brand, J. A., Scottish Election Study, 1979 [computer file]. Colchester, Essex: UK Data Archive [distributor], 1981. SN: 1604, http://dx.doi.org/10.5255/UKDA-SN-1604-1.

British Social Attitudes

NatCen Social Research, British Social Attitudes Survey, 2012 [computer file]. Colchester, Essex: UK Data Archive [distributor], April 2014. SN: 7476, http://dx.doi.org/10.5255/UKDA-SN-7476-1.

NatCen Social Research, British Social Attitudes Survey, 2011 [computer file]. Colchester, Essex: UK Data Archive [distributor], March 2013. SN: 7237, http://dx.doi.org/10.5255/UKDA-SN-7237-1.

National Centre for Social Research, British Social Attitudes Survey, 2010 [computer file]. Colchester, Essex: UK Data Archive [distributor], February 2012. SN: 6969, http://dx.doi.org/10.5255/UKDA-SN-6969-1.

National Centre for Social Research, British Social Attitudes Survey, 2009 [computer file]. Colchester, Essex: UK Data Archive [distributor], February 2011. SN: 6695, http://dx.doi.org/10.5255/UKDA-SN-6695-1.

National Centre for Social Research, British Social Attitudes Survey, 2008 [computer file]. Colchester, Essex: UK Data Archive [distributor], March 2010. SN: 6390, http://dx.doi.org/10.5255/UKDA-SN-6390-1.

National Centre for Social Research, British Social Attitudes Survey, 2007 [computer file]. Colchester, Essex: UK Data Archive [distributor], July 2009. SN: 6240, http://dx.doi.org/10.5255/UKDA-SN-6240-1.

National Centre for Social Research, British Social Attitudes Survey, 2006 [computer file]. Colchester, Essex: UK Data Archive [distributor], April 2008. SN: 5823, http://dx.doi.org/10.5255/UKDA-SN-5823-1.

National Centre for Social Research, British Social Attitudes Survey, 2005 [computer file]. 2nd Edition. Colchester, Essex: UK Data Archive [distributor], October 2007. SN: 5618, http://dx.doi.org/10.5255/UKDA-SN-5618-1.

National Centre for Social Research, British Social Attitudes Survey, 2004 [computer file]. Colchester, Essex: UK Data Archive [distributor], February 2006. SN: 5329, http://dx.doi.org/10.5255/UKDA-SN-5329-1.

National Centre for Social Research, British Social Attitudes Survey, 2003 [computer file]. Colchester, Essex: UK Data Archive [distributor], September 2005. SN: 5235, http://dx.doi.org/10.5255/UKDA-SN-5235-1.

National Centre for Social Research, British Social Attitudes Survey, 2002 [computer file]. Colchester, Essex: UK Data Archive [distributor], March 2004. SN: 4838, http://dx.doi.org/10.5255/UKDA-SN-4838-1.

National Centre for Social Research, British Social Attitudes Survey, 2001 [computer file]. Colchester, Essex: UK Data Archive [distributor], February 2003. SN: 4615, http://dx.doi.org/10.5255/UKDA-SN-4615-1.

National Centre for Social Research, British Social Attitudes Survey, 2000 [computer file]. Colchester, Essex: UK Data Archive [distributor], March 2002. SN: 4486, http://dx.doi.org/10.5255/UKDA-SN-4486-1.

National Centre for Social Research, British Social Attitudes Survey, 1999 [computer file]. Colchester, Essex: UK Data Archive [distributor], January 2001. SN: 4318, http://dx.doi.org/10.5255/UKDA-SN-4318-1.

Social and Community Planning Research, British Social Attitudes Survey, 1998 [computer file]. Colchester, Essex: UK Data Archive [distributor], June 2000. SN: 4131, http://dx.doi.org/10.5255/UKDA-SN-4131-1.

Social and Community Planning Research, British Social Attitudes Survey, 1997 [computer file]. Colchester, Essex: UK Data Archive [distributor], February 2000. SN: 4072, http://dx.doi.org/10.5255/UKDA-SN-4072-1.

Social and Community Planning Research, British Social Attitudes Survey, 1996 [computer file]. 2nd edition. Colchester, Essex: UK Data Archive [distributor], December 1999. SN: 3921, http://dx.doi.org/10.5255/UKDA-SN-3921-1.

Social and Community Planning Research, British Social Attitudes Survey, 1995 [computer file]. Colchester, Essex: UK Data Archive [distributor], January 1998. SN: 3764, http://dx.doi.org/10.5255/UKDA-SN-3764-1.

Social and Community Planning Research, British Social Attitudes Survey, 1994 [computer file]. Colchester, Essex: UK Data Archive [distributor], August 1996. SN: 3572, http://dx.doi.org/10.5255/UKDA-SN-3572-1.

Social and Community Planning Research, British Social Attitudes Survey, 1993 [computer file]. Colchester, Essex: UK Data Archive [distributor], November 1995. SN: 3439, http://dx.doi.org/10.5255/UKDA-SN-3439-1.

Social and Community Planning Research, British Social Attitudes Survey, 1991 [computer file]. 2nd edition. Colchester, Essex: UK Data Archive [distributor], October 1999. SN: 2952, http://dx.doi.org/10.5255/UKDA-SN-2952-1. SN: 2952, http://dx.doi.org/10.5255/UKDA-SN-2952-1.

Social and Community Planning Research, British Social Attitudes Survey, 1990 [computer file]. Colchester, Essex: UK Data Archive [distributor], November 1991. SN: 2840, http://dx.doi.org/10.5255/UKDA-SN-2840-1.

Social and Community Planning Research, British Social Attitudes Survey, 1989 [computer file]. Colchester, Essex: UK Data Archive [distributor], November 1990. SN: 2723, http://dx.doi.org/10.5255/UKDA-SN-2723-1.

Social and Community Planning Research, British Social Attitudes Survey, 1987 [computer file]. Colchester, Essex: UK Data Archive [distributor], February 1989. SN: 2567, http://dx.doi.org/10.5255/UKDA-SN-2567-1.

Social and Community Planning Research, British Social Attitudes Survey, 1986 [computer file]. Colchester, Essex: UK Data Archive [distributor], February 1988. SN: 2315, http://dx.doi.org/10.5255/UKDA-SN-2315-1.

Social and Community Planning Research, British Social Attitudes Survey, 1985 [computer file]. Colchester, Essex: UK Data Archive [distributor], May 1986. SN: 2096, http://dx.doi.org/10.5255/UKDA-SN-2096-1.

Social and Community Planning Research, British Social Attitudes Survey, 1984 [computer file]. Colchester, Essex: UK Data Archive [distributor], 1985. SN: 2035, http://dx.doi.org/10.5255/UKDA-SN-2035-1.

Social and Community Planning Research, British Social Attitudes Survey, 1983 [computer file]. Colchester, Essex: UK Data Archive [distributor], 1984. SN: 1935, http://dx.doi.org/10.5255/UKDA-SN-1935-1.

Eurobarometer

The Mannheim Eurobarometer Trend File 1970–2002, [Computer file]. GESIS Study ZA3521, 2nd edition (2.01), Cologne, Germany.

European Commission: Eurobarometer 66.1 (2006). TNS OPINION & SOCIAL, Brussels [Producer]. GESIS Data Archive, Cologne. ZA4526 data file version 1.0.1, doi:10.4232/1.10980.

European Commission: Eurobarometer 63.4 (2005). TNS OPINION & SOCIAL, Brussels [Producer]. GESIS Data Archive, Cologne. ZA4411 data file version 1.1.0, doi:10.4232/1.10968.

European Commission: European Communities Studies 1970, Part 2: Great Britain. GESIS Data Archive, Cologne. ZA3651 data file version 1.0.1, doi:10.4232/1.10976.

European Social Survey

ESS Round 6: European Social Survey Round 6 Data (2012). Data file edition 1.1. Norwegian Social Science Data Services, Norway – Data Archive and distributor of ESS data.

ESS Round 5: European Social Survey Round 5 Data (2010). Data file edition 3.0. Norwegian Social Science Data Services, Norway – Data Archive and distributor of ESS data.

ESS Round 4: European Social Survey Round 4 Data (2008). Data file edition 4.1. Norwegian Social Science Data Services, Norway – Data Archive and distributor of ESS data.

ESS Round 3: European Social Survey Round 3 Data (2006). Data file edition 3.4. Norwegian Social Science Data Services, Norway – Data Archive and distributor of ESS data.

ESS Round 2: European Social Survey Round 2 Data (2004). Data file edition 3.3. Norwegian Social Science Data Services, Norway – Data Archive and distributor of ESS data.

ESS Round 1: European Social Survey Round 1 Data (2002). Data file edition 6.3. Norwegian Social Science Data Services, Norway – Data Archive and distributor of ESS data.

European Values Study

European Values Study. 2010. European Values Study 2008, 4th wave, Integrated Dataset. GESIS Data Archive, Cologne, Germany, ZA4800 Data File Version 2.0.0 (2010-11-30) doi:10.4232/1.10188.

European Values Study. 2011c. European Values Study 1999 (release 3, 2011), 3rd wave, Integrated Dataset. GESIS Data Archive, Cologne, Germany, ZA3811 Data File Version 3.0.0 (2011-11-20) doi:10.4232/1.10789.

EVS (2011): European Values Study 1990, 2nd wave, Integrated Dataset. GESIS Data Archive, Cologne, Germany, ZA4460 Data File Version 3.0.0 (2011-11-20) doi:10.4232/1.10790.

EVS (2011): European Values Study 1981, 1st wave, Integrated Dataset. GESIS Data Archive, Cologne, Germany, ZA4438 Data File Version 3.0.0 (2011-11-20) doi:10.4232/1.10791.

Other survey datasets

Almond, Gabriel, and Sidney Verba. Civic Culture Study, 1959-1960. ICPSR07201-v2. Ann Arbor, MI: Inter-university Consortium for Political and Social Research [distributor], 2009-02-12. doi:10.3886/ICPSR07201.v2.

Hornsby-Smith, M. P. and Lee, R. M., Roman Catholic Opinion, 1978 [computer file]. Colchester, Essex: UK Data Archive [distributor], January 1982. SN: 1570, http://dx.doi.org/10.5255/UKDA-SN-1570-1.

Bibliography

Adell Cook, E., Jelen, T. G. and Wilcox, C. (1992), *Between Two Absolutes: Public Opinion and the Politics of Abortion* (San Francisco: Westview Press).

Alden, C. (2002), 'Archbishop Lobbies Blair on Iraq', *The Guardian*, August 6. Available at: http://www.theguardian.com/world/2002/aug/06/iraq.religion.

Alderman, G. (1995), 'Jewish Political Attitudes and Voting Patterns in England 1945–1987', in R. Wistrich (ed.), *Terms of Survival: The Jewish World since 1945* (London: Routledge).

Bader, C. D., Desmond, S. A., Carson Mencken, F. and Johnson, B. R. (2010), 'Divine Justice: The Relationship Between Images of God and Attitudes Toward Criminal Punishment', *Criminal Justice Review*, 35(1): 90–106.

Baker, D. L. (1991), 'Turbulent Priests: Christian Opposition to the Conservative Government since 1979', *The Political Quarterly*, 62(1): 90–105.

Barker, D. C., Hurwitz, J. and Nelson, T. L. (2008), 'Of Crusades and Cultures Wars: "Messianic" Militarism and Political Conflict in the United States', *Journal of Politics*, 70(2): 307–22.

Bates, S. (2003), 'No War Can Be Holy Warns the Archbishop ...', *The Guardian*, February 22. Available at: http://www.theguardian.com/uk/2003/feb/22/iraq.politics.

Bates, S. (2004), *A Church at War: Anglicans and Homosexuality* (London: I. B. Tauris).

Baumgartner, J. C., Francia, P. J. and Morris, J. S. (2008), 'A Clash of Civilisations? The Influence of Religion on Public Opinion on U.S. Foreign Policy in the Middle East', *Political Research Quarterly*, 61(2): 171–9.

Baylor Institute for Studies of Religion (2006), *American Piety in the 21st Century: New Insights to the Depth and Complexity of Religion in the US. Selected Findings from The Baylor Religion Survey*. September 2006, Baylor University. Available at: http://www.baylor.edu/content/services/document.php/33304.pdf.

BBC News (2009), 'UK Muslims Split on Taliban Fight', June 25. Available at: http://news.bbc.co.uk/go/pr/fr/-/1/hi/uk/8119273.stm.

Bebbington, D. (1982), *The Nonconformist Conscience: Chapel and Politics, 1870–1914* (London: Allen & Unwin).

Bingham, J. (2013a), 'Gay Marriage Could Signal Return to "Centuries of Persecution", – Say 1,000 Catholic Priests', *The Daily Telegraph*, January 11. Available from: http://www.telegraph.co.uk/news/religion/9795680/Gay-marriage-could-signal-return-to-centuries-of-persecution-say-1000-Catholic-priests.html.

Bingham, J. (2013b), 'Ethnic-Minority Churches Dismiss Cameron's "Diversity" Arguments for Gay Marriage', *The Daily Telegraph*, April 29. Available from: http://www.telegraph.co.uk/news/religion/10024693/Ethnic-minority-churches-dismiss-Camerons-diversity-arguments-for-gay-marriage.html#mm_hash.

Bingham, J. (2013c), 'More than 500 Imams in Landmark Gay Marriage Protest', *The Daily Telegraph*, May 19. Available from: http://www.telegraph.co.uk/news/religion/10066730/More-than-500-imams-in-landmark-gay-marriage-protest.html.

Bingham, J. (2014), 'Church of England Bishops Do Not Speak for Flock on Welfare, Study Suggests', *Daily Telegraph*, 22 February. Available at: http://www.telegraph.co.uk/news/religion/10654828/Church-of-England-bishops-do-not-speak-for-own-flock-on-welfare-study-suggests.html.

Birch, A. H. (1959), *Small-Town Politics: A Study of Political Life in Glossop* (Oxford: Oxford University Press).

Blake, D. (2007), 'British Catholic Leaders Call for "Change of Attitude" Towards Abortions', *Christian Today*, 25 October. Available at: http://www.christiantoday.com/article/british.catholic.leaders.call.for.change.of.attitude.towards.abortions/14185.htm.

Boffey, D. (2011), 'Archbishop Rowan Williams Backs Revolt Against Coalition's Welfare Cuts', *The Observer*, November 19. Available at: http://www.theguardian.com/politics/2011/nov/19/archbishop-rowan-williams-welfare-reforms.

Boomgaarden, H. G. and Freire, A. (2009), 'Religion and Euroskepticism: Direct, Indirect or No Effects?', *West European Politics*, 32(6): 1240–65.

Boorstein, M. and Craighill, P. M. (2014), 'Pope Francis Faces Church Divided Over Doctrine, Global Poll of Catholics Finds', *The Washington Post*, February 9. Available at: http://www.washingtonpost.com/national/pope-francis-faces-church-divided-over-doctrine-global-poll-of-catholics-finds/2014/02/08/e90ecef4-8f89-11e3-b227-12a45d109e03_story.html.

Brown, C. G. (2006), *Religion and Society in Twentieth-Century Britain* (Harlow: Pearson Education).

Bruce, S. (2012), *Religion and Politics in the United Kingdom* (London: Routledge).

Bruce, S. (2013), 'Post-Secularity and Religion in Britain: An Empirical Assessment', *Journal of Contemporary Religion*, 28(3): 369–84.

Budge, I. and Urwin, D. W. (1966), *Scottish Political Behaviour: A Case Study in British Homogeneity* (London: Longmans).

Butler, D, and Stokes, D. (1969), *Political Change in Britain: Forces Shaping Electoral Choice* (Harmondsworth: Penguin).

Butler, D. and Stokes, D. (1974), *Political Change in Britain: The Evolution of Electoral Choice* (London: Macmillan).

Butt, R. (2011), 'Cardinal Keith O'Brien Warns of Threat from "Aggressive Secularism"', *The Guardian*, April 24. Available at: http://www.guardian.co.uk/world/2011/apr/24/cardinal-keith-obrien-aggressive-secularity?INTCMP=SRCH.

Carrell, S. (2010), 'Scotland's Bishops Urge Voters to Back Champions of Christian Values', *The Guardian*, 22 April. Available at: http://www.theguardian.com/politics/2010/apr/22/scotland-bishops-voters-christian-values.

Catterall, P. (1993), 'Morality and Politics: The Free Churches and the Labour Party Between the Wars', *The Historical Journal*, 36(3): 667–85.

Chapman, J. (1986), 'The Political Implications of Attitudes toward Abortion in Britain', *West European Politics*, 9(1): 7–31.

Chaves, M. (1994), 'Secularization as Declining Religious Authority', *Social Forces*, 72(3): 749–74.

Chaves, M. (2011), *American Religion: Contemporary Trends* (Princeton, NJ: Princeton University Press).

Chaves, M. and Anderson, S. (2012), 'Continuity and Change in American Religion 1972–2008', in P. V. Marsden, *Social Trends in the United States, 1972–2006. Evidence from the General Social Survey* (Princeton: Princeton University Press).

Church Urban Fund (2012), *Bias to the Poor? Christian Attitudes to Poverty in this Country*, with Church Action on Poverty. Available at: http://www.cuf.org.uk/sites/default/files/documents/PDFs/Bias_to_the_poor.pdf.

Clarke, H. (1993), *The Church Under Thatcher* (London: SPCK Publishing).

Clements, B. (2009), 'The Sociological and Psychological Influences on Public Support for the European Union in Britain, 1983–2005', *British Politics*, 3(1): 47–82.

Clements, B. (2013), 'Religion and Ethnic Minority Attitudes in Britain toward the War in Afghanistan', *Politics and Religion*, 6(1): 25–49.

Clements, B. (2014a), 'Christian Affiliation in Britain', *British Religion in Numbers*. Available at: http://www.brin.ac.uk/news/2014/christian-affiliation-in-britain/.

Clements, B. (2014b), 'Partisan Attachments and Attitudes towards Same-Sex Marriage in Britain', *Parliamentary Affairs*, 67(1): 232–44.

Clements, B. (2014c), 'The Correlates of Traditional Religious Beliefs in Britain', *Journal of Beliefs & Values: Studies in Religion & Education*, 35(3): 278–90.

Clements, B. (2014d), 'The Religious Sources of Opposition to Abortion in Britain: Assessing the Role of "Belonging", "Behaving" and "Believing"', *Sociology*, 48(2): 364–81.

Clements, B. (2014e), 'Research Note: Assessing the Determinants of the Contemporary Social Attitudes of Catholics in Britain: Abortion and Homosexuality', *Journal of Contemporary Religion*, 29(3): 491–501.

Clements, B. (2014f), 'An Assessment of Long-Term and Contemporary Attitudes towards "Sanctity of Life" Issues amongst Roman Catholics in Britain', *Journal of Religion in Europe*, 7(3–4): 269–300.

Clements, B. and Field, C. D. (2014) 'The Polls – Trends: Public Opinion toward Homosexuality and Gay Rights in Great Britain', *Public Opinion Quarterly*, 78(2): 523–47.

Clements, B. and Spencer, N. (2014), *Values and Voting in the UK: Does Religion Count?* (London: Theos).

Clery, E., McLean, S. and Phillips, M. (2007), 'Quickening Death: The Euthanasia Debate', in A. Park, J. Curtice, K. Thompson, M. Phillips and M. Johnson (eds), *British Social Attitudes: 23rd Report. Perspectives on a Changing Society* (London: Sage).

ComRes (2009), *Pollwatch*, 23 March 2009.

Crockett, A. and Voas, D. (2003), 'A Divergence of Views: Attitude Change and the Religious Crisis over Homosexuality', *Sociological Research Online*, 8. Available at: http://www.socresonline.org.uk/8/4/crockett.html.

Daily Telegraph, 'Majority of Public in Favour of Hanging', 22 December 1964.

Davie, G. (1994), *Religion in Britain since 1945: Believing Without Belonging* (Oxford: Blackwell).

Davie, G. (2015), *Religion in Britain: A Persistent Paradox* (Oxford: John Wiley & Sons).

Davis, N. J. and Robinson, R. V. (1999), 'Their Brothers' Keepers? Orthodox Religionists, Modernists, and Economic Justice in Europe', *American Journal of Sociology*, 104(6): 1631–65.

Denver, D., Carman, C. and Johns, R. (2012), *Elections and Voters in Britain*, 3rd edition (Basingtoke: Palgrave).

Dowley, K. M. and Silver, B. D. (2011), 'Support for Europe among Europe's Ethnic, Religious, and Immigrant Minorities', *International Journal of Public Opinion Research*, 22(3): 315–337.

Durham, M. (1997), '"God Wants Us to be in Different Parties": Religion and Politics in Britain Today', *Parliamentary Affairs*, 50(2): 202–12.

Evans, G. (2002), 'In Search of Tolerance', in A. Park, J. Curtice, K. Thomson, L. Jarvis and C. Bromley (eds), *British Social Attitudes: The 19th Report, 2002/2003* (London: Sage).

Evans, G., Heath, A. and Lalljee, M. (1996), 'Measuring Left-Right and Libertarian-Authoritarian Values in the British Electorate', *The British Journal of Sociology*, 47(1): 93–112.

Field, C. D. (2007), 'Islamophobia in Contemporary Britain: The Evidence of the Opinion Polls, 1988–2006', *Islam and Christian-Muslim Relations*, 18(4): 447–77.

Field, C. D. (2012), 'Revisiting Islamophobia in Contemporary Britain, 2007–10', in M. Helbling (ed.), *Islamophobia in the West: Measuring and Explaining Individual Attitudes* (London: Routledge).

Field, C. D. (2014a), 'Christian Country', *British Religion in Numbers*. Available at: http://www.brin.ac.uk/news/2014/christian-country-and-other-news/.

Field, C. D. (2014b), 'Measuring Religious Affiliation in Great Britain: The 2011 Census in Historical and Methodological Context', *Religion*, 44(3): 357–82.

Field, C. D. (2014c), 'Another Window on British Secularization: Public Attitudes to Church and Clergy since the 1960s', *Contemporary British History*, 28(2): 190–218.

Field, C. D. (2014d), 'No Popery's Ghost. Does Popular Anti-Catholicism Survive in Contemporary Britain?', *Journal of Religion in Europe*, 7: 116–49.

Field, C. D. (2015), *Britain's Last Religious Revival? Quantifying Belonging, Behaving and Believing in the Long 1950s* (Basingstoke: Palgrave Macmilllan).

Field, C. D. (forthcoming), 'Repurposing Religious Surveys', in L. Woodhead (ed.), *How to Research Religion: Putting Methods into Practice* (Oxford: Oxford University Press).

Filby, E. (2013), 'The Death of Tory Anglicanism', *The Spectator*, November 23. Available at: http://www.spectator.co.uk/features/9081451/beyond-belief-7/.

Filby, L. (2010), *God and Mrs Thatcher: Religion and Politics in 1980s Britain*. PhD thesis, University of Warwick. Available at: http://webcat.warwick.ac.uk/record=b2482617~S15.

Francis, L., Robbins, M. and Astley, J. (2005), *Fragmented Faith? Exposing the Fault-Lines in the Church of England* (Carlisle: Paternoster Press).

Francome, C. (1989), *Abortion and Public Opinion* (London: Abortion Law Reform Association and National Abortion Campaign).

Froese, P. and Bader, C. (2008), 'Unraveling Religious Worldviews: The Relationship between Images of God and Political Ideology in a Cross-Cultural Analysis', *The Sociological Quarterly*, 49(4): 689–718.

Froese, P. and Bader, C. D. (2007), 'God in America: Why Theology is Not Simply the Concern of Philosophers', *Journal for the Scientific Study of Religion*, 46(4): 465–81.

Froese, P. and Mencken, F. C. (2009), 'A U.S. Holy War? The Effects of Religion on Iraq War Policy Attitudes', *Social Science Quarterly*, 90(1): 103–16.

Gabel, M. J. (1998), *Interests and Integration. Market Liberalization, Public Opinion, and European Union* (Ann Arbor: University of Michigan Press).

Gallup, G. H. (1976a), *The Gallup International Public Opinion Polls: Great Britain, 1937–1975*, Volume 2 (New York: Random House).

Gallup, G. H. (1976b), *The Gallup International Public Opinion Polls: Great Britain, 1937–1975*, Volume 1 (New York: Random House).

Geddes, A. (2013), *British and the European Union* (Basingstoke: Palgrave Macmillan).

George, S. (1998), *An Awkward Partner: Britain in the European Community* (Oxford: Oxford University Press).

Gerhards, J. (2010), 'Non-Discrimination towards Homosexuality: The European Union's Policy and Citizens' Attitudes towards Homosexuality in 27 European Countries', *International Sociology*, 25(1): 5–28.

Gill, R. (2003), *The Empty Church Revisited* (London: Ashgate).

Gill, R., Hadaway, C. K. and Marler, P. L. (1998), 'Is Religious Belief Declining in Britain?', *Journal for the Scientific Study of Religion*, 37(3): 507–16.

Gledhill, R. (2003), 'Church Insists Iraq War Must Have UN Backing', *The Times*, February 26. Available at: http://www.thetimes.co.uk/tto/news/world/article1970310.ece.

Gledhill, R. and Gibb, F. (2013), 'Christians Back Change in Assisted Suicide Law, Poll Finds', *The Times*, May 1. Available at: http://www.thetimes.co.uk/tto/faith/article3752991.ece.

Glendinning, T. (2014), 'The Public Presence of Religion in Western Europe: Its Social Significance Among Religious Constituencies Lying Between the Secular and Churchgoing Christians?', *International Journal of Social Science Studies*, 2(1): 51–64.

Glendinning, T. and Bruce, S. (2011), 'Privatization or Deprivatization: British Attitudes About the Public Presence of Religion', *Journal for the Scientific Study of Religion*, 50(3): 503–16.

Gover, D. (2011), *Turbulent Priests? The Archbishop of Canterbury in Contemporary English politics* (London: Theos). Available at: http://www.theosthinktank.co.uk/files/files/Reports/TheosTurbulentPriests2.pdf.

Greeley, A. and Hout, M. (2006), *The Truth about Conservative Christians: What They Think and What They Believe* (Chicago: University of Chicago Press).

Green, D. M. (2007), *The Europeans: Political Identity in an Emerging Polity* (Boulder, CO: Lynne Rienner).

Guth, J. (2013a), 'Religion and American Public Attitudes on War and Peace', *Asian Journal of Peacebuilding*, 1(2): 227–52.

Guth, J. (2013b), 'Militant and Cooperative Internationalism Among American Religious Publics', *Politics and Religion Journal*, 7(2): 315–43.

Guth, J. L. (2009), 'Religion and American Public Opinion: Foreign Policy Issues', in C. E. Smidt, L. A. Kellstedt and J. L. Guth (eds), *The Oxford Handbook of Religion and American Politics* (New York: Oxford University Press).

Guth, J. L. (2012), 'Religion and Public Opinion on Security: A Comparative Perspective', in C. Seiple, D. Hoover and P. Otis (eds), *Routledge Handbook of Religion and Security* (New York: Routledge).

Hagevi, M. (2000), 'Religiosity and Swedish Opinion on the European Union', *Journal for the Scientific Study of Religion*, 41(4): 759–69.

Hagevi, M. (2002), 'Religiosity and Swedish Opinion on the European Union', *Journal for the Scientific Study of Religion*, 41(4): 759–69.

Harrop, M. and Miller, W. L. (1987), *Elections and Voters: A Comparative Introduction* (Basingstoke: Macmillan Education).

Hayes, B. C. (1995a), 'The Impact of Religious Identification on Political Attitudes: An International Comparison', *Sociology of Religion*, 56(2): 177–94.

Hayes, B. C. (1995b), 'Religious Identification and Moral Attitudes: The British Case', *British Journal of Sociology*, 46(3): 457–74.

Hayes, B. C. and Dowds, L. (2013), 'Religion and Attitudes Towards Gay Rights in Northern Ireland: The God Gap Revisited', in S. D. Brunn (ed.), *The Changing World Religion Map: Sacred Places, Identities, Practices and Politics* (New York: Springer).

Hayes, B. C. and Moran-Ellis, J. (1997), 'Party Identification and Attitudes Towards Homosexuals in Great Britain', *International Journal of Public Opinion Research*, 7(1): 23–39.

Heath, A. F., Fisher, S. D., Rosenblatt, G., Sanders, D. and Sobolewska, M. (2013), *The Political Integration of Ethnic Minorities in Britain* (Oxford: Oxford University Press).

Heath, A., Jowell, R., Curtice, J., Evans, G., Field, J. and Witherspoon, S. (1991), *Understanding Political Change* (Oxford: Pergamon Press).

Heath, A., Martin, J. and Elgenius G. (2007), 'Who Do We Think We Are? The Decline of Traditional Social Identities', in A. Park, J. Curtice, K. Thompson, M. Phillips and M. Johnson (eds), *British Social Attitudes: 23rd Report. Perspectives on a Changing Society* (London: Sage).

Heath, A., Savage, M. and Senior, N. (2013), 'Social Class: The Role of Class in Shaping Social Attitudes', in A. Park, C. Bryson, E. Clery, J. Curtice and M. Phillips (eds), *British Social Attitudes: The 30th Report* (London: NatCen Social Research). Available at: www.bsa-30.natcen.ac.uk.

Heath, A., Taylor, B., Brook, L. and Park, A. (1999), 'British National Sentiment', *British Journal of Political Science*, 29(1): 155–75.

Heath, A., Taylor, B. and Toka, G. (1993a), 'Religion, Morality and Politics', in R. Jowell, L. Brook and L. Dowds (eds), *International Social Attitudes: The 10th BSA Report* (Aldershot: Dartmouth Publishing).

Heath, A., Evans, G. and Martin, J. (1993b), 'The Measurement of Core Beliefs and Values: The Development of Balanced Socialist/Laissez Faire and Libertarian/Authoritarian Scales', *British Journal of Political Science*, 24(1): 115–32.

Hetherington, M. J. and Weiler, J. D. (2009), *Authoritarianism and Polarization in American Politics* (Cambridge: Cambridge University Press).

Hill, M. (2009), 'Voices in the Wilderness: The Established Church of England and the European Union', *Religion, State and Society*, 37(1–2): 67–80.

Hobolt, S. B., Van der Brug, W., De Vreese, C. H., Boomgaarden, H. G. and Hinrichsen, M. C. (2011), 'Religious Intolerance and Euroscepticism', *European Union Politics*, 12(3): 259–79.

Hoffman, J. P. (1998), 'Confidence in Religious Institutions and Secularization: Trends and Implications', *Review of Religious Research*, 39(4): 321–43.

Hoffman, J. P. (2013), 'Declining Religious Authority? Confidence in the Leaders of Religious Organisations, 1973–2010', *Review of Religious Research*, 55(1): 1–26.

Hoffmann, J. P. and Mills Johnson, S. (2005), 'Attitudes Toward Abortion among Religious Traditions in the United States: Change or Continuity?', *Sociology of Religion*, 66(2): 161–82.

Hooghe, M. and Meeusen, C. (2013), 'Is Same-Sex Marriage Legislation Related to Attitudes Toward Homosexuality? Trends in Tolerance of Homosexuality in European Countries Between 2002 and 2010', *Sexuality Research and Social Policy*, 10: 258–68.

Hornsby-Smith, M. (1987), *Roman Catholics in England. Studies in Social Structure Since the Second World War* (Cambridge: Cambridge University Press).

Hornsby-Smith, M. P. (1989), 'The Roman Catholic Church in Britain since the Second World War', in P. Badham (ed.), *Religion, State and Society in Modern Britain* (Lampeter: The Edwin Mellen Press).

Hornsby-Smith, M. P. and Lee, R. M. (1979), *Roman Catholic Opinion: A Study of Roman Catholics in England and Wales in the 1970s* (Guildford: University of Surrey).

Ipsos MORI (2005a), 'Religious Denomination', May 2005. Available at: http://www.ipsos-mori.com/researchpublications/researcharchive/86/Religious-Denomination.aspx?view=wide.

Ipsos MORI (2005b), 'Voting Intention by Religion 1992–2005', May 2005. Available at: http://www.ipsos-mori.com/researchpublications/researcharchive/poll.aspx?oItemID=2370&view=wide.

Jelen, T. (2003), 'Causes and Consequences of Public Attitudes Toward Abortion: A Review and Research Agenda', *Political Research Quarterly*, 56(4): 489–500.

Jelen, T. G. (2009), 'Religion and American Public Opinion: Social Issues', in C. Smidt, L. Kellstedt and J. Guth (eds), *The Oxford Handbook of Religion and American Politics* (Oxford: Oxford University Press).

Jelen, T. G. and Wilcox, C. (2003), 'Causes and Consequences of Public Attitudes Toward Abortion: A Review and Research Agenda', *Political Research Quarterly*, 56(4): 489–500.

Jones, G. (2005), 'Blair on Defensive as Cardinal Puts Abortion at Heart of Election', *The Daily Telegraph*, 16 March. Available at: http://www.telegraph.co.uk/news/uknews/1485713/Blair-on-defensive-as-cardinal-puts-abortion-at-heart-of-general-election.html.

Jones, J. (2007), 'Among Religious Groups, Jewish Americans Most Strongly Oppose War', Gallup, February 23. Available at: http://www.gallup.com/poll/26677/Among-Religious-Groups-Jewish-Americans-Most-Strongly-Oppose-War.aspx.

Jordan, J. (2013), 'Religious Belief, Religious Denomination, and Preferences for Redistribution: A Comparison across 13 Countries', *West European Politics*, 37(1): 19–41.

Jowell, R. and Airey, C. (eds) (1984), *British Social Attitudes: The 1984 Report* (Aldershot: Gower).

Kendrick, S. and McCrone, D. (1989), 'Politics in a Cold Climate: The Conservative Decline in Scotland', *Political Studies*, 37(4): 589–603.

Kettell, S. (2009), 'Did Secularism Win Out? The Debate over the Human Fertilisation and Embryology Bill', *The Political Quarterly*, 80(1): 67–75.

Kettell, S. (2013) 'I Do, Thou Shalt Not: Religious Opposition to Same-Sex Marriage in Britain', *The Political Quarterly*, 84(2): 247–55.

Kiss, Z. and Park, A. (2014), 'National Identity: Exploring Britishness', in A. Park, J. Curtice and C. Bryson (eds), *British Social Attitudes 31* (London: Sage), pp. 1–17.

Kleiman, M. B., Ramsey, N. and Pallazo, L. (1996), 'Public Confidence in Religious Leaders: A Perspective from Secularization Theory', *Review of Religious Research*, 38(1): 79–87.

Knill, C., Preidel, C. and Nebel, K. (2014), 'Brake rather than Barrier: The Impact of the Catholic Church on Morality Policies in Western Europe, *West European Politics*, 37(5): 845–66.

Koss, S. (1975), *Nonconformity in Modern British Politics* (London: Batsford).

Kotler-Berkowitz, L. A. (2001), 'Religion and Voting Behaviour in Great Britain: A Reassessment', *British Journal of Political Science*, 31(3): 523–54.

Lee, L. (2012), 'Religion. Losing Faith?', in A. Park, E. Clery, J. Curtice, M. Phillips and D. Utting (eds), *British Social Attitudes 28* (London: Sage).

Lee, P. (2012), 'Military Intervention in the Post-Cold War Era', in S. G. Parker and T. Lawson (eds), *God and War. The Church of England and Armed Conflict in the Twentieth Century* (London: Ashgate).

Leege, D. C. and Kellstedt, L. A. (eds) (1993), *Rediscovering the Religious Factor in American Politics* (New York: M. E. Sharpe).

Leustean, L. N. (ed.) (2012), *Representing Religion in the European Union: Does God Matter?* (London: Routledge).

Leustean, L. N. and Madeley, J. T. S. (eds) (2013), *Religion, Politics and Law in the European Union* (London: Routledge).

Lewis, V. and Kashyap, R. (2013), 'Are Muslims a Distinctive Minority? An Empirical Analysis of Religiosity, Social Attitudes, and Islam', *Journal for the Scientific Study of Religion*, 52(3): 617–26.

Lipset, S. M. and Rokkan, S. (eds) (1967), *Party Systems and Voter Alignments: Cross-National Perspectives* (New York: Free Press).

Machin, G. I. T. (1996), 'British Churches and Social Issues, 1945–60', *Twentieth Century British History*, 7(3): 345–70.

Machin, G. I. T. (1998), *Churches and Social Issues in Twentieth-Century Britain* (Oxford: Clarendon Press).

Martin, B. (1968), 'Comments on Some Gallup Poll Statistics', in D. A. Martin (ed.), *Sociological Yearbook of Religion in Britain* (London: SCM Press).

Martin, D. (1989), 'The Churches: Pink Bishops and the Iron Lady', in D. Kavanagh and A. Seldon (eds), *The Thatcher Effect* (Oxford: Clarendon Press).

McAndrew, S. (2010), 'Religious Faith and Contemporary Attitudes', in A. Park, J. Curtice, K. Thomson, A. Phillips, E. Clery and S. Butt (eds), *British Social Attitudes: 2009–2010. The 26th Report* (London: Sage).

McElwee, J. (2013), 'Vatican Asks for Parish-Level Input on Synod Document', *National Catholic Reporter*, October 31. Available at: http://ncronline.org//news/vatican/vatican-asks-parish-level-input-synod-document.

McIver, B. (2012), 'Priests Read the Riot Act on Government's Same-Sex Marriage Plans', *Daily Record*, August 27. Available from: http://www.dailyrecord.co.uk/news/scottish-news/priests-tell-catholics-to-oppose-gay-1281463.

McKenzie, R. and Silver, A. (1968), *Angels in Marble: Working Class Conservatives in Urban England* (London: Heinemann Educational Publishers).

McLeod, H. (2004), 'God and the Gallows: Christianity and Capital Punishment in the Nineteenth and Twentieth Centuries,' in K. Cooper and J. Gregory (eds), *Retribution, Repentance and Reconciliation* (Martlesham: Boydell & Brewer), pp. 330–56.

McLeod, H. (2007), *The Religious Crisis of the 1960s* (Oxford: Oxford University Press).

Medhurst, K. and Moyser, G. (1988), *Church and Politics in a Secular Age* (Oxford: Clarendon Press).

Minkenberg, M. (2009), 'Religion and Euroscepticism: Cleavages, Religious Parties and Churches in EU Member States', *West European Politics*, 32(6): 1190–211.

Minkenberg, M. (2013), 'Religious Parties, Churches and Euroscepticism', in J. Haynes and A. Hennig (eds), *Religious Actors in the Public Sphere: Means, Objectives, and Effects* (London: Routledge).

Moyser, K. (1989), 'In Caesar's Service? Religion and Political Involvement in Britain', in P. Badham (ed.), *Religion, State, and Society in Modern Britain* (Lewiston: Edwin Mellen Press), pp. 343–79.

Mudrov, S. (2014), 'Religion and the European Union: Attitudes of Catholic and Protestant Churches toward European Integration', *Journal of Church and State*, doi: 10.1093/jcs/csu003.

Nelsen, B. F. and Guth, J. L. (2003), 'Religion and Youth Support for the European Union', *Journal of Common Market Studies'*, 41(1): 89–112.

Nelsen, B. and Guth, J. (forthcoming), *Religion and the Struggle for Europe* (Georgetown: Georgetown University Press).

Nelsen, B. F., Guth, J. L. and Fraser, C. R. (2001), 'Does Religion Matter? Christianity and Public Support for the European Union', *European Union Politics*, 2(2): 191–217.

Nelsen, B. F., Guth, J. L. and Highsmith, B. (2011), 'Does Religion Still Matter? Religion and Public Attitudes Toward Integration in Europe', *Politics and Religion*, 4(1): 1–26.

New Humanist (1976), 'Voluntary Euthanasia Wins Two-Third Majority', September–October, 107.

New Humanist (1979), 'Support for Assisted Suicide', February, 137.

Newport, F. (2006), 'Protestants and Frequent Churchgoers Most Supportive of Iraq War', Gallup, March 16. Available at: http://www.gallup.com/poll/21937/Protestants-Frequent-Churchgoers-Most-Supportive-Iraq-War.aspx.

Newport, F. (2009), 'Catholics Similar to Mainstream on Abortion, Stem Cells', Gallup, March 30. Available at: http://www.gallup.com/poll/117154/catholics-similar-mainstream-abortion-stem-cells.aspx.

Norris, P. and Inglehart, R. (2012), *Sacred and Secular. Religion and Politics Worldwide* (Cambridge: Cambridge University Press).

O'Brien, K. (2012), 'We Cannot Afford to Indulge This Madness', *Sunday Telegraph*, March 3. Available from: http://www.telegraph.co.uk/comment/9121424/We-cannot-afford-to-indulge-this-madness.html.

Olson, L. R., Cadge, W. and Harrison, J. T. (2006), 'Religion and Public Opinion about Same-Sex Marriage', *Social Science Quarterly*, 87(2): 340–60.

Park, A., Bryson, C., Clery, E., Curtice, J. and Phillips, M. (eds) (2013), *British Social Attitudes: The 30th Report* (London: NatCen Social Research). Available at: www.bsa-30.natcen.ac.uk.

Park, A., Clery, E., Curtice, J., Phillips, M. and Utting, D. (eds) (2012), *British Social Attitudes: The 29th Report* (London: NatCen Social Research).

Park, A. and Rhead, R. (2013), 'Personal Relationships: Changing Attitudes Towards Sex, Marriage and Parenthood', in A. Park, C. Bryson, E. Clery, J. Curtice and M. Phillips (eds), *British Social Attitudes: The 30th Report* (London: NatCen Social Research). Available at: www.bsa-30.natcen.ac.uk.

Patterson, D., Gasim, G. and Choi, J. (2011), 'Identity, Attitudes, and the Voting Behavior of Mosque-Attending Muslim-Americans in the 2000 and 2004 Presidential Elections', *Politics and Religion*, 4(2): 289–311.

Peele, G. (2012), 'Religion and Conservatism in the United Kingdom', in M. B. McNaught (ed.), *Reflections on Conservative Politics in the United Kingdom and the United States* (Lexington Books).

Pew Research Center (2007), *Muslim Americans. Middle Class and Mostly Mainstream*. Available at: http://pewresearch.org/assets/pdf/muslim-americans.pdf.

Pew Research Center (2011), *Muslim Americans. No Signs of Growth in Alienation or Support for Extremism*. Available at: http://www.people-press.org/files/legacy-pdf/Muslim-American-Report.pdf.

Pew Research Center for the People & the Press (2012), 'Continued Majority Support for Death Penalty', January 6. Available at: http://www.people-press.org/2012/01/06/continued-majority-support-for-death-penalty/.

Potter, H. (1993), *Hanging in Judgment: Religion and the Death Penalty in England* (Continuum).

Pulzer, P. (1967), *Political Representation and Elections in Britain* (London: Allen and Unwin).

Putnam, R. D. and Campbell, J. E. (2012), *American Grace: How Religion Divides and Unites Us* (New York: Simon & Schuster).

Raymond, C. (2013), 'The Continued Salience of Religious Voting in the United States, Germany, and Great Britain', *Electoral Studies*, 30(1): 125–36.

Saad, L. (2012a), 'In U.S., Nonreligious, Postgrads are Highly "Pro-Choice"', Gallup, May 29. Available at: http://www.gallup.com/poll/154946/Non-Christians-Postgrads-Highly-Pro-Choice.aspx

Saad, L. (2012b), '"Pro-Choice" Americans at Record-Low 41%', Gallup, May 23. Available at: http://www.gallup.com/poll/154838/Pro-Choice-Americans-Record-Low.aspx.

Sanders, D. (1999), 'The Impact of Left-Right Ideology', in G. Evans and P. Norris (eds), *Critical Elections: British Parties and Voters in Long Term Perspective* (London: Sage).

Scheve, K. and Stasavage, D. (2006), 'Religion and Preferences for Social Insurance', *Quarterly Journal of Political Science*, 1(3): 255–86.

Schnabel, A. and Hjerm, M. (2014) 'How the Religious Cleavages of Civil Society Shape National Identity', SAGE OpenFeb 2014, 4(1) doi: 10.1177/2158244014525417.

Scott, J. (1998), 'Generational Changes in Attitudes to Abortion: A Cross-National Comparison', *European Sociological Review*, 14(2): 177–90.

Seawright, D. (2000), 'A Confessional Cleavage Resurrected? The Denominational Vote in Britain', in D. Broughton and H. M. T. Napel (eds), *Religion and Mass Electoral Behaviour in Europe* (London: Routledge).

Shakman Hurd, E. (2006), 'Negotiating Europe: The Politics of Religion and the Prospects for Turkish Accession', *Review of International Studies*, 32(3): 401–18.

Sherkat, D. E., Powell-Williams, M., Maddox, G. and de Vries, K. M. (2011), 'Religion, Politics, and Support for Same-Sex Marriage in the United States, 1988–2008', *Social Science Research*, 40(1): 167–80.

Simms, M. (1965–66), 'Abortion and Public Opinion', *Family Planning*, 14.

Smidt, C. E. (2005), 'Religion and American Attitudes Towards Islam and an Invasion of Iraq', *Sociology of Religion*, 66(3): 243–61.

Smidt, C., Kellstedt, L. and Guth, J. (2009), 'The Role of Religion in American Politics: Explanatory Theories and Associated Analytical and Measurement Issues', in C. Smidt, L. Kellstedt and J. Guth (eds), *The Oxford Handbook of Religion and American Politics* (Oxford: Oxford University Press).

Stegmueller, D., Scheepers, P., Roßteutscher, S. and de Jong, E. (2012), 'Support for Redistribution in Western Europe: Assessing the Role of Religion', *European Sociological Review*, 28(4): 482–97.

Steven, M. (2009), 'Religious Lobbies in the European Union: From Dominant Church to Faith-Based Organisation', in L. N. Leustean and J. T. S. Madeley (eds), *Religion, Politics and Law in the European Union* (London: Routledge).

Steven, M. (2011a), *Christianity and Party Politics: Keeping the Faith* (London: Routledge).

Steven, M. (2011b), 'Christianity and British Politics: A Neglected Dimension', in F. Foret and X. Itçaina (eds), *Politics and Religion in Western Europe: Modernities in Conflict* (London: Routledge).

Stonewall (2012), *Living Together: British Attitudes to Lesbian, Gay and Bisexual People in 2012* (London: Stonewall). Available at: http://www.stonewall. org.uk/documents/living_together_2012.pdf.

Storm, I. (2011), 'Ethnic Nominalism and Civic Religiosity: Christianity and National Identity in Britain', *The Sociological Review*, 59(4): 828–46.

Surridge, P., Brown, A., McCrone, D. and Paterson, L. (1999), 'Scotland: Constitutional Preferences and Voting Behaviour', in G. Evans and P. Norris (eds), *Critical Elections: British Parties and Voters in Long-term Perspective* (London: Sage).

Szczerbiak, A. and Taggart, P. (2000), 'Opposing Europe: Party Systems and Opposition to the Union, the Euro and Europeanisation', University of Sussex OERN Working Paper No. 1.

Takács, J. and Szalma, I. (2011), 'Homophobia and Same_Sex Partnership Legislation in Europe', *Equality, Diversity and Inclusion: An International Journal*, 30(5): 356–78.

Tilley, J. (2014), 'We Don't Do God? Religion and Party Choice in Britain', *British Journal of Political Science*, doi: http://dx.doi.org/10.1017/S0007123414000052, pp. 1–21.

Tilley, J., Exley, S. and Heath, A. (2005), 'Dimensions of British Identity', in K. Thompson, A. Park and C. Bromley (eds), *British Social Attitudes – The 21st Report: Continuity and Change Over Two Decades* (London: Sage), pp. 147–67.

Thorup Larsen, L., Studlar, D. T. and Green-Pedersen, C. (2012), 'Morality Politics in the United Kingdom: Trapped between Left and Right', in I. Engeli, C. Green-Pedersen and L. Thorup Larsen (eds), *Morality Politics in Western Europe Parties, Agendas and Policy Choices* (Basingstoke: Palgrave Macmillan).

Twitchell, N. (2012), *The Politics of the Rope: The Campaign to Abolish Capital Punishment in Britain, 1955–1969* (Bury St Edmunds: Arena Books).

Unnever, J. D., Bartkowski, J. P. and Cullen, F. T (2010), 'God Imagery and Opposition to Abortion and Capital Punishment: A Partial Test of Religious Support for the Consistent Life Ethic', *Sociology of Religion*, 71(3): 307–22.

Unnever, J. D. and Cullen, F. T. (2006), 'Christian Fundamentalism and Support for Capital Punishment', *Journal of Research in Crime and Delinquency*, 43(2): 169–97.

Unnever, J. D., Cullen, F. T. and Applegate, B. K. (2005), 'Turning the Other Cheek: Reassessing the Impact of Religion on Punitive Ideology', *Justice Quarterly*, 22(3): 304–36.

Unnever, J. D., Cullen, F. T. and Bartkowski, J. P. (2006), 'Images of God and Public Support for Capital Punishment: Does a Close Relationship with a Loving God Matter?' *Criminology*, 44(4): 835–66.

van der Brug, W., Hobolt, S. B. and de Vreese, C. H. (2009), 'Religion and Party Choice in Europe', *West European Politics*, 32(6): 1266–83.

VanHeuvelen, T. (2014), 'The Religious Context of Welfare Attitudes', *Journal for the Scientific Study of Religion*, 53(2): 268–95.

Village, A. and Francis, L. J. (2008), 'Attitude Toward Homosexuality among Anglicans in England: The Effects of Theological Orientation and Personality', *Journal of Empirical Theology*, 21(1): 68–87.

Voas, D. (2003), 'Is Britain a Christian Country?', in P. Avis (ed.), *Public Faith?* (London: SPCK).

Voas, D. (2007), 'Surveys of Behaviour, Beliefs and Affiliation: Micro-Quantitative', in J. A. Beckford and J. Demerath (eds), *The Sage Handbook of the Sociology of Religion* (London: Sage).

Voas, D. and Crockett, A. (2005), 'Religion in Britain: Neither Believing Nor Belonging', *Sociology*, 39(1): 11–28.

Vollard, H. (2006), 'Protestantism and Euro-scepticism in the Netherlands', *Perspective on European Politics and Society*, 7(3): 276–97.

Wilcox, C. and Wolpert, R. (2000), 'Gay Rights in the Public Sphere: Public Opinion on Gay and Lesbian Equality', in C. A. Rimmerman, K. D Wald and C. Wilcox (eds), *The Politics of Gay Rights* (Chicago: University of Chicago Press).

Wilson, B. (1966), *Religion in Secular Society: A Sociological Comment* (London: Watts).

Wilson, M. J. (1999), '"Blessed are the Poor?" American Protestantism and Attitudes Towards Poverty and Welfare', *Southeastern Political Review*, 27(3): 421–37.

Wilson, M. J. (2009), 'Religion and American Public Opinion: Economic Issues', in J. Guth, C. A. Smidt and L. A. Kellstedt (eds), *The Oxford Handbook of Religion and American Politics* (New York: Oxford University Press).

Woodhead, L. (2013a), 'What We Really Think', *The Tablet*, November 9, pp. 12–13.

Woodhead, L. (2013b), 'Endangered Species', *The Tablet*, November 16, pp. 6–7.

Woodhead, L. (2013c), 'A Gap is Growing within the Church', *Church Times*, September 20. Available at: http://www.churchtimes.co.uk/articles/2013/20-september/comment/opinion/a-gap-is-growing-within-the-church.

Woodward, W. and Bates, S. (2007), 'Anglicans Back Catholics in Gay Adoption Row', *The Guardian*, January 24. Available at: http://www.theguardian.com/uk/2007/jan/24/gayrights.religion.

Wozniak, K. H. and Lewis, A. R. (2010), 'Reexamining the Effect of Christian Denominational Affiliation on Death Penalty Support', *Journal of Criminal Justice*, 38(5): 1082–9.

Yates, N. (2010), *Love Now, Pay Later? Sex and Religion in the Fifties and Sixties* (London: SPCK).

YouGov (2003a), 'February Euro Tracker (prepared for the *Sunday Times*)', 20–21 February. Available at: http://d25d2506sfb94s.cloudfront.net/today_uk_import/YG-Archives-Fin-sTimes-EuroTracker-030224.pdf.

YouGov (2003b), 'Survey Results – Iraq (prepared for *The Mail on Sunday*)', 27–28 February. Available at: http://d25d2506sfb94s.cloudfront.net/today_uk_import/YG-Archives-Ira-mos-AttIraq-030301.pdf.

YouGov (2007), 'YouGov Survey Results – Catholics for Choice', 14–16 November. Available at: http://iis.yougov.co.uk/extranets/ygarchives/content/pdf/For%20website.pdf.

YouGov (2012), 'Sunday Times Survey Results', 26–27 January. Available at: http://cdn.yougov.com/cumulus_uploads/document/5bal45p4b2/YG-Archives-Pol-ST-results-27-290112.pdf.

YouGov (2013), 'EMEA Survey Results', 21–27 February. Available at: http://cdn.yougov.com/cumulus_uploads/document/auqvjc212x/Eurotrack-February-2013.pdf.

Index

Note: Page numbers in bold type refer to figures and those in italic type refer to tables. Page numbers including an 'n', for example 243n4 refer to notes. If a note number appears twice on the same page, the chapter referred to is in brackets after the page number and note number, for example 242n2(Ch5).

Printed and bound in Great Britain by
CPI Group (UK) Ltd, Croydon, CR0 4YY